AN ILLUSTRATED HISTORY OF
THE UNITED STATES

UNIFORM WITH THIS VOLUME

An Illustrated History of
ENGLAND

An Illustrated History of
FRANCE

An Illustrated History of
GERMANY

The original translation by Denver and Jane Lindley
has been adapted and revised for this edition
by Helen Katel.

AN ILLUSTRATED HISTORY OF

THE UNITED STATES

by André Maurois

WITH A NEW POSTSCRIPT BY

Malcolm Cowley

THE VIKING PRESS

NEW YORK

Histoire des États-Unis
© Librairie Hachette, 1968
An Illustrated History of the United States
Revised English-language translation and up-dated text
© The Bodley Head Ltd, 1969
All rights reserved
Published in 1969 by The Viking Press, Inc.
625 Madison Avenue, New York, N.Y. 10022
Library of Congress catalog card number: 69–12671
Printed and bound in England by Jarrold & Sons Ltd, Norwich
The text of this book is a condensed version,
with revised English-language translation,
added material, and up-dated text,
of a book originally published in the United States
by Harper & Brothers under the title *The Miracle of America*,
Copyright 1944 by André Maurois

CONTENTS

ONE OF THE OLDEST MAPS OF NEW ENGLAND. SEVENTEENTH
CENTURY. *British Museum, Map Crown CXX. 27.*

I
Europe Discovers America

The Country and the People

Less than five centuries ago the peoples of Europe, Asia, and Africa were not aware of so much as the existence of those lands that today are called America. Between them and the European and Asiatic centers of civilization lay oceans of such size that navigators had neither the idea, nor the daring, nor the means of crossing them. The only territories relatively close to the Old World were situated to the north in Arctic regions difficult to reach. Over immense distances was scattered a population which today could be gathered together in a few New York City blocks. The crucial consequence was that these virgin lands became a proving ground for experiments. Because of this meeting of an unexploited continent and an advanced civilization, social history suddenly took a new turn.

The results of this meeting would have been less startling if the climate of America had not been so favorable to Europeans. And, further, it was a continent easy to penetrate. America was turned toward Europe as Europe toward America. The deeply indented east coast of the New World, rich in natural harbors and navigable rivers, was hospitable to mariners. The hilly barriers were by no means insurmountable and did not present a serious obstacle to the advance of the white man. On that east coast were the mouths of a number of good navigable rivers, which furnished natural means of access. Furthermore, the Mississippi and its tributaries unified an immense territory. Thanks to these waterways, the coast would be able to exchange its products with the interior as soon as the latter was cleared. In the north, toward the region that today is Canada, lay another giant system of lakes and rivers, which issued into the valley of the Saint Lawrence, and as a finishing touch in this natural design, between the Mississippi system and that of the Saint Lawrence the distance was very small.

The continent was colonized principally by Europeans, although they acquired new characteristics there. For almost three hundred years it was the peculiarity of America to have a moving frontier that retreated toward the west. On this extreme fringe of civilization the harshness of life, the

struggle against the forest and the Indian, the abundance of land, and the necessity of mutual aid created a new type of man: the pioneer, generous, independent, and rugged, who recognized no inequalities save those of physical strength and enthusiasm for work. In this setting men of very different countries came to resemble one another. All showed a spirit of cooperation that could hardly be found in Europe. On the frontier envy was curtailed by equality in the face of danger. Because government could not reach them, the pioneers fell into the habit of governing themselves. One's neighbor was not a rival but a partner. From this there resulted a gaiety and good will that astonished, and still astonish, the Europeans accustomed to parochial feuds. From this also came a new phenomenon: the easy acceptance of liberty. In the old countries liberties were conquests wrung by individuals from established governments; on the American frontier it was the government that was going to have to wrest rights from the individual.

When the first Europeans landed in America, they encountered tribes that were at different levels of civilization but all of which seemed to belong to the same race. The explorers called these natives Indians because the geographers of that day placed the Indies on the western shore of the Atlantic Ocean.

The Indians of North America had not, like the Aztecs or the Incas, conquered or built up empires. Many of them had remained nomads. Those of the great central plains lived almost entirely upon

TB 20

FEATHERED INDIANS. German sixteenth-century engraving. It is a somewhat embellished illustration of accounts by the first Portuguese explorers and conquerors. The bird feathers were worn only as a headdress; here they also adorn the neck, shoulders, forearms, waists, and even the ankles. The caravels in the background are more realistic. *New York Public Library, Stokes Collection.*

BISON HUNT. *Contrary to the artist's naïve picture, hunters did not work alone, but went in a group, in order to surround the animal. From* Cosmographie Universelle, *by André Thevet, 1575. Bibliothèque Nationale. Hachette photo.*

immense herds of buffaloes, which thronged the prairie by the millions. For draft animals the Indians used dogs. In certain localities and particularly in the Southwest (Arizona and New Mexico), the tribes had become sedentary since prehistoric times and lived in many-storied towns, the pueblos, which recall the ksours of the Sahara. A pueblo was an immense building made of stone rooms superimposed one upon the other in banks and ventilated from above. The Pueblo Indians cultivated maize, successfully carried on irrigation, and had domesticated the turkey; each village possessed a flock of turkeys. Before the era of the Pueblos there had been another civilization, that of the Basket Makers, who had carried the art of basketry to a high point. Almost all the Indians were acquainted with tobacco; some smoked it, others chewed it or used it as snuff.

Certain tribes owned pipes of stone or clay; some packed the tobacco into little stone cylinders and thus produced the first cigarettes.

The social life of the northern Indians was simple. Some of the tribes had a chief, a sachem; some a council of elders. Sometimes, as in the case of the Iroquois, several 'nations' formed a confederation governed by a grand council of fifty sachems and under the command of two permanent chieftains. The priests (or medicine men) had two essential functions: to heal the sick and to bring rain. Toward a captive, cruelty was the rule. He was tortured, burned, sometimes eaten. The custom of scalping, that is to say, the removal of the hair and scalp of an enemy, was not usual in pre-Columbian times.

The influence of Indian civilization on North America has been rapidly effaced. Nevertheless, the

RUINS OF A PRE-COLUMBIAN INDIAN VILLAGE IN NEW MEXICO. *U.S. Department of the Interior. National Park Service photo.*

European colonists learned from the Indians how to cultivate certain plants and how to adapt to their life in the woods. Moreover, commerce with the Indians guided the first explorers to the continent. Clearings made in the primeval forests by the herds of buffaloes became the Indian trails; the latter, followed by the first traders, were transformed into roads, which were later paralleled by railways. The Indian village gave rise to the trading post, which in its turn gave way to the fort, and it to the town. Such was the history of Albany, Pittsburgh, Detroit, Chicago, Saint Louis, and Kansas City. And finally the Indian made a contribution by bringing the pioneers closer together. He was long the enemy, almost mythical and yet dangerously real, whose threatening presence saved the white men in America from the implacable mutual hatreds of the white men in Europe.

The Spaniards and the French in America

Christopher Columbus, a Genoese, the son of a weaver and for a time a weaver himself, had studied cosmography and loved the sea. He had navigated. He had will power, enthusiasm, and a good deal of vanity as well as imagination. After several voyages he settled in Portugal and proposed to the king an expedition to the Indies by sailing west. But the king of Portugal was at that time completely absorbed in his African project; Columbus was forced to fall back on the Spanish sovereigns. Ferdinand and Isabella kept him in suspense for a long time, sending him from junta to junta. Columbus demanded the rank of admiral, the viceroyalty of all lands he might discover, and a tenth part of the riches found. Meticulous officials bargained with him over this hypothetical fortune. Finally he triumphed, and the port of Palos received orders to fit out three caravels for him. On August 3, 1492, the 'Admiral' left Spain with three light vessels, the *Santa Maria*, the *Pinta*, and the *Niña*, and a crew of ninety men, among whom—a symbolic detail—were Italians, Spaniards, an Englishman, and a Jew. The voyage was relatively easy and lasted five weeks. On October 12 there appeared a shore that Columbus named San Salvador. The grass there was as sweet as 'that of Andalusia in the month of April.' The whole crew sang *Gloria in Excelsis Deo*. Columbus believed he was in the Indies; he had actually discovered one of the Bahama Islands.

The discoverer did not have even the legitimate recompense of bestowing his name on his discovery. Immediately after him sailors, soldiers, and adventurers hastened on the quest for gold, pearls, and a passage to the Indies. In 1493 Pope Alexander VI, 'having learned that our well loved son Christopher Colonus [*sic*] setting out in search of unknown continents had discovered peoples who believed in God and could be led into the Catholic faith, had decided for the purpose of exalting and disseminating that faith' and in order to avoid all conflict between the two Catholic powers, to divide the new worlds in advance between Spain and Portugal. And so he had a line traced on a globe of the world and assigned to Portugal all countries that might be discovered east of that line, to Spain all countries situated to the west.

Meanwhile, caravels and galleons were crossing the Atlantic. One of these expeditions was joined in 1499 by a Florentine, Amerigo Vespucci, who upon his return wrote a letter under the title of *Mondus Novus*, which became famous throughout Europe. It was reproduced in the *Cosmographiae Introductio* of Martin Waldseemüller, professor at Saint-Dié, who was the first to suggest that the name of America should be given to the continent discovered by 'Americus'. The conquerors followed the discoverers and took part in prodigious adventures. In the seventeenth and eighteenth centuries the Spaniards established themselves solidly in the region of the Pueblo Indians, giving it the name of New Mexico because the great buildings resembled from a distance the structures of the Aztecs.

Spain treated her American empire not as a colony but as a province. There were two realms, New Spain and Peru, each with its viceroy. Although the government was administered by Spain, the Indians were allowed a certain autonomy. The task of assimilating them was entrusted to the Church. Jesuits, Dominicans, and Franciscans established on the frontiers of the colony missions that were half farms and half monasteries. In these gracious structures of Spanish design the natives, attracted by gifts, were instructed by Spanish priests in the true religion, the arts of building and European agriculture, the breeding of cattle, and the manufacture of useful objects. Whenever a mission became successful, it was transformed into an agricultural and industrial colony; it became an Indian pueblo, and the missionaries moved on to play their role at a more distant place. Thus the frontier advanced peaceably; the Indians forgot their native language, and the Inquisition had great trouble in finding heretics.

French sailors were among the most adventurous in Europe. Normans and Bretons had always loved danger. When the pope divided the New World between the sovereigns of Spain and Portugal, the king of France asked jokingly by what legal right the heritage of Adam had been conveyed to his dear cousins.

In 1529, after making peace with Spain, Francis I, like Henry VIII of England, fell to dreaming of galleons loaded with gold. In 1534 he helped Jacques Cartier of Saint-Malo to sail for the New World in search of a northwest passage to the Indies.

Cartier took with him sixty French sailors. He touched at Newfoundland, then, continuing west, entered a bay into which flowed a mighty river, which he called the Saint Lawrence. The Indians

CHRISTOPHER COLUMBUS. By Sebastiano del Piombo. *Metropolitan* ▶ *Museum of Art, New York. Francis G. Mayer photo.*

INDIANS IN FLORIDA, 1564. By Jacques Le Moyne. This painting is believed to be the only original work of Le Moyne's that has survived. It depicts the Indian chief Athore showing Laudonnière the marble column erected by Jean Ribault two years earlier. This column, engraved with the arms of France, was all that remained of Ribault's ill-fated attempt to plant a colony there. *Collection: James Hazen Hyde.*

whom he met used the word Canada to designate a country or city. Cartier took some of them back to France with him, and they learned French and so became interpreters on subsequent voyages. Although he returned from this first voyage without either gold or news of the Indies, the king allowed him to equip three vessels and return to Canada the following year. The voyage was so difficult and so long that Cartier could not return before the stormy season and had to spend the winter in a land of extreme cold. The Indians of Stadacona (Quebec) informed him that a little farther up the river there was an important encampment at Hochelaga. Today it is the site of Montreal. Cartier found there a few huts and corn fields. He wintered in a little fort that his men had built, and very nearly died of cold and

hunger. The sailors who returned to Saint-Malo the following spring were not very enthusiastic, and the king subsidized no further voyages. For a period of sixty years the idea of a New France slumbered.

Nevertheless, once the religious wars had subsided and Henry IV was on the throne, certain Frenchmen recalled the unexplored country where the banner of France had once been planted. A certain de Chastes, commander of the fort at Dieppe, formed a partnership with Samuel de Champlain, an explorer of great courage and experience, and secured the monopoly on trade with Canada. Champlain found Hochelaga in ruins. On de Chastes's death, his monopoly passed into the hands of de Monts, who made an agreement to form a company and transport at least one hundred

ATTACK ON AN ENTRENCHED CAMP. Three French harquebusiers helped by Indian mercenaries advancing upon the camp defenders. In back of the fascine-reinforced hedge, the two chieftains' hammocks. *From* Voyages du Sieur de Champlain, *1613. Bibliothèque Nationale. Hachette photo.*

colonists a year. He recruited volunteers, and in 1604 two ships sailed, one by way of the Saint Lawrence, the other farther to the south to a region that was called Acadia. The second group, among whom was Champlain, spent the winter on an island (Sainte Croix), ran short of water and vegetables and was decimated by scurvy. When the ice and snow melted, the survivors founded the town of Port Royal on the coast. Champlain had gone to Quebec and had made friends with the Hurons and Algonquins. He provided them with French muskets to use against their enemies; the Iroquois; they assisted him in exploring the surrounding country. This New France was an empire.

The beginnings of the colony were distressing. Nothing dampened the courage of Champlain. At length Richelieu came to power. He understood that France might hope for an imperial future and accordingly founded the Company of New France. At once a large flotilla was formed and sent to Canada. But it was the time of the wars with England. The ships were intercepted by privateers, and the company, at the very start, lost part of its capital. A little later the colony itself was conquered by the British. But in accordance with the Treaty of Saint-Germain-en-Laye, signed in 1632, it was returned to France. In 1672 the king, full of hope for the future of New France, sent out an excellent governor, Count de Frontenac, whose plan was to build forts at strategic points commanding the mouths of the waterways. The first, Fort Frontenac, was situated at the place where Lake Ontario flows into the Saint

PARISIAN FILLES DE JOIE BEING FORCIBLY SENT TO THE FRENCH
COLONY OF NEW ORLEANS. The India Company first attempted to
recruit girls and women volunteers to settle the French Louisiana city,
but its plan failed. Women of doubtful virtue were then forcibly shipped
off. This has been described in a famous passage of *Manon Lescaut*. This
popular engraving shows the scene in a rosier light: La Belle Angélique
and Marie du Tire-Boudin from the rue St. Honoré are smiling and singing
as they say farewell to the Salpêtrière doctors and to their clients. *Musée
Carnavalet. Hachette photo.*

THE 'MAYFLOWER II'. By John Leavitt. *Plymouth Plantation, Plymouth, Massachusetts.*▶

Lawrence. He gave command of it to Robert Cavelier de la Salle, a native of Rouen, for whom he had a high regard. Then in 1678 he directed La Salle to build Fort Niagara. It was a handsome structure in the style of Marshal Vauban, on the walls of which one can still read the names of Normans and Poitevins, the Frenchmen who constituted the first garrison.

Robert Cavelier de la Salle, a daring Norman, dreamed, like all explorers of his time, of reaching the Western Sea. With the missionaries of Saint Sulpice, he had already gone as far as Lake Erie, and it is probable that he proceeded from there into the basin of the Ohio. Everywhere, the Indians talked to him of the Great River (the Mississippi), and he wondered whether this might not be the road to the west. But two other Frenchmen, Jacques Marquette and Louis Joliet, reached the Great River and realized that it went, not toward the Indies, but toward the Gulf of Mexico. La Salle proposed to follow it as far as its mouth. He built a ship, the *Griffon*, and launched it on Lake Erie, where this 'floating fort' filled the Indians with amazement; later he reached the junction of the Illinois and the Mississippi; in 1682, with extraordinary courage, he descended the Mississippi to its mouth, raised there a pillar ornamented with fleurs-de-lis, and unfurled the banner of the king. The return was difficult; it was necessary to ascend the river; but La Salle succeeded in returning to Canada. In 1684 he went to France and urgently advised Louis XIV to create a colony at the mouth of the Mississippi, which should be called Louisiana in honor of the king. Later on, by joining together Canada and Louisiana, France would acquire an immense empire. It was a vast and noble project; it would have given France practically all North America. The king understood this and entrusted four vessels to La Salle, but this time La Salle was unable to find the mouth of the Great River. He wandered miserably along the coast and was finally assassinated by one of his own men.

This great man's project did not die with him. Fort Maurepas was built by the French near the Mississippi, and Jean Baptiste Le Moyne, Sieur de Bienville, agent of the India Company, founded there a city that was called Nouvelle-Orléans in honor of the regent, the Duke of Orléans. A French colony began to develop; it is described in *Manon Lescaut*. In order to populate it, the company resorted to blameworthy methods: 'women of doubtful virtue' were picked up by constables and shanghaied. In order to people Nouvelle-Orléans, ancient Orléans was swept clean. There were revolts, and constables were killed. Saint-Simon talks about them in his *Mémoires*. Once Nouvelle-Orléans was founded, the next step was to create a line of forts in the valley of the Mississippi to join those that Canada was constructing along the Ohio. Then the hopes of La Salle, of Joliet and Marquette, would finally be realized. But what power in France after Louis XIV lasted long enough to pursue such grand designs?

New England differed from England in many ways, whereas New France was a transplanted cutting from Old France. In Quebec, the little French capital, a court and salons were set up. Precedence was fixed by birth, and it was inflexible. Priests wore cassocks. The congregation leaving mass on Sunday in the rural parishes made a picture of provincial France. On their trips among the Indians, the missionaries carried with them in valises little portable altars and embroidered chasubles. La Salle, attending mass in a virgin forest, wore a suit of scarlet embroidered in gold. The *coureurs des bois* alone had adopted a local costume—fur cap, buffalo-hide vest, moccasins, snowshoes; and, like the natives, they let their beards grow. The Indians got along well with the French, whose gaiety amused them and whose gallantry aroused their admiration. The Indians respected the missionaries for teaching them many useful things, even how to build better forts with little towers at the four corners to guard the approaches. They had high regard for the peasants who so valiantly cleared the ground. So much work, courage, and good nature should have made the colony prosperous, and it was. But it developed too slowly to have any chance of surviving. In 1754, when the neighboring English colonists numbered more than a million, Canada had barely eighty thousand inhabitants. This dangerous disparity was the result of the bounty of France, whose citizens had no desire to leave her, and the royal government's abhorrence of heretics.

INTERCESSION OF A JESUIT MISSIONARY ON BEHALF OF THE WOUNDED. Secular and ▶ regular priests, and especially the Jesuits, were influential during the 'conquest' of America. Although they were not able to prevent civilians—old people, women, and children—from being decimated, they did obtain humane treatment for the wounded. *From* New Voyage in a Country Larger than Europe, *by Louis Hennepin, 1698. Library, Chantilly Jesuit Seminary. Hachette photo.*

When Pope Alexander VI so generously divided the unexplored countries between Spain and Portugal, England was not even mentioned. There was nothing surprising about this omission. England at that time was a little kingdom without naval strength, torn by political and religious strife. Nevertheless, as early as the time of Christopher Columbus she had in Henry VII a king who believed that the future of his people was on the sea and who built a fleet and an arsenal to protect his adventurous merchants. The successors of Henry VII faithfully carried on his naval program. In Queen Elizabeth's time a daring mariner, Sir Francis Drake, in time of peace assaulted the Spanish forts, disembarked on the Isthmus of Darien, attacked the mule trains transporting gold from Peru, and brought the treasure back to England. One of Elizabeth's favorites, Sir Walter Raleigh, and his half-brother, Sir Humphrey Gilbert, had the idea of founding a colony in North America. In 1584 Raleigh equipped an expedition that landed on an island near the coast of what today is North Carolina. The land was named Virginia in honor of Elizabeth, the Virgin Queen. After two or three voyages Raleigh left on the Island of Roanoke a small group of English people consisting of eighty-nine men and seventeen women. When a ship with provisions arrived at Roanoke two years later, there was no trace of the colony. No one ever discovered what became of these unfortunate people. But Raleigh said with assurance in 1602 that some day there would be an English nation in Virginia.

After the defeat of the Armada the myth of Spanish invincibility collapsed. There was no longer any reason to respect Spain's monopoly in the New World. Nevertheless, to attack her possessions would have been a tremendous undertaking; it was simpler to settle in those regions where Spaniards had not yet come. Virginia became the style again. By 1606 two companies, the London Company and the Plymouth Company, had been formed, but only the first survived. Toward Christmas 1606 three of its vessels, the *Godspeed*, the *Susan Constant*, and the *Discovery*, sailed from the port of London with one hundred forty-three colonists. The company had given the emigrants a sealed box which was not to be opened until they were in Virginia and which contained the names of seven of their number who were to form the local council of the colony and elect the president. There was no question of a free government. The charter was the property of the company, not of the colonists. The emigrants, moreover, had only a very vague idea of what they were going to find. When early in May they finally entered Chesapeake Bay, they saw a wooded coast covered with cedars and cypress, wild forests, and blue birds with scarlet wings. The mysterious box was opened and the council set up. It was decided to proceed up the river, which was named the James in honor of the king, and to found the first settlement about thirty miles inland in order to be safe from surprise attack by the Spaniards.

The president elected by the council of Jamestown was Edmund Wingfield. But the most remarkable person in the little colony was Captain John Smith, a young man of good family who had been an adventurer from the age of sixteen. With his handsome face tanned by the sun and his black beard trimmed to a point, John Smith was an Elizabethan of the great tradition. The Indians had at first welcomed the small fleet with a hail of arrows; then they had grown accustomed to the colonists and had exchanged their corn for beads and hatchets. Soon the captain of the flotilla set sail for England, and the colonists were left alone.

In the spring of 1610 the sixty survivors, reduced to the appearance of skeletons, were about to abandon the colony and return to England, when a new flotilla appeared. The colony was saved.

Salvation came in an unexpected way, from tobacco. England had hitherto bought tobacco from the Spaniards. But why should she not produce it herself? John Rolfe, a colonist, planted some that had been imported from the Antilles. At once this crop became the rage. In 1618 the harvest was twenty thousand pounds; in 1627, five hundred thousand pounds; in 1662, twenty-four million pounds. Despite the success of tobacco, the development of Virginia was slow. The creation of the colony had been a commercial enterprise under royal patronage, but in 1620 there appeared in America, farther north, a new type of British colony. In this early part of the seventeenth century

THE TOBACCO PLANTER. The first English Pilgrim Fathers in America were often better suited for theological argument than for the thankless toil of the pioneer. Besides, tobacco did not grow well in the arid soil, and the black slaves brought in by force were always falling sick or dying. *From* Pleasant Places in the World, *by P. Van der Ux. Bibliothèque Nationale. Hachette photo.*

England was torn by bitter conflicts. Political and religious hatreds attained a paroxysm of violence seldom equaled in that country. Three groups of Churches contended for members: the Anglicans, the Presbyterians, and the Separatists. The Separatists considered as 'unclean things' both the Church of England and the Presbyterian Church, and were persecuted by both those denominations. The Separatists sought a land where they might have freedom to pray in peace; the company was looking for colonists. They made a deal. Thus one hundred and two 'Pilgrims,' who by the way were not all Separatists, embarked on the *Mayflower* in September, 1620. On November 21, after a frightful voyage, the Pilgrims, instead of arriving in Virginia, found themselves within sight of Cape Cod, where they had no concession or rights of any kind. Before disembarking, the forty-one men of the expedition,

the so-called Pilgrim Fathers, met in the ship's cabin and signed a pact, or covenant, in which they swore to remain together and to obey the laws established by common consent for the common good. Having elected one of their number, John Carver, governor, the passengers of the *Mayflower* founded the village of Plymouth, whose early days were to be as difficult as those of Jamestown. The colony of Plymouth survived for some time, but it did not prosper. In 1691, when it united with the Massachusetts Bay Colony, it numbered only seven thousand colonists. This second colony did not hold the same religious principles as the Pilgrims of Plymouth, but it borrowed from them one important idea: that of assigning the lands to members of the community as freeholds. The colony of Plymouth vegetated, then disappeared, but its influence continued to grow after it was gone.

The group of dissidents who in 1629 obtained a royal charter for 'the Government and Company of Massachusetts Bay in New England' had among their members a number of landed gentlemen and prosperous merchants; in religion they were low-Church Anglican; their leader was a well-known lawyer, John Winthrop, and the capital had been subscribed without difficulty by the members themselves. John Winthrop and his companions were by no means democrats. They wished to found a holy community where they would be free to worship God according to their understanding.

The first group had numbered one thousand immigrants; many more followed. The times in England were hard. Political and religious refugees found their way either to the West Indies or to America. By 1634 Boston, which John Winthrop had founded on the bank of the Charles River, numbered four thousand inhabitants. Numerous small towns surrounded it. The communities of Massachusetts differed from those of Virginia. The soil required hard labor; tobacco did not grow well; Negroes did not become acclimated. Only small farms, cultivated by the farmer and his family, prospered, and these farms had to be grouped in villages or towns to assure common defense against the Indians. The New England town was a modification of the English manor. The charter had been drawn up in such a way that at the outset John Winthrop and a dozen assistants governed alone. Then, as a result of complaints, it was decided that in voting taxes the council would be assisted by two delegates from each town. And so the first assembly was formed, which was later to be divided into two houses, the assistants of the governor forming a sort of Upper House and the delegates a Lower House.

Roger Williams, 'a pious young man filled with divine madness,' arrived from England in 1631 and became a preacher in Salem. He, together with some friends, founded a settlement on Rhode Island, to which he gave the name of Providence. Rhode Island was to be a colony of complete religious freedom, a refuge for people of sensitive conscience. Many such came there, particularly the Baptists. To this founder of political liberalism, America owes an enormous debt. Anne Hutchinson, an impassioned woman who had caused a division in the whole Massachusetts colony through religious controversy, went to Rhode Island, where she founded the Portsmouth colony. In 1643 she was killed by the Indians, an event in which the magistrates of Massachusetts recognized the justice of God. Other discontented groups, also coming from Massachusetts, established the colony of Connecticut. The most famous of these groups was led to Hartford by 'the grave and judicious' Thomas Hooker. Other Puritans, led by John Davenport, founded New Haven on the banks of Long Island Sound. They decided that divine law, as delivered by Moses, should be their code, whence came the famous blue laws that enjoined strict observance of the Sabbath, denied trial by jury, and prescribed the death penalty for adulterous couples, as well as other inhuman severities. Before long they were made less severe. In 1662 the various settlements in Connecticut united and obtained an extremely liberal charter, since the king and Parliament demanded no control over the assembly and government elected by the colony. In this way Connecticut and Rhode Island became the first independent Colonial states. They achieved this in the seventeenth century through flexibility and decency, and by not attracting attention. Boston, a hundred years later, had to fight for the same rights.

It was not only to the companies but to individuals as well that the Crown granted Colonial charters, for instance, to Sir George Calvert, a Catholic gentleman.

The king, being unable to employ Sir George in England because of his religion, created him Lord Baltimore and conferred upon him, in fee simple, the lands situated between the Potomac and the fortieth parallel. In homage and gratitude to his queen, Henrietta Maria, Baltimore called the new domain Maryland. When Calvert died, without having been able to return to America, the charter passed to his son. It was completely feudal in nature. The proprietor was the overlord, head of the Church, and captain general of the armed forces. He had the sovereign right to create manors, hence a nobility. Baltimore began by offering a thousand acres to any gentleman who would bring five men to Maryland, and the colonists came. A Catholic and

WILLIAM PENN. By Francis Place. *Historical Society of Pennsylvania.*

the subject of an Anglican king, he was constrained to be cautious, and he gave orders that Protestants were to be treated kindly and with justice. His wise religious policy succeeded rather well; in Maryland was to be seen the miracle of the Roman Church and the Protestant Episcopal Church living on friendly terms. Following the Glorious Revolution of 1688, the Church of England was established in Maryland, and the Catholic Church was no longer authorized to hold public worship. This measure made the Catholics in Maryland enemies of the Crown and made Lord Baltimore a Protestant. As payment for this conversion he retained ownership of his lands; the governmental authority, however, passed to the Crown.

What Charles I had done for Lord Baltimore, Charles II, after his restoration, tried to do for such faithful royalists as Clarendon, Monk, Shaftesbury, and Sir George Carteret, former governor of Jersey. He gave them a vast territory south of Virginia that in his honor they named Carolina (which soon was divided into North Carolina and South Carolina). These great gentlemen conceived the strange notion of having a constitution drawn up by John Locke, who was the fashionable philosopher of that period. He drafted an amazing document in which he laid out the future classes in the state as an engineer might lay out roads. A fifth of the land was to remain in the possession of the founders, a fifth was to go to the new nobility who were to be created and who would have it farmed by serfs, and the rest was to be in the hands of independent farmers. In 1729 the Carolinas passed to the Crown. Lord John Berkeley and Sir George Carteret had also bought from the Duke of York in 1664 the territory between the Hudson and the Delaware, which they called New Jersey, in memory of the island Sir George had once governed. There they founded the city of Elizabeth, and Puritans from Connecticut founded Newark. But difficulties of all sorts discouraged the proprietors, and in 1702 New Jersey in its turn became a colony of the Crown.

The Society of Friends, to whom the name of Quakers had been given because they trembled with emotion when the Spirit took possession of them, was a religious group that had pushed Puritan Protestantism to its logical extreme. The Quakers were pacifists. They shocked the conformists as much by their virtues as by their beliefs. England had persecuted them; many of them emigrated to the Colonies, where they also were persecuted and a few of them were even hanged. They needed a concession from the Crown, but the king could not give a charter to so hated a sect. Finally William Penn, the son of an admiral who had helped to restore Charles II, to whom the Crown owed sixteen thousand pounds, and who had grown to respect the Quakers, obtained from the king in 1681 a personal charter. It gave him proprietary rights to a tract of land stretching between Massachusetts and Maryland, and as large as England and Wales combined. He decided to assemble the Quakers there, organize a free government, and try the 'Holy Experiment' of a country where love and not violence should reign.

In 1682 he visited his state and named it Pennsylvania. The beauty of the forests and rivers enchanted him. He called the capital Philadelphia, city of brotherly love. The Holy Experiment was a success. The Quakers' principles proved useful to them. Because they treated the Indians with kindness, the Indians were friendly to them. Because they dealt fairly, they succeeded in their enterprises. Because they were tolerant, various groups of immigrants came to them. Scotch-Irish Presbyterians, German Lutherans, and Welsh settled in Pennsylvania. Around 1750 Franklin found that the population was one-third Quaker, one-third German, and one-third 'other.' Philadelphia had become a little city of red-brick houses that recalled the most delightful aspects of England. Penn had hoped that his capital would be at once city and country. And so it was. Although the Quakers were no longer a majority, they were elected to all important offices because they were so greatly trusted. This harmony was first disturbed when Penn, a friend of the royal family, gave his support to James II, a Catholic sovereign. The Scotch and Welsh in the colony became indignant. When Penn died, his son (who had been converted to Anglicanism) lost all prestige. Between the proprietor and the assembly a conflict broke out, which continued until the Revolution. The Holy Experiment had lasted as long as experiments usually last, but the Quakers remained, and remain today, loyal

PHILADELPHIA AROUND 1752-54. *Historical Society of Pennsylvania.*

to their faith, one of the simplest and noblest in the world.

The colony of New York was Dutch before it was English. In 1609 a ship of the Dutch East India Company, the *Half Moon*, Henry Hudson, captain, had discovered a magnificent bay into which flowed a fine river, which Hudson named after himself. At the mouth of the river he disembarked on a long island of granite that the Indians (who had given Hudson their usual gifts-and-arrows welcome) called Manhattanick—'the island where we were drunk.' High wooded cliffs bordered the river. The Dutch sailed as far as a point just below where Albany stands today. When they returned, their stories, and especially the furs they brought back, excited lively interest. Other expeditions followed that of Hudson. The village of New Amsterdam was founded on the tip of Manhattan. In 1621 the Dutch West India Company received by charter the right to exploit New Netherland and purchased the island of Manhattan from the Indians for sixty guilders.

The development of the colony was rapid. The Dutch were enterprising, intelligent, aggressive, and accustomed to liberty. To encourage immigration, the company granted vast domains to anyone who would bring fifty persons over. As a matter of form, the land was legally purchased from the Indians by the payment of a few pieces of silver. All along the valley of the Hudson there arose fine houses adorned with family portraits. The Van Cortlandts, Van Rensselaers, Beekmans, and Schuylers owned thousands of acres, and the formation of this feudal class aroused much discontent among less wealthy colonists. In 1646, to restore harmony, the company sent out an energetic and picturesque director, Pieter Stuyvesant. He had a wooden leg (they called him Old Silver Nails) and the soul of a dictator.

New Amsterdam had grown very fast. But the

NEW AMSTERDAM IN 1650. Dutchmen were the first to establish themselves on the island of Manhattan, which they had bought from the Indians in 1626. There they created the city of New Amsterdam, which became so prosperous that Charles II of England soon demanded all of the New Netherland territory. In 1664 he sent an expeditionary force commanded by Colonel Richard Nicolls to back his demand. He then gave the territory to his brother the Duke of York, hence the city's new name, New York. *Museum of the City of New York.*

English took no pleasure in seeing this Dutch enclave in their New World. In 1653, when the two countries were at war, the Dutch prepared to defend themselves and built across the island of Manhattan a wall that has given its name to Wall Street. Suddenly Charles II claimed the territory of New Netherland on the somewhat feeble pretext of the discovery of these lands by John Cabot in 1498. It was an old story, but in 1664 an English fleet anchored in the Hudson gave it novelty. Five hundred soldiers under the command of Colonel Richard Nicolls supported the demand for capitulation. Stuyvesant saw that he was lost; his people demanded that he surrender and said that to resist was madness; the governor knew this was true. He surrendered, and without losing a man England acquired a flourishing colony. The king gave it as a present to his brother, the Duke of York, and the city of New Amsterdam became New York, while Fort Orange took its new name from another of the duke's titles—Albany. A final colony, far to the south, completed the British domain. It was founded by a philanthropist, General Edward James Oglethorpe, who wished the colony to be strictly moral. Wesley and Whitefield went there to preach. The sale of rum was forbidden. But while morality prohibited alcohol, the climate demanded it. Little by little, the colonists fled to more lenient places. In 1737 there were five thousand; in 1742, five hundred. Finally, the philanthropists gave up, Georgia became a royal province, and the colonists returned.

Thus, one after another and in various ways, eight Colonies founded by chartered companies (nine if Delaware is counted as a separate state) had become Colonies of the Crown; two (Pennsylvania and Maryland) still belonged to proprietors; two (Rhode Island and Connecticut) administered their own affairs independently. As a matter of fact, by 1750 all had a large measure of independence. All at the bottom of their hearts, were contemptuous of a power so distant and so ignorant of their needs. All were tasting with relish in their assemblies a liberty that was to some degree rebellious. The only significant difference between them was that which distinguished the North from the South. In the North puritanism had given a population primarily of merchants and artisans the morality best calculated to assure their temporal success.

But the South was no less necessary than the North to the equilibrium of America. There the large plantations where a family produced almost everything it needed had developed a different independence from that engendered by puritanism, but one no less impatient of authority. These southern leaders around 1750 resembled the country gentlemen of England. Perhaps they were even closer than their English counterparts to the old English tradition.

The first point to be noted about the economic life of the English Colonies in America is their unmistakable prosperity. Growth in population is its most striking index. In 1640 the Colonies had twenty-five thousand inhabitants; in 1690, two hundred thousand; in 1770, about two million. Thus the population had increased tenfold between 1690 and 1770. This prevents us from lightly condemning British methods. Some would reply that the success had been won, not thanks to those methods, but in spite of them. This point deserves further examination.

Second point: this prosperity came chiefly from agriculture, hunting, and fishing. Cities were few; only five of them in 1790 had more than eight thousand inhabitants (Philadelphia was the first); and they represented together only 3.3 per cent of the population. More than nine-tenths of the Americans worked on the land. The others were merchants, shipowners, sailors, miners, and artisans. Factories remained few and unimportant; England discouraged their growth.

The plantations in America and other places allowed the cultivation on British soil of products that England otherwise would have had to buy abroad, in accordance with the mercantile system; hence, the supporters of this system fostered the Colonies, but only on the condition that they should not go beyond the role assigned to them. The plantations were not to aspire to produce anything but raw materials. A colonist who became rich was not allowed to invest his money in manufacturing. The Navigation Act of 1651 required that the exports of the Colonies to England should be carried in English ships. The Staple Act of 1663 decreed that all imports from foreign countries into

GENERAL EDWARD JAMES OGLETHORPE. The philanthropic general to whom Georgia owes its existence soon placed the entire colony in grave danger. In 1737 his advisers, who were even more puritanical than he, demanded a ban on the sale of rum, and within less than five years nine-tenths of the settlers fled. The ban had to be rescinded. *Oglethorpe University, Georgia.*

the Colonies should first pass through an English port and there pay duty. Thus English commerce with the Colonies was protected against all competition from outside. The Act of 1660 reserved certain products—tobacco, sugar, cotton, indigo, etc.— exclusively for the English market. In the eighteenth century this list was added to: furs in 1722, molasses in 1733. Wheat and fish were not on the list, but could not be exported except via an English port, which prevented, for example, any direct exchange between the Colonies and the French or Spanish Antilles or between the Colonies and Portugal.

Did the Colonies on the whole suffer from these restrictions? They had in return the protection of the English fleet and the English market for their tobacco. In 1620 a proclamation had prohibited the planting of tobacco in England. But the effects of the mercantile system varied in different regions. The South, whose products were tobacco, rice, and indigo, all necessary to England, could easily exchange them for the manufactured goods it

needed. The South did not grow rich, but it managed to live. In the North the mercantile system appeared more dangerously absurd. The North produced wheat, meat, and fish, which England did not need. How then should the Yankees pay for the textiles, furniture, clothes, and shoes they required? By sending exports to other countries. This was the only way, but the Navigation Acts made this trade difficult.

In fact, the so-called triangular trade was the only operation open to the northern colonists. A Boston merchant would buy wheat, sell it in Portugal in exchange for a cargo of wine, and exchange the wine in England for cloth and hats, which he would import to America. This operation was allowed on the condition that it pass through a British port, both coming and going. The triangular trade led to the formation in the North of powerful commercial houses such as Hancock and Faneuil in Boston, De Lancey in New York, and Logan in Philadelphia. To the great merchants and

[31]

ship-owners who had their own vessels, it was a temptation to disregard the English laws and trade directly with Europe, or even to buy their molasses in the French or Spanish Antilles in contempt of the law. This contraband assured such big profits that almost all practiced it.

Time of the Wars

The Europeans who had sought refuge on the new continent believed they had escaped from the endemic feuds of Europe. But the quarrels quickly overtook them. Conflict was inevitable on the European continent; in America it was no less so. There the English occupied the best part of the coast, and their Colonies were prosperous. But the French explorers had turned the British flank. French forts on the Ohio threatened to cut off the English Colonies from the hinterland, and if the French in Canada succeeded in making connection with their fellow countrymen in Louisiana, France would become mistress of the continent. Thus local rivalries made common cause with dynastic rivalries. As for the Indians, they astutely watched these quarrels of the white man, hoping to profit by them, either as opportunities for pillage or to defend their independence.

Upon the accession of William III, the Iroquois, encouraged by the English with whom they were allied, attacked the village of Lachine near Montreal in August 1689 and perpetrated a frightful massacre. The aged Frontenac, hurriedly summoned from retirement, was sent to Quebec as war governor. He would have liked to take the offensive, descend the valley of the Hudson, and march upon New York; but not having sufficient equipment for so ambitious a project, he, in turn, instigated Indian raids against the British frontier. The massacre of Schenectady was the reply to that at Lachine. Sir William Phips, a rich Puritan of Massachusetts, determined to lead a crusade, first against Port Royal in Acadia, where he succeeded in taking possession of the city, then against Quebec. He went up the Saint Lawrence with a fleet and more than ten thousand men, anchored near Quebec, and sent an ultimatum to Frontenac. Phips then tried to disembark his troops but failed. He returned to Boston much discomfited, not understanding how Heaven could permit this triumph of the Papists. Meanwhile in Europe, Louis XIV was forced to defend himself against the powerful coalition formed by William III. In eight years of campaigning the latter failed to defeat France, and at Ryswick in 1697 Louis XIV was able to sign a peace that was not too unfavorable. He was forced to recognize William III, but France retained her colonies. Unhappily, it was a peace that even those who signed it considered only a truce.

When the War of the Spanish Succession, known in America as Queen Anne's War, brought Queen Anne of England into conflict with Louis XIV, the Americans of Boston renewed their operations against Port Royal and for a second time took possession of Acadia. A large expedition was sent from London to Quebec. Through the fault of a bad general and an incompetent admiral, this campaign was a total failure. But in Europe France was losing the war. The Peace of Utrecht (1713) was less disastrous than might have been feared a few years earlier. In America France lost Hudson's Bay, Acadia, and Newfoundland. Meanwhile, Canada was saved once more.

The War of the Austrian Succession, which in America is called King George's War (1744–1748), brought no changes.

Englishmen such as Lord Fairfax owned properties in the West so vast that they had not as yet even been surveyed. It was Lord Fairfax who first took with him on a surveying trip a young Virginian, George Washington, a relative of his by marriage. This Washington, an orphan, was a planter's son and an agreeable young man, brave and self-possessed, who enjoyed both the gay life of the great houses of the South, with its dancing, hunting, clambakes, and barbecues, and the rough life of the forests. The wild savagery of the West attracted young Washington. Having been appointed official surveyor of the county, he spent long periods among the Indians and pioneers. In his profession, he became something of a soldier and was one of the first to realize the threat to the future of Virginia represented by the advance of the French in the Ohio region. The whole commerce of the interior of the continent was carried by two rivers, the Mississippi and the Saint Lawrence, and both were in the hands of the French.

The role played by France in the discovery and

Combat entre deux Vaisseaux Anglois et François.

colonization of the American continent had been one of capital importance. Not only had Marquette and Joliet, and after them La Salle, opened up the route of the Great Lakes to the Mississippi and established the portages that made it possible to reach the Father of Waters through the valley of the Illinois or the Wisconsin, but a Frenchman from Belgium, Father Louis Hennepin, in 1680 had discovered and christened the Falls of Saint Anthony (today Minneapolis) in the upper valley of the river. Another Frenchman, Daniel Greysolon, Sieur Duluth, had founded a post at the spot where today stands the city named in his memory, Duluth. Near the Detroit River a Gascon gentleman, Sieur Antoine de la Mothe Cadillac, had built a fort. How could he have dreamt that some day, at this very place, thousands of workers would produce cars named Cadillac in memory of him? The Middle West remains dotted with French names: Prairie du Chien, Des Moines, Saint Louis. The entire valley of the Mississippi is like a triumphal way bordered by monuments erected in honor of great Frenchmen, these monuments being huge cities. Farther to the north, other Frenchmen had ascended the valley of the Missouri. La Vérendrye was the first white man to see the Rocky Mountains. The daring of the French explorers was deserving of admiration, but to the English colonists on the coast it was disturbing. The French in Canada coveted New York, which would give them an ice-free winter route. New York, well aware of this feeling, saw in it a constant danger.

The danger was all the more threatening because the Colonies could never agree. If Virginia became ardent, Pennsylvania remained hesitant. To both, London gave orders to take up arms if the French

[33]

[35]

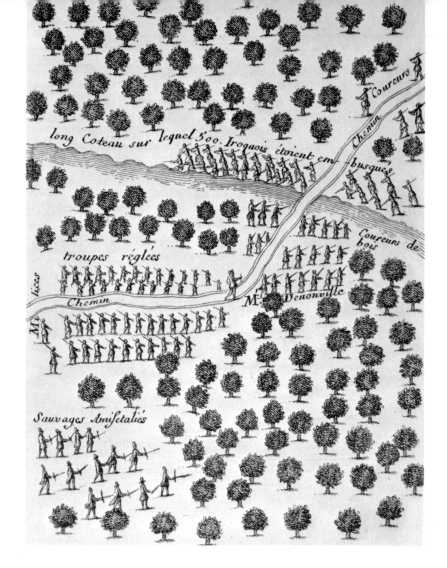

Long Coteau sur lequel 500 Iroquois étoient em busqués

Chemin
Coureurs
troupes réglées
Coureurs de bois
Mr. Denonville
Chemin
Milices
Sauvages Amisetaliés

CARTOON BY BENJAMIN FRANKLIN. 1754. ▶
This was often reprinted in Colonial newspapers until 1789. *Historical Society of Pennsylvania.*

TAKING AN IROQUOIS VILLAGE. A French regiment, with the support of 'friendly and allied Savages,' is getting ready for an assault on the Iroquois warriors who are waiting for them on a hillside. *From* New Voyages of Baron de Labrontan in Northern America, *1703. Bibliothèque Nationale. Hachette photo.*

invaded English territory. Well and good, but what would constitute a violation of the frontier? Canada and Louisiana belonged to France, and the territory to the east of the Alleghenies to England; to whom did the territory of the Indian Six Nations belong? To the Iroquois? Then the English, who were their allies, had the right to trade there. Nevertheless, the French all along the Ohio Valley nailed to the trees little panels bearing the arms of France and buried in the ground plaques with the fleur-de-lis. Representatives of the Colonies and the Iroquois met in a congress at Albany, where Benjamin Franklin tried to make them adopt a plan for union, with a common council for defense. This aroused jealousy and separatism on all sides. The Colonial assemblies rejected Franklin's plan, however, because they refused to limit their sovereignty; their lordships of the Board of Trade rejected it because they thought it was too democratic. Common sense was thus overridden, as it always is so long as danger does not seem imminent.

The war had not been declared, but it had begun. During the winter of 1754–1755 France and England made great preparations. A French army, commanded by Dieskau, was sent to Canada; an English army, under the command of Braddock, was sent to Virginia. Each of the two countries begged the other to explain these troop movements; each replied that the sole object of its preparations was to maintain the peace. But General Braddock had been ordered to take Fort Duquesne and General Dieskau to prevent him. When Braddock and his army had, with great difficulty, made their way into the forest, cutting a road as they went, and when they encountered there a mixed troop of French and Indians, the regular and disciplined formation of the British soldiers became the very cause of their destruction. Braddock was killed; two-thirds of his officers and one-half of his men perished. The frontier was open to the Indians.

Terror took possession of the Colonies, and with reason. The Indians turned against the vanquished.

JOIN, or DIE.

Massacres and scalpings began again. Washington, who had emerged with honor from the Braddock affair, during which he had had two horses killed under him, was named at the age of twenty-three colonel and commander of all the troops in Virginia. In Pennsylvania the assembly voted to make war against the Indians and went so far as to promise bounties for scalps. This counter-savagery led a number of Quakers to resign from the assembly, so that the majority at Philadelphia became non-Quaker. Despite this, a conflict broke out between the assembly and the governor of Pennsylvania. Disputes such as these, following upon a serious defeat, threatened England's position in America. Braddock's disaster had reduced the prestige of the army. The conflicts between English officers and American militia, between the Colonies and their proprietors, created a state of mind that might one day become dangerous.

England's failures were retrieved when William Pitt came to power. He conducted the war like a despot, but he won it. To Canada he sent General Jeffrey Amherst, who was forty, and James Wolfe, who was only thirty. A great man was commanding the French armies. He was the Marquis de Montcalm, an ideal type of Frenchman, not unlike Turenne, courageous, simple, and generous. For a long time Montcalm held the Lakes successfully, but in 1758 Fort Duquesne fell, and then Fort Frontenac. In honor of Pitt, Fort Duquesne was renamed Pittsburgh. The English now had the advantage of numbers. Their Colonies were fifteen times as populous as those of France. They controlled the sea and had the support of the Iroquois. Amherst took Louisbourg. Wolfe, with an army of thirty thousand men, laid siege to Quebec. Montcalm received no reinforcements. Wolfe, by a daring maneuver, scaled the cliff at night and at dawn attacked Montcalm's infantry on the Plains of Abraham. Montcalm, fighting desperately and bravely, was killed in the battle, as was Wolfe also (1759). The next year Montreal was taken. Canada and its inhabitants, who in practice were so completely French, were lost to France.

The Treaty of Paris stripped France of almost all her colonies. She lost Canada, India save for certain business establishments, and Senegal save for Gorée. The territory on the east bank of the Mississippi went to England, while by a secret treaty Louisiana was ceded to Spain, which was bound to France by a family alliance and on whose friendship the French minister Choiseul was counting for revenge.

Scenes from Colonial Life

In 1763 the English Colonies in North America had altogether about 1,250,000 inhabitants of the white race and about 230,000 Negroes. The Indians had been driven back into the forests, but at many points the frontier was no more than a day's journey from the coast, and the colonists remained aware of the presence on the fringe of their civilization of the savage, capricious, and fearless tribes. Among the whites, distinctions of class existed, but they were less precise than in England. The emigrants had almost all belonged to the middle classes. A planter, the head of a respected family who sent his son to Oxford, shone at the governor's receptions, painted a coat of arms on his carriage, and reigned over a community of slaves, might have had as ancestor, three or four generations back, a poor fellow who had sold himself as a servant in order to pay for his passage. In the North the governing class had at first been dominated by the clergy. Then the great merchants and ship-owners had taken precedence and formed a sort of gentry. The sacred cod, dispenser of riches, figures in more than one coat of arms. In Massachusetts only a few families owned their own carriages, but the stagecoach and the saddle horse were in common use. When Daniel Leonard, a Boston lawyer, dared to wear gold embroidery and harness two horses to his carriage, he ruined his career. In New York some descendants of the burghers wore powdered perukes, silk stockings, and swords. The

governor entered Trinity Church followed by a Negro who presented him with his prayer book on a velvet cushion. An artisan or farmer was Goodman, his wife was Goodwife. A laborer was designated by his name alone. Below him came the servants and finally the slaves.

As a matter of fact, the class system could not be oppressive in a country where one need only move west to escape from it. To every heart that longed for equality, the frontier offered a primitive society where only courage and hard work counted. The indentured servants who had paid for their passage by contracting before they embarked to work for five years could, once the five years were up, turn themselves into pioneers. If they were successful, they founded families of landowners; if they failed they became 'poor whites'; but in the South slavery established a sort of equality between whites, whether exalted or humble. The mind of the South was obsessed by fear of the Negroes. Slavery had become an institution there. At the start it had not been recognized by law and was established in fact before it had legal standing. In 1755 there were in South Carolina ten thousand blacks to six thousand two hundred whites. The planters could not get along without Negroes, and they were afraid of them; there resulted a division of sentiment and violent race feeling.

In New England, where slaves were fewer and gave no cause for alarm, race feeling was less strong. In compensation, poor whites there suffered from inequality of rank. The arrogance of the Boston ministers and of the great merchants was more insulting than that of an English duke because their manners were worse.

Although suffrage was restricted, political life was becoming active. Each of the Colonies had a legislature made up of two houses. In Connecticut and Rhode Island the governor was elected; in the other Colonies he was appointed by the Crown or by the proprietors. On occasion he might buy his appointment. Often the position of the hapless governor was very difficult. The local assembly voted his pay; if displeased, it would withhold his

TOWN MEETING IN A NEW ENGLAND COMMUNITY. Town meetings ▶ were held in meeting-houses. They were attended by the representatives of active citizens working in the Colony and by proprietors' representatives. Debates were rather stormy at times. *Library of Congress, Washington.*

living expenses. For a century and a half the Crown tried unsuccessfully to reorganize the administration of the Colonies. But the Parliament of London was far away, and its decisions were so slow in arriving that the colonists laughed at them. 'This year,' one of them said, 'you complain to Parliament; next year Parliament sends someone to make an investigation, and the following year the government will have been changed.'

In each New England community the center of political life was the meetinghouse with its steep roof and graceful steeple, an edifice half religious, half political, and a symbol of life in these provinces. Preparation was made for the town meetings in private gatherings in the taverns or by small juntas, committees of active citizens.

The electors, few in number, represented only a small part of the population. But everyone, including those who did not vote, was interested in the contests carried on by active citizens to defend the charter of the colony, to resist the claims of the proprietor, or to hold the governor in check. Independent sects, in the tradition of Plymouth, by their doctrine of the equality of all believers, prepared people's minds for the idea of a republican 'commonwealth,' while in the forests along the frontier, free from all restraint, a new people was growing up, composed of all races, and was quietly forging in action a wholly American doctrine of liberty.

Outside New England the Episcopalians formed the most powerful Church. Some of the Dutch and some of the Huguenots had joined it. But in the South the system of great plantations created enormous parishes, which bred indifference because of the miserable state of the roads. Tithes were paid in tobacco. The Congregational Church was a power in its northern domain and was supported by taxation in Massachusetts. For a long time it had been intolerant, and how could it have been otherwise? Had not the Puritans left England to establish 'a rampart against the antichrist'?

The excess of evil brought its own remedy. The Salem witchcraft trial had aroused many good people, and as was to happen later in France as a result of the trials of La Barre and Calas, it bred some measure of tolerance. Judge Sewall, who had condemned the unfortunate 'witches,' five years later made a public apology. Cotton Mather, himself a fierce Puritan, was not altogether sure of the sanctity of this butchery. The eighteenth-century ideas of the natural goodness of man were beginning to threaten the Calvinist doctrine of predestination. Puritanism grew milder; in many families it survived simply as a salutary discipline of conduct. Around the middle of the century all observances became less strict. Franklin seldom went to church, because Sunday was his day for reading and work. When he did go, he found the sermons dry and uninteresting. 'My mother,' Franklin said, 'grieves that one of her sons is an Arian; another, an Arminian. What an Arian or an Arminian is, I cannot say that I very well know. The truth is I make such distinctions very little in my study.' It was a novelty to hear a son of New England say that he made 'such distinctions very little in my study.' Boston, a city formerly closed to the sons of Belial, now had Episcopal and Baptist churches. In 1718 Cotton Mather himself took part in the ordination of a Baptist minister and in 1726 he boasted of admitting to communion in his Church members of other denominations. This period of indifference was followed by a religious renaissance. It was called the Great Awakening. Traveling preachers shook the masses by their eloquence and, by breaking up the parishes in favor of new sects, produced a sort of religious revolution.

The personal life of the Americans was governed by the English common law. This made the husband the absolute master of the household. Jefferson, who was living in Paris, was shocked by the visits that unattended women paid upon men in the government, 'unbelievable as it may seem,' he said, 'to inhabitants of a country where the sex does not endeavor to extend itself beyond the domestic line.' At that time women married very young and often died in childbirth. The widower remarried, for to live in chastity was grievous and to live in sin dangerous. In the South pretty Negro women sometimes submitted to the claims of the planter. But a white servant who misbehaved had her time of bondage prolonged by one year. In Virginia and in Maryland divorces were rare, since the Catholic Church and the Episcopal Church did not allow them; in Connecticut and Massachusetts, on the other hand, the law was based on the Bible, which

permits repudiation. Among the Quakers marriage required only a promise of fidelity made before witnesses. The father of a family possessed, at first, complete power over his children, but the ease with which sons could find land or a calling of their own rapidly weakened this paternal authority. The last traces of feudalism such as the right of primogeniture and entailed estate, disappeared. As happens in all provincial and monotonous societies, burials were pretexts for celebration, although ministers thundered against the custom.

In the South social life had great charm. The large houses afforded a generous hospitality. Balls were given to which all the planters of the neighborhood came on horseback or in barouches to dance jigs or reels or other country dances. In 1674 a tailor and another artisan were fined for racing their horses, 'a sport reserved for gentlemen.' In the eighteenth century there was a jockey club in Virginia. The country fairs attracted booths and games of all kinds. In the clubs and taverns and in the private houses there was a great deal of drinking—rum, brandy made from various fruits, beer, and cider. Card-playing was very popular. For a long time the only method of smoking was the pipe, copied from the Indians; in 1762, after his return from Cuba, General Israel Putnam introduced the cigar, but it was not until 1800 that cigars were made in America. In Virginia and around New York rich huntsmen rode to hounds, importing their foxes from England. The taste for music was growing. In Charleston the Saint Cecilia Society gave concerts and brought over French musicians. In Massachusetts the theater was not allowed until after Puritanism had lost its hold; and in Philadelphia not until 1754, because the Quakers were opposed to it. The center of life was the home and family. The interiors of the houses were modeled after those of England and Holland, but were less elaborate.

The problems of education were not easy to solve. Distances, especially in the South, were an obstacle to the success of schools. In 1636 the town meeting established the Boston Latin School. In 1642 a Massachusetts law made parents responsible for having their children taught. In 1647 another law decreed that every community of fifty families should have a grammar school, that is, a secondary school that prepared for college. The law was not always observed, but little by little the number of grammar schools increased. Daughters of schoolmasters opened dame schools, where girls learned to read, count, sew, and knit. For boys there were elementary schools. Franklin went to a grammar school for a year and then got his true education by himself with remarkable success. In the other colonies the charge of education was left to the parishes. Too often, all that was required to secure the right to teach was to rent a room, put benches in it, and procure a mahogany cane to inspire slow minds. The South imitated the methods of the English: elementary schools for the poor; tutors for rich children, who completed their education in college, sometimes in England. The quality of the average speech delivered in the colonies shows that, for the better minds, lack of schools did not entail lack of culture.

Harvard College was founded in 1636. The General Court that year voted four hundred pounds to establish a college and the following year selected for its location Newtown, whose name was changed to Cambridge in order to put the institution under the patronage of the great English university. In 1638 'it pleased God to excite the heart' of a Mr. John Harvard, a pious gentleman and a friend of letters, to give half his fortune, which was in all seventeen hundred pounds, for the creation of a college and its library. He started the latter by a gift of two hundred sixty volumes. These rules for admission were agreed on: 'When a student shall be capable of understanding Cicero (or any other classic Latin author) on sight, and also of speaking or writing in Latin in prose or in verse, then only admit him to the college.' Neither an examination in English nor a knowledge of history, geography, or arithmetic was required. At college, in addition to Latin, the students were to learn Greek and Hebrew and take part in theological discussions. A Dutchman who visited Harvard at the time it was starting wrote: 'We found there eight or ten young men sitting in a circle and smoking tobacco. The smoke filled the room. . . . We asked them how many professors they had and they replied: "Not one. There is not enough money to pay for them. . . ."'

This state of affairs did not last. The charter of 1650 created a corporation that administered the

WILLIAMSBURG, THE FIRST SOUTHERN STATES UNIVERSITY TOWN. This document, discovered in Oxford in 1928, made it possible to reconstruct the town's main edifices as shown here. Top: William and Mary College. Center, right: the college dean's house. Bottom: the Capitol, another view of the college, and the governor's palace. *U.S.I.S.* (*United States Information Service*).

college from that date on. Harvard became rich through gifts and legacies. Later, the South had its own college, William and Mary, founded in 1693 and named in honor of the English sovereigns. A Doctor Blair had gone to England to seek support for this college, intended to form religious souls. The answer he frequently received was: 'Damn your souls! Make tobacco.' But he brought back from his trip a charter and a gift from the royal couple. Yale was founded in 1701 as a rival to Harvard, and in 1746 the Presbyterians in their turn started the College of New Jersey, which later became Princeton University.

Benjamin Franklin, sensible, witty, and moderate, was the great writer of his period and was a sort of American Voltaire, but a Voltaire combined with Sancho Panza. If he did not have the mad poetry of *Candide*, he possessed gifts of irony and satire, and his common sense amounted to genius. The puritanism of New England (where he was born) left no trace in his character. It has been said of him that he was much less interested in saving his soul from eternal fire than in saving his neighbor's house from burning up. Men's actions, not their beliefs, seemed to him the measure of their value. He shared with Voltaire a taste and respect for the sciences. In politics he was open-minded, reasonable, humorous, witty, incapable of hating his adversaries, and always ready to accept a fair compromise. Franklin took liberties in words and in deeds and had a lively sense of humor. He did not fear platitudes when they were also truths, nor did he fear epigrams: 'Keep your eyes open before marriage,' he advised, 'and half-shut afterward.' Or again: 'There are more old drunkards than old doctors.' He contributed to American culture, not only by his works, but by creating the first public libraries, improving stoves and lamps (both helpful for reading), and facilitating the circulation of newspapers when he was postmaster general.

The first American newspapers were newsletters written by hand. Then John Campbell, who sent news from Boston to several people, found it more convenient to print his letters under the title of the *Boston News-Letter*. On April 24, 1704, Sewall notes in his journal: 'I gave Mr. Willard the first newsletter which has ever crossed the river.' Other journals were started in Philadelphia and Boston, one of which was the conservative *Boston Gazette*, the other the *New England Courant*, which was very radical and was edited by James Franklin, Benjamin's brother. James Franklin was a fearless and imprudent young man who published satires against the Mathers and got himself arrested several times. Later Benjamin Franklin bought the *Pennsylvania Gazette*. The *New York Weekly Gazette* was controlled by Governor Cosby, a corrupt and dictatorial man; when he came into conflict with his managers, the latter started a rival paper, the *New York Weekly Journal*, which was published by John Peter Zenger, a German. The governor in a rage ordered that the *Journal* be burned by the public executioner. The mayor declared the order illegal. Zenger was arrested and prosecuted for libel and sedition. At the trial there appeared for the defense, to the great surprise of all, Andrew Hamilton, an illustrious and venerable lawyer from Philadelphia, who eloquently defended the freedom of the press. The verdict was: 'Not guilty.' Zenger was acquitted in a tumult of applause, and when Hamilton returned to Philadelphia he was received with high honors, flag-draped windows, and the thunder of cannon. The word *liberty* was evidently dear to Americans.

Conclusion

The inhabitants of the New World had not created a civilization; they had transferred from beyond the oceans the civilization of the Old World. In their minds, as in those of Europeans, centuries of culture and experience were alive. In South America the culture and experience were Spanish; in Canada they were French; in New England and Virginia they were essentially English. It is true, other races were mixed with the first Anglo-Saxon colonists. Germans, Swiss, Scots, and Irish formed a tenth part of the population. But language, laws, and ideas came from England.

In 1763 many Americans were patriotic Britons, proud of belonging to a nation that had just won a great war and conquered Canada. There was no question of rebellion. When they said 'home' they meant the Old Country, which had given, to many of them, flesh and blood and, to all, their powers and rights.

The religious and philosophic ideas of the colonists differed in certain respects from those of the English. The Dissenters had fled England in order to find tolerance and liberty. They were terrified as soon as anyone talked of 'establishing' the Church of England in America. Episcopalian clergymen went to England to be ordained, but Congregational ministers were potential rebels against authority. When the Bishop of London talked about a Colonial Episcopate, Samuel Adams thundered against these tyrants, the bishops, and conjured up the specter of papism. The cynicism of the dandies and fops of London aroused the indignation of the Puritans. 'Chastity is certainly not the style in England,' one of them said, and went on to ask how a corrupt aristocracy could govern honest Protestants. Franklin himself, on one of his rare bad days, said that compared with such people, every Indian was a gentleman.

But of all the misunderstandings, the most serious was the economic one. England, in establishing the Colonies, had expected from them the products that she lacked: spices, wines, silk. She had pictured their production as supplementing her own. But what did the Colonies send: fish, which she hardly needed; tobacco, which disappeared in smoke; and a few masts for ships. It was a great disappointment, and the tropical possessions in the West Indies were much better thought of in the mother country. On his side, the colonist was irritated to see restrictions imposed on his commerce

VOLUNTEER FIREMEN IN NEW YORK. Notice of a fire-▶ extinguishing drill, addressed to the citizens who were members of the Hand-in-Hand Company. It was signed by Isaac Roosevelt, a surname that was soon to become famous. *New York Public Library.*

Sir   New York 3.d March 1762.

You are hereby notified of a Meeting of the
Hand-in-Hand Fire Company at the House
of Mr Crawley, at the City Arms, on
Thursday next at Seven o'Clock in the Evening

To The Rt. Honble. The Earl of Sterling.

Isaac Roosevelt. Clerk.

and prohibitions pronounced against his industries. Franklin said: 'Great Britain would, if she could, manufacture and trade for all the world; England for all Britain; London for all England, and every Londoner for all London. . . .' The Colonies had trouble in seeing themselves as 'markets destined to enrich all the merchants of the City'; they wanted to exist for themselves; they thought their interests were just as important as those of some English shire. They did not pause to consider what they owed to England—the capital that had given them their start, the British fleet that made their continued existence possible. In 1763 the colonists were faithful subjects of the king and never dreamed of denying him their loyalty. But once in a while they had the uncomfortable feeling that they were second-class citizens, governed by the Crown, not for their own good, but for that of more privileged subjects. In the eyes of an English minister, Colonial commerce was a small question bound up with a thousand others. In the eyes of the colonists, it was the condition of their existence. Nevertheless, even among the malcontents, there was hardly any talk of the combined American Colonies as a nation. They were more conscious of the things that separated them than of the things that united them. Communication between them was difficult. Bad roads, forests, and Indians were the obstacles. Quarrels about the frontier divided them: Maryland, Pennsylvania, Virginia, Connecticut, and New York vied with each other for land. But without their realizing it, the bond that united them was already strong. A planter on the Potomac looked very different from a Boston merchant, and their interests might perhaps diverge. On the other hand, a pioneer on the Virginia frontier and a pioneer on the Pennsylvania frontier resembled each other. Scottish farmers on the extreme fringe hardly knew to what colony they belonged. All had engaged in the same struggle against the forest; all had the same love of independence; all felt the same impatience at certain official attitudes. 'To have had common glories in the past,' says Renan, 'to possess a common will in the present, to have accomplished great things together, and to wish to accomplish more, these are the essential conditions for being a people.'

The labor question was a grave problem in a constantly growing country. From the Indian nothing could be expected; he clung to his independence, and the harshest of masters could not profitably exploit him. Immigrants (Germans fleeing from the devastated Palatinate, Irishmen fleeing from poverty) were fairly numerous, but these farmers or artisans came for the purpose of starting establishments of their own; they left their native lands to be free, not to serve new masters. Thus labor immediately became dear. An English traveler noted that the price of a cake was higher in Boston than in London, although milk and flour were cheaper. Young girls who agreed to be housemaids married at twenty, and the new couples set out for the frontier. The solutions were: for the pioneers in the West, mutual aid and neighborliness; for the whole coast, indentured servants; for the South, first indentured servants and later slavery. The indentured servants were so called because they signed contracts of from three to five years, written in duplicate on a piece of paper, the edges of which were notched, or 'indentured.' Slavery would never have existed in America if it had not been an ancient African institution. In Guinea prisoners had always been sold as slaves, and the tribal chiefs found it quite natural to hand them over to white captains. When the Treaty of Utrecht allowed the English to trade with the Spanish colonies, slave trading became a considerable branch of commerce in which the most respectable shipowners of Liverpool, Saint-Malo, and New England took part. Small ships of fifty tons made the voyage from Boston (or Rhode Island) to the slave coast. The business was profitable. One bought eight thousand gallons of rum in New England; with that one procured in Guinea thirty-five Negro men, fifteen Negro women, and several boys and girls, plus a little gold dust; one traded them in the West Indies for molasses, which was carried to New England to be distilled into rum. This barter of alcohol for human flesh and blood produced a handsome profit. It has been estimated that between 1750 and 1800, the slave traders imported into America approximately seven thousand five hundred blacks a year.

Slavery was not immediately sanctioned by law, but all the Colonies tolerated it. Even William Penn and Roger Williams, who were men of virtue, owned slaves. In the North (for economic and not moral reasons) the Negroes were seldom anything but domestic servants, but in the South the cultivation of tobacco and later of cotton led to such growth of slavery that soon the planters were dismayed by this enormous 'foreign body' beside which they had to live.

In 1760 Franklin published a booklet entitled *Information for those Desirous of Coming to America*. In it he described with exactness and common sense the economic situation of the Colonies: 'The truth is, that though there are in that country few people so miserable as the poor of Europe, there are also very few that in Europe would be called rich; it is rather a general happy mediocrity that prevails. There are few great proprietors of the soil, and few tenants; most people cultivate their own lands, or follow some handicraft or merchandise; very few are rich enough to live idly upon their rents or incomes, or to pay the highest prices given in Europe for paintings, statues, architecture and other works of art. . . . Of civil offices, or employments, there are few; no superfluous ones, as in Europe. . . . It cannot be worth any man's while who has a means of living at home, to expatriate himself, in hopes of obtaining a profitable civil office in America. . . . Much less is it advisable for a person to go thither, who has no other quality to recommend him but his birth. . . . It is a commodity that cannot be carried to a worse market than that of America, where people do not inquire concerning a stranger: "What is he?" but "What can he do?" . . . In short, America is the land of labor, and by no means what the French call *Pays de Cocagne*.' Americans did not yet know that together they had accomplished a great thing; on the day when they realized it, they would feel the desire to accomplish more.

HARVARD COLLEGE AT THE TIME
OF ITS FOUNDING. The college,
which was founded through a donation
by the pious John Harvard, very soon
became one of the most famous
private universities. The name of the
small town of Newtown, Massachusetts, where it had been started, was
deemed unworthy of such an honor,
and was changed to Cambridge. *Massachusetts Historical Society. Francis G.
Mayer photo.*

PHILADELPHIA

Ameriquam

Commerce d'Angleterre

Anglois

Hollandois

Espagnol

Fran...

MAL LUI VEUT MAL LUI TOURNE DIT LE BON HOMME RICHA

Sujet Mémorable des Révolutions de l'Univers

ENGLAND THREATENED BY COMPETITION. The meek British lion
dozing in the foreground is letting a puny dog insult him. The 'Englishman' is wringing his hands at the sight of a milch-cow (representing
British trade) surrounded by four very busy figures—a Dutchman, a
Spaniard, a Frenchman, and an American. The first three have milked her,
and the fourth is sawing off her horns. In the background the port of
Philadelphia, where a British vessel, its flag tattered, appears to be in
trouble. *Bibliothèque Nationale. Giraudon photo.*

II
At the Crossroads

Post-war Problems

A peace, even a victorious peace, creates as many problems as it solves. The Peace of Paris (1763) raised more than one problem for America. France had been eliminated from the immense basin of the Mississippi; but the French, as much by their alliances with the Indians as by their forts and outposts, had hitherto maintained order in that region. Who henceforth was to play that role? It could be only the British Army. The problem of pacifying the West had not yet been solved.

What would the English government do with the immense territory it had acquired? Many Colonials hoped that this domain would be opened to them, and that farmers, speculators, and trappers could make their fortunes there. That was the *laissez-faire* solution. It was not without danger. In October 1763 the government announced that four new provinces would be created: Quebec, East Florida, West Florida, and Grenada. As for the territory bordered by the Alleghenies, the Mississippi, and the Great Lakes, it was to become an Indian reservation. No one was allowed to make a home-stead there or to buy or sell land without special license, and those living there were ordered to leave. The colonists were enraged.

When, after 1763, England began to demand more of the Colonies, many blamed the new king, George III, and his autocratic ideas; but the problem went deeper than that. 'Great Britain adopted a new imperial policy because she had conquered a new empire.' A French population in Canada and the necessity of guarding a long frontier against the Indians required the presence in America of at least ten thousand men. But expenditures for the Colonies had already risen to four hundred twenty thousand pounds, and the quitrents produced barely sixteen thousand pounds. To this the colonists replied that one could not ask plantations still in swaddling clothes to guarantee the costs of their support. 'As long as he is still in his childhood,' said James Wilson, 'a subject cannot be expected to fulfill all the duties of his allegiance. One must wait before demanding this accomplishment until he arrives at the age of discretion and maturity.'

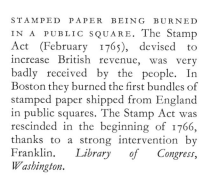

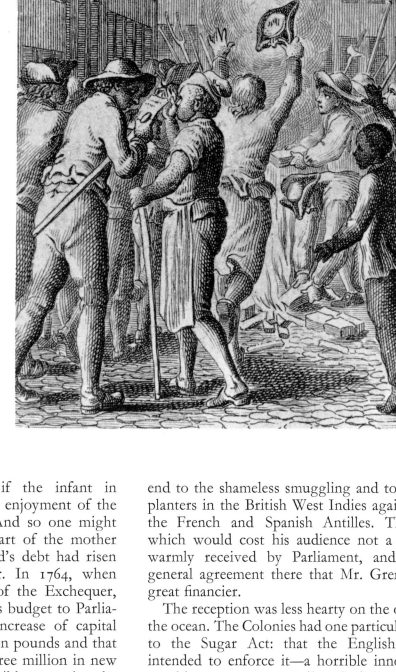

This argument lost cogency if the infant in swaddling clothes demanded the enjoyment of the liberties of a full-grown man. And so one might excuse some irritation on the part of the mother country, especially since England's debt had risen sharply as a result of the war. In 1764, when Grenville, the new Chancellor of the Exchequer, with his prolix skill explained his budget to Parliament, he announced that the increase of capital debts amounted to seventy million pounds and that it would be necessary to raise three million in new taxes. Two solutions were possible: to raise the property tax in England, or to increase the revenues from colonial customs. The landed gentry who constituted the Commons would feel a natural and lively preference for the second method. Grenville made his choice accordingly. The Sugar Act was intended both to increase revenue by putting an end to the shameless smuggling and to protect the planters in the British West Indies against those in the French and Spanish Antilles. This budget, which would cost his audience not a penny, was warmly received by Parliament, and there was general agreement there that Mr. Grenville was a great financier.

The reception was less hearty on the other side of the ocean. The Colonies had one particular objection to the Sugar Act: that the English authorities intended to enforce it—a horrible innovation. Up to this moment smuggling had been tolerated. Armed patrols, inquiries, and searches appeared unbearable. And in 1765 Grenville repeated the offense. It was necessary, he said, to defend the Colonies by collective and permanent measures. Who was able to organize this military and naval defense? The Colonies themselves? Thirteen

[55]

governments had never organized anything, and Franklin admitted that union was necessary but impossible. His Majesty's government? Then it would need new resources. What resources? The Treasury suggested a stamp tax. Would the Americans object? Their agents in London were consulted by Grenville, who inquired of them with what sauce the Americans would like to be eaten. As for himself, he thought that a stamp tax was the easiest to digest, but if the Americans preferred some other condiment, he was ready to study their preference. Franklin suggested a return to the old method of the English kings, who used to ask the Colonies themselves to vote the necessary sums.

'Can you agree on the proportion each Colony should raise?' asked Grenville. Franklin had to admit that he could not. Nothing remained for Parliament but to vote the Stamp Act, which it did in February 1765.

This act decreed that thenceforth stamps sold by appointed agents should be used in America for all documents, licenses, announcements, journals, almanacs, playing cards, etc. Franklin was far from imagining the tempest that the Stamp Act would raise in America. It was not that the burden was crushing. Stamps varied in price, depending on the importance of the document, from one penny to six pounds. It was the principle of the measure that

BURIAL OF THE STAMP ACT. English cartoon on the abrogation of the Stamp Act. In the center of the procession George Grenville, the originator of the unpopular law, holds the dead infant in his arms. The coffin is inscribed, 'Born in 1765, Died in 1766.' *John Carter Brown Library, Brown University.*

A SOCIETY OF PATRIOTIC LADIES AT EDENTON IN NORTH CAROLINA. Cartoon by P. Dawe. The women of Edenton '. . . having resolved *not* to drink any more *tea,* nor wear any more British cloth' until all laws aiming at enslaving their country were abrogated, formed an association and signed a pledge to this effect. *Metropolitan Museum of Art.*

shocked Americans. They had always admitted the right to impose customs duties because that was a regulation governing the *external* commerce of the Colonies; they refused to pay *internal* taxes voted by a Parliament in which they were not represented. In 1765 Patrick Henry, a young lawyer, proposed five resolutions concerning the Stamp Act and submerged a Virginian assembly 'in the torrents of his eloquence.' The 'old families' listened to him with irritation. When he said: 'Tarquin and Caesar each had his Brutus, Charles the First his Cromwell; and George the Third . . .' cries of 'Treason!' interrupted him. The loyal subjects of His Majesty had no liking for such violent language. Franklin advised the abrogation of the Stamp Act pure and simple. 'Suppose,' one of the members of the House of Commons, where he was testifying, asked him, 'that the Stamp Act is retained; will the bad humor of the Americans go so far as to make them purchase poor merchandise elsewhere in preference to ours?' *Reply:* 'Yes, I believe so . . .' *Question:* 'What has hitherto been the pride of the Americans?' *Reply:* 'To follow British styles.' *Question:* 'What is their pride now?' *Reply:* 'To wear their old clothes until they can make others themselves.' It is hard to tell whether it was Franklin's testimony that won the day for the Americans. Be that as it may, the clarity of his exposition, the

[57]

simplicity of his replies, and their moderation enabled Parliament to save its face. The Stamp Act was rescinded and Franklin, who a year earlier had been the traitor of traitors, became a popular hero in America. King George III, who had a high regard for his own majesty, hesitated a long time before signing this capitulation. But his ministers represented to him the grave discontent of the City: Parliament, by a declaratory act, maintained its theoretic rights; the king gave in; and in the spring of 1766 America celebrated this victory in all its taverns by innumerable toasts to liberty.

Second Round

In 1767 the Chancellor of the Exchequer was Charles Townshend, a charming and paradoxical man, as witty as he was indiscreet. Townshend, in a speech that was much relished by the House, said, in effect: 'We have had enough of this. The Assembly in New York must be suspended until it is ready to quarter troops. Since the customary reprisal of the Americans is to refuse to vote their governors' pay, we must assure the latters' salaries by taxes levied upon the Americans. What taxes? Since the Americans prefer, no one knows why, external taxes, well and good. They shall have external taxes.' No sooner proposed than voted. This time the British Parliament believed itself on firm ground. The wildest American radical had never disputed Parliament's right to levy customs duties. . . . The radicals in Boston were now wondering whether Townshend's acceptance of the principle of external taxes had not concealed a trap. But this time the argument was harder for them to sustain than in the case of the Stamp Act. On what pretext could they oppose what the colonists had accepted for one hundred fifty years? John Dickinson, a dignified and honest Whig lawyer and the author of *Letters from a Farmer in Pennsylvania*, a series of masterly political essays, found a way of doing it. He explained that the danger of the tax was not so much in the tax itself as in the intention of those who levied it. Taxation designed to regulate commerce was legitimate; taxation intended to produce revenue and to pay officials was not. Benjamin Franklin, who possessed a clear and honest mind, which is dangerous in time of revolution, thought these distinctions not very

clear. He would have found it simpler to say: 'Either Parliament can make all laws for America; or it cannot make any.' This formula had the advantage of stating the true problem, which was that Americans at the bottom of their hearts no longer wanted to accept *any* law from England, and thus of forcing America and England to seek some new formula of imperial union. But Franklin was the only one to see this larger aspect of the question.

The colonists had already made the discovery that, in the eyes of the English merchants, a refusal to trade constituted the strongest of arguments. It was this embargo that had led to the abrogation of the Stamp Act; they made use of the same method to deal with the new taxes. In 1769 the imports from England to New York fell from four hundred eighty-two thousand pounds to seventy-four thousand pounds. In Boston the tension mounted dangerously. The Massachusetts Assembly, which had sent circular letters to the other Colonies, urging common action for the defense of their liberties, received an order in the king's name to annul this resolution. On the evening of March 5, 1770, a fire alarm drew into the streets of Boston a large crowd composed in part of young boys. It had snowed; a snowfight began, and soon the motionless red sentries became targets. One of the soldiers peppered by snowballs called for help; the guard turned out; the crowd attacked. Shots were fired, and when the scuffle was over five bodies lay on the snow. This is one account of what was called the Boston Massacre. Incidents multiplied in all the Colonies and kept irritation alive. The boycott was extended; in 1769 English exports to the Colonies had dropped by a million pounds. It was evident that Lord North, the prime minister, hoped to follow a policy of appeasement. This policy found allies in America. But the radicals were biding their time, and at their head was Samuel Adams, whom Governor Thomas Hutchinson, his victim, called sometimes the 'Machiavelli of chaos,' sometimes the 'incendiary in chief.'

Samuel Adams, the oracle of the people of Boston, was the son of a businessman who, after a long period of prosperity, had been partially ruined by a decree of the British government against a bank in which he held interests. This was

ENGLISH TEA BEING THROWN INTO THE SEA. Young men disguised as feathered
Mohawk Indians stole onto the *Dartmouth*, one of the merchant vessels anchored in
the port of Boston, and threw the cargo of tea overboard. This picturesque demonstration was the climax of a series of patriotic speeches accompanied by punch drinking.
Another demonstration, presided over by Samuel Adams, was attended by a quieter
audience. But it was the fake Mohawk Indians who were to remain famous, and a few
leaves of the tea—out of the 18,000 pounds thrown into the sea—are on exhibition in a
Massachusetts museum. *U.S.I.S.*

THE BOSTON MASSACRE. A mere fire alarm started the bloody scuffle of March 5, 1770. Young boys harassed the 'red sentries' and frightened the guards by throwing snowballs at them. Shots were fired in the ensuing scuffle; five members of the crowd were killed. The incident set off an uninterrupted series of violent demonstrations throughout the Colonies. *Metropolitan Museum of Art.*

the first grievance against England. The son had finished ruining the paternal business and in 1762, at the age of forty, had decided to consecrate his talents henceforth exclusively to the interests of the community. His financial integrity was never in doubt. The glitter of gold never seduced him. Samuel Adams ate little, drank little, slept little, thought much, and asserted even more. In his youth he had loved clubs, discussions over theories, and political maneuvering. Another name that Hutchinson gave him was 'Master of the Marionnettes.' Indeed, he used to spend entire days talking to the Boston shopkeepers and artisans in the doorways of their places of business or in the taverns, and this long-standing familiarity gave him great influence over their opinions. Samuel Adams had no equal in proving to the happy citizens of New England that they were miserable slaves suffering from British tyranny. His enemies said that he was intellectually the most dishonest of men and that he did not know it. It may be that he did know it and did not care. He sincerely wished to defend liberty, but he was incapable of granting it to those who did not think as he did. He condemned intolerance, and practiced it without remorse; nor did he have any great scruples in vilifying the servants of the Crown. In his manhood he had chosen as subject for his Master of Arts thesis at Harvard: 'Whether it be lawful to resist the supreme Majesty if the Commonwealth cannot otherwise be preserved?' and decided in the affirmative. Trained in Puritan scholasticism, he conceived the world as the theater of an eternal battle between liberty and tyranny. Tyranny could not be conquered except by the sovereignty of the people; liberty could not be saved except by equality. Samuel Adams was not willing to accept even parliamentary government and saw in the town meeting, where he had won his own triumphs, the one true democracy. The idea of a reconciliation with England filled him with horror. How could he live without that hatred? Between 1770 and 1773 the British government took no further action, and Samuel Adams also should have grown calmer. But he could not give up this struggle, for the struggle was within himself. On the contrary, it was during this period that he was most active in spreading his propaganda against 'our implacable enemies.' The underground

agitation continued and spread. All that was needed was an incident to provoke a crisis.

In May 1773 the East India Company, crushed by debt and close to bankruptcy, had accumulated in London a stock of seventeen million pounds of tea. In an attempt to save the company, and also as a means of suppressing the sale of Dutch tea, the British government agreed to exempt that company, and that company alone, from all export duties from England. It is difficult to imagine a more stupid project, or one better calculated to provoke disturbances in an already nervous mercantile community. When the company's first ship, the *Dartmouth*, was tied up at a dock in Boston, a large meeting organized in the Old South Meetinghouse brought together an excited crowd. Samuel Adams and Josiah Quincy denounced England, George III, Parliament, the government, and the company. 'This meeting,' said Samuel Adams finally, 'can do nothing more to save the country.' These were strong words to use in a rather small matter, but Samuel Adams knew his audience. At the same time, a group of young men held another and gayer meeting, with much drinking of punch. They dressed themselves up as Mohawk Indians. When the punch had produced its effect and the bright-colored feathers had been donned, the Mohawks ran down to the dock, boarded the *Dartmouth*, and threw the tea overboard, defying King George III to interrupt their 'tea party.' Eighteen thousand pounds of tea were washed up by the tide on neighboring beaches. A few leaves of this historic tea are today preserved in a glass bowl in a Massachusetts museum.

But the government of King George III possessed more arrogance than skill. It took a strong line. 'The bets are down,' said the king. 'The Colonies must now triumph or submit.' In spring, 1774, Parliament voted the five laws that America called the five 'intolerable acts.' The first completely closed the port of Boston until reimbursement should be made for the tea, which was to have the result of depriving Bostonians of their livelihood, and thus turning even peace-loving ones into revolutionists. The second revoked the charter of Massachusetts, gave the king the right to appoint the members of the council, and prohibited town meetings. The third transferred to England the

criminal trials arising out of the application of these laws. The fourth concerned the quartering of troops in Massachusetts towns. The fifth, called the Quebec Act, accorded religious liberty to the Catholics of Canada and substantially extended the limits of the province of Quebec, which, in the eyes of the citizens of New England, was a monstrous attempt to establish autocratic government in the Colonies, perhaps even to win French Canada over to the side of the Crown thus instituting on the American continent a balance of power. Finally, General Gage was named governor of Massachusetts. He was a soldier who believed in strong measures, and he had said to George III: 'They will be lions whilst we are lambs, but if we take the resolute part, they will undoubtedly prove very meek.' The measures enacted by the Tories could not but delight American radicals, whom they furnished with what they had hitherto most lacked—legitimate grievances. From the beginning of the affair Chatham and Franklin had advised the Bostonians to pay for the lost tea and put an end to the incident. This attempt at appeasement had exasperated and enraged Samuel Adams: 'Franklin may be a great philosopher but he is a bungling politician.'

Toward Independence

The five 'intolerable acts' aroused the indignation of Americans. All the Colonies rushed to the succor of the city of Boston 'starved' by the closing of the port. The people of Connecticut gave sheep; those of the Carolinas, rice. It was decided that a Continental Congress, whose members were to be chosen by the Committees of Correspondence or the Security Committees, should meet in Philadelphia in September 1774 to study the means of common resistance. Both Samuel Adams and his cousin John Adams, together with John Hancock, were delegates from Massachusetts.

For the many prominent men who were loyal Englishmen at heart, this was a difficult situation. They had no wish to abandon the unfortunate Bostonians; they had no desire to sacrifice their relations with the Empire, their business affairs, and their tranquillity to the passions of radicals who

VIEW OF BOSTON, 1768. By Paul Revere.

actually were distasteful to them. Their only hope was that 'if they showed their fists perhaps George III would respond by holding out his hand.' To satisfy those who favored Platonic protestation, Congress drew up a petition to the king, which asked for a return to the state of 1763. But to satisfy the radicals, the moderates had to endorse the Continental Association, which recommended to the Colonies that they break off all commercial relations with England.

A second Continental Congress met at Philadelphia in May 1775. A number of political personalities were emerging throughout the Colonies. John Adams proudly wrote that a conclave of cardinals assembled for the election of a pope could not offer better specimens. And he was right. Qualities of style and thought in this assembly would have done honor to a British Parliament of the best period. The important men of the First Congress were reunited here plus several others; the Adamses were present and John Hancock and the Lees of Virginia and other Virginians, Washington, Jefferson, and John Dickinson, 'A shadow, tall

but slender as a reed, pale as ashes.' Franklin and Morris, the first a liberal, the second a conservative, represented Pennsylvania. It was then that men in America began to be labeled *Tories* or *Patriots*. But these words for a long time had no precise meaning. If *Tory* meant *being faithful to the king*, then nine-tenths of the Americans were Tories as late as 1775; if *Patriot* meant *one who favored a break with England*, it was, in the eyes of the English and their friends, a debatable definition.

After Lexington, where the insurgents had attacked English troops that were trying to take a powder depot, a spontaneous truce occurred. Each of the adversaries tried to prove that the other had been the first to fire. The Congress in Philadelphia carried on its debates amid administrative difficulties. How was it to govern thirteen Colonies that were jealous of one another and not one of which was willing to participate in the costs? General Gage, for his part, wrote reports and did nothing. The British government sent seven thousand men under the command of Generals Howe, Clinton, and Burgoyne. To the radicals, General and Admiral

[63]

THE BUNKER HILL HAIR STYLE. An American cartoonist, inspired by the historical hairdos then current in France (*Frégate, Belle-Poule*), invented this eccentric style to commemorate the Battle of Bunker Hill, in which very severe casualties were suffered by the English. *Library of Congress, Washington.*

Howe became 'the two hateful brothers dedicated to the annals of infamy.' As for the American militia after Lexington, they came and camped around Boston, bottling up Gage's army in the city. In June 1775 Gage discovered that the Americans had fortified two hills close to Cambridge on the other side of the Charles River—Breed's Hill and Bunker Hill. The circle was growing tighter. Gage thought he would have no trouble in breaking out. He led veteran soldiers against men who, for the most part, had never been under fire and who were short of powder. Under Howe's orders, the thin red line bristling with bayonets climbed bravely to the assault of Bunker Hill. It was a massacre. The Americans, protected by a barricade, held their fire until the last moment, then shot at point-blank range. When the bullets gave out, they used screws and nails. In three assaults, the English lost a thou-

sand men out of three thousand five hundred, and a large number of officers. Finally they turned the position, and the Americans abandoned the hill, but it was a disastrous victory. The American General Greene said that they had a great deal more land they would willingly sell at the same price.

When the Congress in Philadelphia received the news of Bunker Hill, it had just chosen a commander in chief. This is always a difficult problem for a coalition army. Each important Colony thought that it had the right to command. Now there was one who seemed indicated in all respects; that was George Washington. He possessed military experience, the authority that comes from fortune and birth, and a magnificent presence that compelled respect. He was unanimously designated. His short speech of acceptance was perfect. He said he felt unequal to this task but would do his duty; he

THE BATTLE OF BUNKER HILL. By
John Trumbull. On June 17, 1775, the
English forces clashed with the Americans
who had fortified Breed's Hill in Boston,
Massachusetts. (The site is joined by a
ridge to Bunker Hill, whose name has
been given to the battle.) When they ran
out of bullets, the Americans retorted to
the British firearms and bayonets with such
projectiles as nails and screws. Both sides
claimed victory, the attackers because
they occupied the position and the
attacked because they inflicted heavy
losses on the English. *Howland S. Warren
Collection. Francis Mayer Ektachrome photo.*

BATTLE OF LEXINGTON, APRIL 19, 1775. The regular troops in orderly ▶
formation are firing at the Americans, whose front-line men, in the foreground, are falling. The others are already retreating in disarray. This is
the British official view of the clash. The American insurgents (termed
'provincials' in the British caption) are in a sorry plight, while the commander of the Royal Grenadiers, erect on his mount, in full view in the
center, does not hesitate to expose himself to enemy fire. In itself a mere
skirmish, the Battle of Lexington is of great historic significance because it
started the War of Independence. *Connecticut Historical Society, Hartford,
Connecticut.*

◀ GEORGE WASHINGTON. By Charles Willson Peale. The hero of the War of Independence shown here in the uniform of colonel of the Virginia Militia. *Washington and Lee University, Lexington, Virginia.*

THOMAS PAINE. By J.W. Jarvis. This completely unknown English citizen rallied a hesitant public opinion around the struggle for independence with his pamphlet *Common Sense. National Gallery of Art, Washington.*

would accept no salary save for the reimbursement of his expenses.

Washington made the trip from Philadelphia to Boston on horseback in fifteen days. On the way he learned of the Battle of Bunker Hill, and his first question was: 'Did the militia fight?' 'Yes.' 'The liberties of the country are safe.' On July 2 he was at Cambridge. In March 1776 Washington had a great success at Boston. Thanks to the cannon he had seized from Fort Ticonderoga, he was able to take possession of Dorchester Heights, one of the hills that dominate Boston. Howe had to retake it or evacuate. A frontal attack, like that at Bunker Hill, would have been a slaughter. General Howe did not wish useless bloodshed. He decided to embark his army and take it to Halifax. One hundred seventy sailing vessels, a veritable forest of masts, carried away the English and their partisans. At the same hour Washington made a triumphal entry into Boston at the head of his troops. Most of the loyalists who left that day were never to see their country again.

It was King George III who forced the colonists to cross their Rubicon. In his speech from the throne in October 1775 he said that England would never renounce her Colonies, that she would exact respect by force of arms, but that she would treat with indulgence her erring children if they sought the king's pardon. The unhappy sovereign could not understand how little disposed George Washington, with a thousand like him, would be to seek amnesty in the role of prodigal sons. This was the first blunder. The second was to announce a policy based on strength at a time when the British Parliament had no strength.

The Speech from the Throne had been an insult to Americans; the sending of foreign mercenaries was a provocation; the taking of Boston was an encouragement. After this, public sentiment, which had hitherto been reserved, swung over in favor of a break. The publication of a pamphlet, 'Common Sense,' the work of Thomas Paine, an unknown Englishman, brought about the crystallization of resistance.

Washington had forcefully expressed himself in favor of independence, and his entry into Boston gave him great prestige. Virginia followed him, partly for political reasons, partly for economic

THE DECLARATION OF INDEPENDENCE. Third name in fourth column, Benjamin Franklin, and fourth name in last column, John Adams, future President of the United States. *Library of Congress, Washington. U.S.I.S.*

DECLARATION OF INDEPENDENCE. By John Trumbull. Signed on July 4, 1776, it bore the signatures of the representatives from the thirteen states. *Yale University Art Gallery, New Haven.*

ones. New England was completely in accord. It was decided that the preparation of a declaration of independence should be entrusted to a committee of which John Adams, Thomas Jefferson, and Benjamin Franklin were to be members. Jefferson was a delegate from Virginia who had made a name for himself in the Congress. A man of thirty-three, already famous in his own section, he feared 'the morbid violence of discussions' and remained silent during the meetings, but in committee and in conversation he was 'prompt, frank, explicit and decisive.' These qualities had resulted in his being chosen one of the committee; they had the further result of prompting the committee to entrust him with drawing up the Declaration. On July 2 all the states except New York, which abstained from the vote, decided to break with England, and on July 4 the Declaration was adopted. Couriers bore it immediately to the four corners of the new nation.

The Declaration of Independence was addressed to the whole world: 'When in the Course of human Events, it becomes necessary for one People to dissolve the Political Bands which have connected them with another, and to assume among the Powers of the Earth, the separate and equal Station to which the Laws of Nature and of Nature's God entitle them, a decent Respect to the Opinions of Mankind requires that they should declare the causes which impel them to the Separation.' There followed a statement of the principles on which the Declaration was based: 'We hold these Truths to be self-evident, that all Men are created equal, that they are endowed by their Creator with certain unalienable Rights, that among these are Life, Liberty, and the Pursuit of Happiness.' This part of the Declaration, inspired by Locke, and also Rousseau, has served as a basis for all democratic movements in the world, beginning with the French Revolution. It affirms that the object of all government is to guarantee the rights of man; that all government derives its powers from the consent of the governed; that if a government fails to guarantee these rights, the duty of the people is to modify or abolish it. The rest of the document, of less permanent value, was

a long list of grievances: the denial of representation, oppressive laws, acts of war. King George III was violently attacked, somewhat to the displeasure of John Adams: 'I never believed George to be a tyrant.' But Jefferson loved tirades and fiery eloquence. The document concludes by stating that the Colonies have appealed to England for justice and have not been heard, and that 'We, therefore . . . Declare, That these United Colonies are, and of Right ought to be, Free and Independent States.'

Military Operations

It was the cannons' turn to speak. The British government had a reasonable plan for the war in America. England had control of the sea and so could take possession of the harbors and waterways. Of the latter the most important was the Hudson, the key to the campaign. If the English got control of that, they could cut the Colonies in two, thus rendering the administration of the new nation difficult and resistance impossible. Hence this plan: General Howe was to go by sea from Halifax to New York, take possession of this port, and proceed up the Hudson River; an army coming from Canada by way of Lake Champlain was to reach the river at Albany. By the juncture of these two forces the Colonies would be divided. Meanwhile a third army, commanded by Lord Cornwallis, was to land at Charleston and rally the southern loyalists. The fate of Cornwallis's army was quickly decided; for it was not even able to get ashore at Charleston, where it was welcomed by gunfire. 'We never received such a drubbing in our lives,' said one of the English sailors. This fleet, badly damaged, beat a hasty retreat, and at New York joined Howe's, which had come from Halifax.

Washington, who understood the importance of the Hudson Valley just as well as the English, had moved his army from Boston to New York by land and had established his headquarters in that city in April 1776. Fort Washington and Fort Lee had been built to defend the entrance to the valley at the point where the George Washington Bridge now

GENERAL JOHN BURGOYNE. By Joshua Reynolds. After the English troops under Cornwallis failed to land, Sir John Burgoyne and Richard Howe were put in command. Burgoyne was no more successful than Cornwallis, and capitulated in Saratoga on October 17, 1778. *Frick Collection, New York.*

RICHARD HOWE. By John Singleton Copley. Convinced that the taking of Philadelphia, the real 'capital' of the new American nation, would end all resistance, Howe vainly kept trying to capture the city. This enabled Washington to isolate Burgoyne and force him to capitulate. *National Maritime Museum, Greenwich.*

stands. Washington's army numbered less than twenty thousand men; Sir William Howe's army, which had been brought from Halifax, was about thirty thousand strong, and the fleet gave him the advantage of mobility. The commander of this fleet was Lord Howe, a crusty but kindly man, taciturn and timorous, whom his men had nicknamed Black Dick. Howe was in an advantageous position, for he had the means of landing his army wherever he wished in Washington's rear. What could the latter do? Nothing. He had neither enough troops to guard all the coast nor troops mobile enough to be rapidly transported to a threatened position. It was madness to try to defend New York, but such were the orders of Congress. Washington had detached some of his men and posted them on Long Island. This was a dangerous position for the Americans; they were dependent upon water transport for their communications and the enemy had control of the sea. On August 22 Howe dispatched half his army, under cover of night, across Long Island to take Brooklyn from the rear. He attacked at daybreak with complete success,

and the Americans lost two thousand men. They retreated, fighting as they went, but Washington's position on Manhattan was hardly better. The English fleet landed troops on the east shores of Manhattan at the place where Thirty-fourth Street is today. On that day Howe could have cut off the retreat of a part of the American army, but he stopped for luncheon at the house of Mrs. Murray on Murray Hill, and during this time four thousand Americans under Israel Putnam were able to escape. Then Washington placed the larger part of his army on the right bank of the Hudson, and by a series of skillful maneuvers eluded the attacks of Howe, who attempted each time to turn the American position by landing, and found each time that the Americans had withdrawn farther to the north. Finally Howe abandoned his plan, returned to Manhattan, and attacked Fort Washington. There he seized about three thousand men as well as cannons and ammunition. Fort Lee was abandoned in time, and what remained of the American army beat a retreat across New Jersey. Lee, whom Washington had left with seven thousand men on the Hudson

[75]

farther to the north and whom he now ordered to join him, carefully refrained from moving and viewed without displeasure the difficulties that encompassed Washington, whom he considered feeble and incompetent. Soon Washington had no more than four thousand men with him. Washington, informed by his spies of Howe's movements, conceived the idea of an audacious stroke, and on Christmas Day he crossed the Delaware and seized Trenton. Then, when Lord Cornwallis was sent to drive him out, instead of fleeing and recrossing the Delaware, Washington allowed the enemy to advance and then boldly took up his position athwart the English lines of communication at Princeton. Cornwallis, in a panic, fearing to be cut off, beat a precipitate retreat. The skillful tactics of Washington had earned him his first victory. The colonel of militia was not a bad general.

But all these campaigns were not *the* campaign. The plan in London remained unalterable. Sir John Burgoyne was to come down from Canada with an army; Sir William Howe was to proceed up the Hudson with another army. They were to meet at Albany, and the war would be over. Lord George Germain, Secretary of State for the Colonies, in his office at Whitehall, approved the plan for the army in Canada and sent a copy to Howe. But he overlooked two things: the first was to order Howe to go and meet Burgoyne; the second is that it is impossible, from a distance of several thousand miles, to foresee what difficulties there may be in an operation that involves penetrating virgin forests and crossing unexplored country. Howe had decided to take Philadelphia. It was a natural strategic mistake for a European to make, for whom the capital of a nation is its heart. But America was a body with thirteen hearts. During the entire spring of 1777 Howe had hesitated. He was ill informed about the condition of Washington's forces. To venture into New Jersey might mean to risk the re-enactment of the Cornwallis fiasco at Princeton. He tried in vain to draw Washington onto open ground, failed to do so, and thus squandered a large part of the year 1777. Finally in July he mysteriously embarked his army, leaving Clinton in New York. Where was he bound? Washington greatly feared that he was going to reoccupy Boston, which was very poorly defended at that time. At last, after five weeks of waiting, he learned that Howe had landed on the shores of Chesapeake Bay. And so it was Philadelphia that the English general was once more threatening. And he was going there by sea. Washington was delighted at this news. He had already sent General Gates with a small army against Burgoyne. As soon as it became clear that Howe was at a distance, this task became easy. 'Now let all New England turn out and entirely crush Genl Burgoyne!' wrote Washington. While this operation was going on, Howe would take Philadelphia but he would lose the campaign.

At the start everything went well. Burgoyne took possession of Ticonderoga, which commanded the route through Lake Champlain. He captured prisoners and seized one hundred twenty-eight cannon.

But at the end of a month, Burgoyne's troops were hungry and discouraged. The course of wisdom would have been to strike obliquely toward New England, where at least he would have found a civilized country. But the orders of the War Office were explicit. He must proceed to Albany and there meet Howe. While the unhappy Burgoyne, through adherence to discipline, was hurrying to destruction, Howe was at sea with his army sailing toward Chesapeake Bay. Soon Burgoyne's situation became desperate. He shut himself up at Saratoga and awaited his fate. On October 17 Burgoyne capitulated. Five thousand men laid down their arms. Gates had promised them the honors of war and permission to embark at Boston for England. Congress disavowed him. Burgoyne's army wandered for a long time along the roads and finally through the fields of Massachusetts. When, later on, peace had been signed and a move was made to repatriate the army, it was discovered that it no longer existed. The soldiers had become colonists. The virgin continent possessed such powers of assimilation that it transformed into citizens those who had come as enemies.

France Enters the War

Louis XVI succeeded Louis XV, and Vergennes succeeded Choiseul. To aid the Colonies without

◄ BRITISH TROOPS DEFEATED AT SARATOGA. By Lavis de Ramberg, 1785. Five thousand men of Burgoyne's army laid down their arms, and General Gates promised them honorable terms. *Charles Allen Munn document, Metropolitan Museum of Art.*

BATTLE OF PRINCETON. Painting by
Mercer. After crossing the Delaware,
Washington confidently waited for Lord
Cornwallis to counterattack, and thus carry
out his orders, which were to destroy
Washington's newly established bridgehead.
Washington even daringly pretended he was
coming to meet the English troops, by
taking positions athwart their lines of
communication in Princeton, on January 3,
1777. The maneuver succeeded, and Cornwallis retreated forthwith. *Historical Society
of Pennsylvania. Francis G. Mayer Ektachrome
photo.*

[78]

going as far as war, this was Vergennes' program. But how was it to be carried out? It was necessary to find some individual who might at need be disavowed and charge him with the task of secretly furnishing supplies. There was a man who seemed especially made to play this role, a man rich in ingenuity, poor in capital, daring in action and a steadfast friend of liberty. This was Caron de Beaumarchais, a writer of genius and an adventurer by profession. In London Beaumarchais had met an American, Arthur Lee, who had talked to him about the needs of his fellow countrymen and the ease with which this great nation could pay, in tobacco and other commodities, for what it bought. Arthur Lee was a dangerous liar; but Beaumarchais, who did not know this, immediately saw the possibility of a glorious and profitable transaction. On his return, he made his report to Vergennes, and it was decided that Beaumarchais should found a fictitious business house: Rodrigue Hortalez et Cie, and that the French government and the Spanish government should each contribute one million pounds to the imaginary Hortalez, who was to make use of this capital to buy uniforms, cannon, and powder for the Americans. It is easy to imagine the joy that the author of *The Barber of Seville* would derive from the task of creating out of whole cloth and lodging in a fine hotel in the Faubourg du Temple a Spanish merchant as powerful as he was fictitious. Life became a comedy madder than any on the stage. Actually, Beaumarchais, the secret agent, was more active than secret. Lord Stormont, who had got wind of the affair, went to Vergennes and inquired whether France was supporting the enemies of England. Vergennes replied with imperturbable gravity that there could be no question of that.

Meanwhile the United States Congress and its Committee of Foreign Correspondence (which was functioning as the State Department), learning of the favorable sentiment in France, began to think about making use of it. It was decided to send Silas Deane to Paris. Vergennes received the American envoy, told him that, since France was at peace with England, he could not officially act but that he would close his eyes to everything that was done unofficially. He urged Silas Deane to negotiate with Rodrigue Hortalez, that is to say with Beaumarchais, to whom the French arsenals would

deliver excellent cannon, first effacing, to be sure, from a sense of decency and prudence, the king's arms. The mythical Hortalez evinced incomparable energy, delivered materials of war sufficient to equip about twenty-five thousand men, but was never paid. The misunderstanding was not cleared up during Beaumarchais's life, and he died in poverty in 1799. Volunteers came in throngs. Many things drew them toward America: the nobleness of the cause, their rancor against England, desire for adventure, the virgin forests, the beautiful Indian girls, the hope of rapid advancement. But the Americans were justly irritated to find themselves commanded by Europeans who did not even speak their language. The volunteers, who expected to be greeted with grateful enthusiasm, were filled with consternation at the coolness of their reception. But the best of them, as always happens, triumphed over troublesome prejudices.

Such was the case of the young Marquis de Lafayette. This nineteen-year-old officer belonged to two of the great families of France, one by birth, one by alliance, for at the age of sixteen he had married Marie-Françoise de Noailles, daughter of the Duke d'Ayen and granddaughter of the Duke de Noailles. It was at Metz that he had first heard the Duke of Gloucester, who was the brother and enemy of the English king, talk about the American Revolution. The Duke said that right was on the side of the Colonies; at Metz he made two converts, the Count de Broglie and the young Lafayette. Broglie conceived at that time the idea of making America the scene of France's revenge against England, but he was too important a personage to go in any capacity save that of commander in chief. Lafayette with two of his friends, the Viscount de Noailles and the Count de Ségur, went to Silas Deane and asked to be accepted for service.

Silas Deane had not yet enlisted recruits of such quality, and he was so dazzled that he promised a commission as major general to a boy. But when the Duke d'Ayen learned of his son-in-law's plans, he raised a great uproar. Lafayette secretly bought a ship, *La Victoire*, fled to Bordeaux, then to Spain with other officers, and ordered the captain to set sail for North America. After fifty-four days at sea he landed at Georgetown, in South Carolina. From

WASHINGTON'S FOOD PROBLEM. While the British were enjoying the comforts and pleasures of Philadelphia, Washington's tattered army was half-starved and half-frozen at bleak Valley Forge. *Historical Society of Pennsylvania.*

there he proceeded to Philadelphia, where he was coldly received by a member of Congress who treated him as an adventurer. It was discouraging. Lafayette wrote to Congress that after the sacrifices he had made for the cause, he believed he had the right to request two favors; that of serving without pay and at his own expense and that of serving as a volunteer and ordinary soldier. The tone was proud. The Marquis de Lafayette was appointed major general in the United States Army. He was not yet twenty years old.

He joined Washington at the time when Howe was marching against Philadelphia and took part in the confused and indecisive Battle of Brandywine, where he conducted himself well and was wounded. When, after the loss of the city, Washington established his winter quarters at Valley Forge, not far from Philadelphia, Lafayette followed him.

Washington had at once been attracted to the young man and had adopted him. They were born to understand each other.

Naturally the great desire of Congress was to secure a treaty of alliance with France. On December 17, 1777, Franklin was informed that Louis XVI had decided to recognize the independence of the United States and to sign a treaty of commerce and friendship. In exchange for this alliance France demanded no special return. She did not want to take anything that the Americans might regret in the future; she did not desire any territory. The only condition was that neither ally should make a separate peace. 'Such was the bounty of the King,' the American commissioners acknowledged, that nothing was proposed to them that they could not accept in a spirit of perfect equality. It would have been to England's interest to prosecute the war

[81]

LAFAYETTE'S VISIT TO MOUNT VERNON. By Thomas P. Rossiter.
The Bettman Archive.

GEORGE WASHINGTON AT YORKTOWN. By George Washington ▶
Parke Custis, Washington's foster son. *Alexandria-Washington Lodge
No. 22, A.F. and A.M., Alexandria, Virginia.*

[82]

vigorously and bring it to a quick conclusion. But the England of George III was not that of Pitt. It would have been easy for Sir William Howe to wipe out Washington at Valley Forge, where he then had only two thousand hungry and half-naked men, but he did not do it. The first French fleet was commanded by Count d'Estaing, a newly appointed admiral who had made his career in the army. He was a man 'of brilliant conceptions and feeble execution.' He tried to take Newport. It was a failure. At the end of 1778 Lafayette had asked for and obtained a leave of absence to go to France. He wished to reawaken enthusiasm for the American cause, whose defeats and Count d'Estaing's unfavorable comments had inevitably dampened. Washington willingly let him go, believing that he was more useful as a propagandist than as a soldier. He was well received at Versailles. The queen herself was eager to see him and hear him speak of 'our good Americans.' His presence alone and the emotion it excited were the best propaganda. To Maurepas and Vergennes he convincingly explained the situation in America. They decided to send six thousand men to be placed at the personal disposal of General Washington to use as he saw fit. But since Lafayette was too young and inexperienced, command of the expedition was given to the Count de Rochambeau. Lafayette, however, was to precede the troops and announce to Washington the success of his mission (February 1780).

Because the Minister of the Navy was Monsieur de Sartines, 'whose watch was always slow,' Rochambeau and his army were at Brest long before the transports. These arrived by such slow degrees that Rochambeau finally decided to wait no longer and left with fifty-five hundred men but without his cavalry. He had fine regiments and officers who bore the greatest names in France: Montmorency, Custine, Chartres, Noailles, Lauzun. In July 1780 the convoy arrived without losses within sight of Rhode Island; at Newport the troops were well received.

The French officers of all ranks made themselves agreeable by that courtesy which characterizes the French nation. Rochambeau had an opportunity to see Washington himself at Hartford. The French general staff were delighted by the American commander in chief. He seemed to them frank, dignified, a little sad, and very impressive in manner: 'A true hero.' Lafayette served as interpreter.

The two generals, Rochambeau and Washington, agreed to ask the king of France for reinforcements. To win the war, they would need thirty thousand men and control of the sea. France's response was generous. It was brought by the ship *La Concorde* on May 16, 1781. Six million pounds in gold were sent to Washington, thus enabling him at length to pay his army. Moreover, Admiral Count de Grasse had left for the West Indies with a large fleet, and through all the summer he would be at Washington's disposal. There was urgent need of preparing plans for this campaign at once. Washington suggested an attack on New York, which remained, in his eyes, the strategic center of the Colonies. Rochambeau hesitated; he would have preferred a campaign against Cornwallis, who was winning Pyrrhic victories in the South against Greene. The advice of Rochambeau prevailed. The French army and the American army, now united, crossed New Jersey on their way to Virginia. In Philadelphia they learned that twenty-eight French ships of the line had just arrived in Chesapeake Bay and had landed three thousand men who had joined Lafayette. Cornwallis had expected Rodney's fleet; he saw Admiral de Grasse's instead. Soon sixteen thousand men were besieging Yorktown. An English fleet under Admiral Graves tried to break the blockade of the city. But Admiral Graves was defeated in Chesapeake Bay and had to beat a retreat toward New York. There remained only one hope for Cornwallis: the arrival of Clinton with an army to relieve him. But Clinton delayed. He finally embarked on October 19. That was the day

◀ THE TAKING OF BRANSTON HILL BY THE MARQUIS DE BOUILLÉ. Drawing by Le Paon. *Blérancourt Museum. Photographic Archives.*

when Yorktown surrendered. The English army
filed past between two lines of victors, the one
French, the other American, in a respectful silence.

The Making of the Peace

The capture of Yorktown was not an event of such
importance that it must inevitably have led to peace.
A great country like England, which had as yet
thrown only a small part of its resources into this
war, could easily have continued the struggle if
it had been willing to accept the necessary sacrifices.
But English public opinion was becoming hostile to
this campaign. Great orators—Chatham, Burke,
Fox—were making it unpopular; the Whigs called
Washington's army 'our army' and discouraged
enlistments; Dr. Johnson and Edward Gibbon,
whom the ministry employed to defend its policy,
did not have the same prestige. The merchants
wept for their lost clients and hoped for a reconciliation. After all, what did it matter whether the
Colonies were independent so long as they were still
markets? Congress, for its part, favored peace
provided it was an honorable one. In 1779 it had
decided to send a plenipotentiary to Paris, and
hesitated for some time between John Adams,

Jay, and Franklin. Franklin had been much maligned
in Congress, as he had been throughout his career,
and John Adams inspired more confidence than did
Jay in New England, which wanted its fishing
rights adequately safeguarded during the peace
negotiations. And so Jay was appointed minister
to Madrid, and Adams was instructed to prepare
plans for the peace, but he was to act in accord with
Franklin and Jay. In addition to the fishing rights
and independence, the thorny points were: the
western frontier of the United States, the navigation
of the Mississippi, and indemnity to the loyalists.
The last was particularly delicate because England
could not honorably abandon her loyal subjects
who had lost everything for her, while in the eyes
of the colonists these worthies were traitors,
justly stripped of their possessions. The advice and
opinions of the French government were simple.
The government wanted peace. The war had been,
and still was, costly to France whose finances were
already compromised. France had no territorial
ambition; she wanted neither to get back Canada
nor to see it annexed by the United States. But she
had made commitments to Spain, and Spain
refused to make peace until Gibraltar was restored
to her. Meanwhile the United States was giving

[87]

DAVID TWINING'S RESIDENCE. By Edward Hicks. It is typical both of the naïve art of the early American school and of the patriarchal life of the United States proprietors in the years just after the War of Independence. The master still wears the habit of the heroic days of the devout Mayflower Pilgrims. *Colonial Williamsburg photograph.*

[88]

very little thought to Spain, and none at all to Gibraltar. It wanted independence, an indemnity or in place of that, Canada, and a settlement of the western boundary question and that of the fishing rights. As for England, since Yorktown she had, at heart, accepted defeat. Lord George Germain had gone to take the news of the surrender to Lord North at 10 Downing Street. A friend asked him afterwards: 'How did he take it?' 'How did he take it? As he would have taken a ball in the breast. For he opened his arms, exclaiming wildly as he paced up and down the apartment during a few minutes: "O God! It is all over!"' The king began by saying that he hoped no one would think that these events would alter his principles. The poor king never suspected that in saying that, he had given an excellent definition of folly. But 'facts are stubborn things.' In February 1782 a motion in favor of peace was defeated in Parliament by a single vote. Lord North's ministry was replaced by Rockingham's ministry, a Whig cabinet in which Fox was foreign secretary.

Lord Shelburne, minister of the Colonies in the new Whig ministry, was an old friend of Franklin and the most liberal of men. The astute and courteous Franklin sent a note of congratulations, and a secret negotiation began between the two men. The English offered the Colonies their independence on the condition that the peace between France and England should honor the Treaty of Paris. The negotiation had been made easier by the defeat of Spain at Gibraltar and that of Admiral de Grasse in the West Indies. England had become once more mistress of the seas. France's promise not to make peace before restoring Gibraltar to Spain fell by force of circumstances. Vergennes tried to persuade the English to exchange Gibraltar for Florida, but failed.

There remained only one means of satisfying Spain: to find a compensation for her in America. Spain had large interests there, and she had watched, not without uneasiness, the birth of the United States so close to Spanish Mexico. If the American Colonies were freed from England and had at their disposal the immense territory situated between the Alleghenies and the Mississippi, what developments might not follow? Count Avenida wrote to the king of Spain: 'This federal republic is but a pigmy in the cradle. A day will come when it will be a great and even a formidable colossus on this continent. Freedom of conscience and the facilities for increase in population which are given by immense territories, as well as the advantages of the new government, will attract the farmers and artisans of all countries. In a very few years we shall observe to our regret the tyrannical existence of the colossus.' And so Vergennes suggested a division of the Indian territories into English and Spanish zones of influence. This was greatly displeasing to Jay, who wanted a frontier for the United States on the Mississippi.

On the question of independence there was no longer any disagreement. England gave up the territories between the Alleghenies and the Mississippi. And this river was to be the dividing line between the United States and the Spanish possessions. Navigation of the Mississippi was to be open to both Americans and English. England was to keep Canada. The frontier between the United States and Canada was somewhat vaguely drawn. The Americans were to retain fishing rights on the banks of Newfoundland and the Gulf of Saint Lawrence. All private debts on both sides were to remain due and were to be paid in undepreciated currency. There remained the question of the loyalists. England demanded that their civil rights and confiscated property be restored. The Americans simply promised 'to recommend to the States' measures of reparation. It was an empty promise and the English knew it very well, but it saved their face. By the treaty France regained Saint Pierre and Miquelon and some concessions in India and Africa. Spain got Florida. All this was unimportant. The United States was the only real beneficiary of the war.

The treaty was signed in September 1783. At this time an English army was still in occupation of New York. It waited before withdrawing until the last loyalists, both in that city and in Charleston, had been assembled for evacuation. These unfortunates were the chief victims of the war. England was losing only a few Colonies; the loyalists had lost everything. Finally, on November 25, 1783, the last English vessel left the port of New York. The English consoled themselves by predicting the most gloomy future for the United States.

III
The Birth of a Nation

The Constitution

Washington took leave of his troops in New York on December 4, 1783. He proceeded on horseback to Annapolis, where Congress was in session, and there solemnly resigned his powers as commander in chief. The weakness of Congress mollified fears; it also created dangers. This assembly had issued paper money, the continental dollar. What value could this dollar have when the states, the sole owners of the real wealth, would not accept responsibility for it? The infant industries that had been created in America during the war possessed neither capital nor reserves. The states called *United* declared commercial wars on one another. New York raised trade barriers against New Jersey; Connecticut boycotted New York. Within the same state one class opposed another.

It was far from true that nothing went well during these so-called critical years. The country's wealth was enormous; the war damage was negligible; there were considerable spoils to be divided. But the postwar Americans saw only their woes, and they suffered from them. They were irritated and harassed

by grievances. One of the most difficult problems for the Confederation had been the division of the immense territory that extended to the west between the Alleghenies and the Mississippi. How should these lands be distributed to the pioneers? In 1784 Jefferson devised a plan. He divided the Western Territory into ten states that were to become parts of the Union as soon as the density of their population justified it. The plan was rejected, in part because the southern states were opposed to the clause dealing with slavery. Congress decided to organize the new territories only when powerful private interests demanded it. In March 1786 certain citizens met in Boston and founded the Ohio Company of Associates, which offered to buy immense territories for a million dollars payable in continental certificates. They retained a skillful negotiator, the Reverend Manasseh Cutler, to represent them in Congress and to secure the establishment of a territorial government. The Reverend Manasseh Cutler was not much impressed by the disinterestedness of Congress; he was able to arrange the concession desired by his group only by drawing into the affair some very prominent men who turned into speculators. Out of five million acres granted the Company, three and a half million had to be used to compensate political support. It was scandalous, but only at that price could the Company obtain its concession, in 1787.

The Northwest was temporarily given a governor (who was, as it happened, General St. Clair, president of Congress), judges, officials. For the future it was decided: (*a*) that territories containing less than five thousand inhabitants should be administered by Congress; (*b*) that territories containing more than five thousand but less than sixty thousand inhabitants should have the right of governing themselves by elected assemblies, but not the right of being represented in Congress; (*c*) that with more than sixty thousand inhabitants the new state should be admitted to the Union on an equal footing with the original states; (*d*) that civil and religious liberty and trial by jury should be guaranteed to the inhabitants of the territories. The Northwest Ordinance is of capital importance. Through it, the federal principle triumphed over the colonial principle on the American continent. Every new populated district that entered the Union was to become, after a trial period, a member of the Union. No nation had ever applied to its future annexations principles as generous as these. A convention assembled in Philadelphia in May 1787 with a slowness that was owing to the difficulties of travel. It was, as Jefferson said, an 'assembly of demi-gods.' George Washington was unanimously chosen as President; he was seated on a dais, and his authority, combined with the dignity of his bearing, lent the deliberations incomparable distinction. The most intelligent man at the convention was probably the young delegate from New York, Alexander Hamilton; but the stiffness of his manner kept him from eloquence and his ideas from popularity. He was a partisan of federal unity even at the cost of states' rights. He had no confidence in the common sense, intelligence, or good will of the masses. His was a strong and pessimistic mind, and he believed that force and self-interest alone control men's actions and that institutions survive only if it is to the interest of the rich and influential classes to maintain them. James Madison, the delegate from Virginia, had hardly more illusions about humanity than Hamilton. 'If men were angels,' he said, 'there would be no need of government at all.' But he managed to refrain from such cutting statements as Hamilton's. Therefore he had much greater authority than Hamilton, and became known as the Father of the Constitution. Very different from most revolutionary assemblies, this one was realistic and objective. The men who composed it almost all had large economic interests to defend. The distinguished men who met at Philadelphia had at heart the future of the country that they had jointly founded. The gravity of their mission filled them with a quasi-religious feeling. The enterprise was new; it was great; it demanded reflection and solemnity. And so the founders provided themselves with a setting of silence and mystery. All the sessions took place behind closed doors.

The Constitution of the United States, an excellent document, is essentially a compromise between the necessity of creating a republican government in order to keep the support of the people and a desire to provide against demagogy in order to retain the confidence of the notables. In the plan as it was adopted equal powers were balanced against each other. The President was to play the roles that in England belonged to the king and the prime minister. Some even desired that he should be called His Majesty the President. In actual fact, the President of the United States was (and remains) much more powerful than the king of England. He was to be chosen by a special body of electors, selected in each state as the legislature should decide and equal in number to the total number of senators and representatives of that state in the

JAMES MADISON. By G.P.A.Healy. A delegate of the State of Vir- ▶ ginia, he played a large role in drafting the final text of the Constitution of the United States of America. Care was wisely exercised to strike a just balance between the interests of the people and those of the officials. *Blérancourt Museum. Hachette photo.*

United States Congress. The fact that George Washington was the first President helped to invest the office with an immense and merited prestige. A vice-president was to be chosen at the same time as the President. Two Houses were to represent the nation. Certain timorous spirits would have liked to remove both from popular election. 'The people,' said Elbridge Gerry, 'are the dupes of pretended patriots.' But Hamilton himself recognized that it was essential that at least one of the Houses (the House of Representatives) should be directly elected by the people. At that time there was no question of universal suffrage. In the America of 1787 the property qualification for voting caused no great outcry because of the great number of small property owners.

Although the new Constitution admitted the principle of popular sovereignty, it did nothing to assure the people as a whole of their civic rights. It was later, through amendments, that universal suffrage was established in the United States. Election to the Senate, which was to take the place of the House of Lords, was left to the legislatures of the states. There was a long discussion as to whether, in calculating the number of representatives from each state, slaves should be taken into account. The South demanded it. The North thought the demand scandalous. Finally a compromise was adopted: the slaves, although they did not have the right to vote, should be counted to the extent of three-fifths of their number in calculating the number of seats for each state. This was absurd, but all compromises are absurd, being designed to mollify feelings and not to satisfy the intelligence.

Justice was elevated above the majority rule. *Vox justitiae, vox Dei.* This was a genuine safeguard for the minority against a demagogic majority; but later, frequent complaints were to be heard about the tyranny of the judiciary power in America.

A problem full of danger was the division of authority between the federal and state governments.

The powers and functions of the Federal Government were enumerated in the Constitution. It had the right to raise taxes for the payment of debts and to assure the defense of the United States; to borrow money; to regulate commerce between the states and with foreign countries; to coin money; to establish a postal service; to declare war; to raise armies and militia. All the powers not enumerated were reserved to the states. Meanwhile the people in whose name the Constitution was being proclaimed knew nothing about it. It had to be submitted to Congress, and to the conventions in each state. Then began a very lively opposition. The nation split into Federalists and Antifederalists. The Antifederalists said that the lawyers, the savants, and the rich men had reached an understanding for the purpose of making poor illiterate people swallow this pill, the Constitution.

The Parties and Federalism

The first election put into office the men who had forged the Constitution. The electors chosen by the nation unanimously selected George Washington as the first President of the United States; John Adams became vice-president. In Hamilton and Jefferson, whom Washington had just made colleagues, were incarnated two opposed and contradictory political philosophies. No historian has been able to speak of these two men without drawing parallel portraits because in this case the parallel is in the nature of their beings. Hamilton represented the party of resistance; Jefferson the party of movement. Jefferson, the rich planter, the owner of numerous slaves, was a democrat; Hamilton, the illegitimate child, the man without fortune, without slaves, was an aristocrat. Hamilton, who had French blood and a wholly French logic, admired the British tradition; Jefferson, who had no French blood, admired Diderot and Rousseau. Hamilton wanted to make the United States an industrial country; Jefferson,

THE CONSTITUTION OF THE UNITED STATES OF AMERICA, September 17, 1787. The two ▶ excerpts on the opposite page are respectively the preamble, which proclaims the aims of the Constitution as being to 'establish justice, insure domestic tranquility, provide for the common defence, promote the general welfare, and secure the blessings of liberty to ourselves and our posterity,' and the last page, which bears the signatures of the members of the Constitutional Convention, in particular those of James Madison and President George Washington. *U.S.I.S.*

[94]

We the People

of the United States, in order to form a more perfect Union, establish Justice, insure domestic Tranquility, provide for the common defence, promote the general Welfare, and secure the Blessings of Liberty to ourselves and our Posterity, do ordain and establish this Constitution for the United States of America.

Article. I.

Section 1. All legislative Powers herein granted shall be vested in a Congress of the United States, which shall consist of a Senate and House of Representatives.

Section 2. The House of Representatives shall be composed of Members chosen every second Year by the People of the several States, and the Electors in each State shall have the Qualifications requisite for Electors of the most numerous Branch of the State Legislature.

No Person shall be a Representative who shall not have attained to the Age of twenty five Years, and been seven Years a Citizen of the United States, and who shall not, when elected, be an Inhabitant of that State in which he shall be chosen.

Representatives and direct Taxes shall be apportioned among the several States which may be included within this Union, according to their respective Numbers, which shall be determined by adding to the whole Number of free Persons, including those bound to Service for a Term of Years, and excluding Indians not taxed, three fifths of all other Persons. The actual Enumeration shall be made within three Years after the first Meeting of the Congress of the United States, and within every subsequent Term of ten Years, in such Manner as they shall by Law direct. The Number of Representatives shall not exceed one for every thirty Thousand, but each State shall have at Least one Representative; and until such enumeration shall be made, the State of New Hampshire shall be entitled to chuse three, Massachusetts eight, Rhode Island and Providence Plantations one, Connecticut five, New York six, New Jersey four, Pennsylvania eight, Delaware one, Maryland six, Virginia ten, North Carolina five, South Carolina five, and Georgia three.

When vacancies happen in the Representation from any State, the Executive Authority thereof shall issue Writs of Election to fill such Vacancies.

The House of Representatives shall chuse their Speaker and other Officers; and shall have the sole Power of Impeachment.

Section. 3. The Senate of the United States shall be composed of two Senators from each State, chosen by the Legislature thereof, for six Years; and each Senator shall have one Vote.

Immediately after they shall be assembled in Consequence of the first Election, they shall be divided as equally as may be into three Classes.

Article. VII.

The Ratification of the Conventions of nine States, shall be sufficient for the Establishment of this Constitution between the States so ratifying the Same.

done in Convention by the Unanimous Consent of the States present the Seventeenth Day of September in the Year of our Lord one thousand seven hundred and Eighty seven and of the Independance of the United States of America the Twelfth In Witness whereof We have hereunto subscribed our Names,

Attest William Jackson Secretary

G°. Washington — Presid. and deputy from Virginia

Delaware
Geo: Read
Gunning Bedford jun
John Dickinson
Richard Bassett
Jaco: Broom

Maryland
James McHenry
Dan of S.t Tho.s Jenifer
Dan.l Carroll

Virginia
John Blair —
James Madison Jr.

North Carolina
W.m Blount
Rich.d Dobbs Spaight.
Hu Williamson

South Carolina
J. Rutledge
Charles Cotesworth Pinckney
Charles Pinckney
Pierce Butler.

Georgia
William Few
Abr Baldwin

New Hampshire
John Langdon
Nicholas Gilman

Massachusetts
Nathaniel Gorham
Rufus King

Connecticut
W.m Sam.l Johnson
Roger Sherman

New York
Alexander Hamilton

New Jersey
Wil: Livingston
David Brearley
Wm. Paterson
Jona: Dayton

Pennsylvania
B Franklin
Thomas Mifflin
Rob.t Morris
Geo. Clymer
Tho.s FitzSimons
Jared Ingersoll
James Wilson
Gouv Morris

THE PEACEABLE KINGDOM. By Edward Hicks, *ca.* 1848. One of the
many versions of this scene painted by Hicks, here with a background
vignette celebrating Penn's peace treaty with the Indians. *Philadelphia
Museum of Art.*

an agricultural country. While Jefferson was in France, Madison represented him in Congress. In response to Jefferson's complaint that there was no bill of rights in the Constitution, Madison got the first Congress to vote and the states to ratify a series of amendments that constituted the most complete guarantee of human liberties that had ever been given to a society. Much more extensive than the English Declaration of Rights, the American Bill of Rights assured religious tolerance by forbidding Congress to make any law to establish any religion or to prohibit the practice of any. Religious beliefs thus became a question that concerned the individual alone. Among other guarantees were freedom of speech, freedom of the press, and freedom of assembly, as well as the right of people to bear arms. This splendid document was as important as the Constitution itself and afforded the most efficacious protection against the growth of tyranny. As Secretary of the Treasury, Hamilton was first concerned with drawing up a balance sheet, which he did in the form of a report to Congress that has remained famous as a model of style, clarity, and intelligence. This balance sheet showed that the Federal Government owed abroad about twelve million dollars; at home, forty-four million dollars; and that the debts of the states amounted to twenty-two million dollars. Hamilton maintained that all these debts should be funded at par, including the debts of the states, because they had been contracted for the common cause and the Federal Government should pay the interest. In August 1790 Congress, thanks to the support of Virginia, voted all of Hamilton's measures. To pay the interest on the debt he counted on import duties, an excise tax on distilled liquors, and the sale of the western lands.

Alexander Hamilton's dream was to reconstitute in America a governmental, economic, and financial edifice modeled on that of England. A bank with a capital of ten million dollars was established on February 25, 1791, and in 1792 the monetary system of the country was organized. The dollar was given a fixed value in gold and the decimal system was adopted for coinage.

In 1792 Washington had been re-elected; there had been no opposition. In 1796 he refused to be a candidate. Opposed in principle to the idea of a third term, he had moreover been made indignant by his treatment at the hands of unbridled partisans. The almost religious respect that at first had been accorded him had been followed by violent abuse. Some said that he had never been a general; others that he had misappropriated state funds! Washington complained with justice that he was attacked in terms so excessive and indecent that they would hardly have been merited by a Nero or a common pickpocket. Worn out and discouraged, he would, he said, have preferred the tomb to another term as President. Once he had made this decision he announced it to the public in an eloquent farewell message. Washington being, by his own wish, eliminated from the contest, John Adams became the logical candidate of the Federalists. Hamilton remained the head of the party, but he was young, unpopular, and aggressive; he had no chance of being President and he knew it. His love of England also would have sufficed to make him distasteful to the electors. John Adams, on the contrary, though he admired British institutions, now passed for an Anglophobe, and he had really become one as he was also a Francophobe, a Europaphobe, and an Adamsophile. On the Republican side, as the frail and timid Madison did not wish to run, Jefferson was clearly the leading candidate. Hamilton, who did not like Adams, hoped that Thomas Pinckney, the other Federalist candidate, would instead be elected President. Aaron Burr was (beside Jefferson) the Republican candidate. Son of a president of Princeton and grandson of the great preacher Jonathan Edwards, an able soldier during the Revolution, Burr had returned, like Hamilton, to the practice of the law and had taken part in the political life of New York State with brilliant success. He was a man of much charm, adored by women. All nameless children of New York were attributed to him. Aaron Burr was one of the first to discover the advantage to be gained by making use of the strength of the Tammany Society in New York elections. The Tammany Society was a demagogic group principally opposed to the propertied classes. Aaron Burr made use of it against the Federalists. When the election came, Burr had thirty votes, Pinckney fifty-nine, Jefferson sixty-eight, and Adams seventy-one. And so Adams was elected, but by a margin of only three votes, for which he was never able to console himself. Adams was very intelligent

[97]

TRANSFER OF NEW ORLEANS TO THE UNITED STATES. Swiss nineteenth-century school. It was Thomas Jefferson, a Francophile, who had the idea of negotiating with France for the purchase of Florida and New Orleans. *Blérancourt Museum. Photographic Archives.*

and, despite his pride, sincerely devoted to his country. But his ingrained Calvinism and his political experience combined to give him a sorry opinion of human nature. He believed that self-interest and not ideas actuated men, that the first concern of every man is his dinner and the second his love affairs. He did not believe in equality. Every democracy, he said, carries within it an aristocracy as clearly defined as that of France, Rome, or England. If power is given to the multitude, he added, there will be no limit to its demands. A new aristocracy will take the old aristocracy's place and treat their former comrades just as severely as their former masters treated them. A republic, according to the new President, should observe the golden mean and stick to the middle of the road between tyranny and anarchy, the extremes that always threaten human societies.

At the very start Adams found himself faced by a Franco-American crisis of major importance. Monroe, the new minister in Paris, had been received at the bar of the Convention and had given warm expression to the sympathy of the United States for the French Revolution. The State Department had rebuked him for this demonstration, which was inconsistent with neutrality, and eventually recalled him. There followed a great uproar in France. The Directory refused to receive Charles C. Pinckney, Monroe's successor, and a number of American ships were seized by French men-of-war on the high seas. It was, in fact if not in law, a break in diplomatic relations. The Treaties of Alliance of 1778 were denounced, and an army was raised. Washington was summoned from his retirement to take command. Adams had hoped to do what he liked with the old man, but encountered the firm will and meticulous precision of Washington. Jefferson sent word secretly to warn Talleyrand that a war would lead to the immediate ascendancy of English influence in the United States. Talleyrand understood, played for peace, and won; for Adams, who wished to avoid war at all costs, suddenly decided to send a new minister to France. He had consulted neither Hamilton nor his cabinet, and both were infuriated. Only one hope remained for the Francophobes: the defeat of the Directory and its General Bonaparte by reactionary Europe. At Marengo, Bonaparte destroyed this hope as well, and on September 30, 1800, a commercial treaty between France and the United States put an end to the quarrel. All the rest of his life Adams said that he wished no other inscription on his tomb but this: 'Here lies John Adams who in the year 1800 took upon himself the responsibility of peace with France.'

Meanwhile, in 1798, at the height of the crisis, the Federalists had obtained the passage of laws designed to strengthen the country in time of war. Among these measures was the Naturalization Act, which required fourteen years' residence (instead of five) in order to become an American citizen; the Alien Act, which authorized the President to deport any alien he considered dangerous; and the Sedition Act, which provided punishments for persons who opposed the execution of the laws, wrote, uttered, or published false or defamatory articles about the President and the government, or incited to revolt. The Republicans, not being a majority in Congress, were unable to prevent the passage of the Federalist measures. But in those states where the Republicans were powerful, the measures had been declared unconstitutional. In respect to the Alien Act the resolutions were in error, for immigration was within the competence of the Federal Government; but the Sedition Act infringed liberties guaranteed by the Constitution. Adams thought he was certain to be elected President a second time in 1800, as Washington had been. He was the only one who thought so. A campaign of extraordinary violence began. Hamilton and his friends represented Jefferson, the gentleman farmer of Monticello, as a man with a knife between his teeth, 'an atheist in religion, a terrorist in politics.' Jefferson won nevertheless.

The Time of Jefferson

Some historians think that the election of Jefferson was a second American revolution. This is an overstatement, but it is true that with Jefferson a new political philosophy came into power. Much as the new President differed from his predecessors in doctrine, he remained in manner a cultured and genial Virginian. His popularity surprised such men as Hamilton, and even Washington, for he was neither an orator nor a soldier. It was owing to the fact that the masses instinctively knew Jefferson had confidence in them. Optimism is the most American of sentiments. In regard to human nature Jefferson was an optimist, Adams a pessimist, and that is why Americans voted for Jefferson.

Major L'Enfant, a Frenchman, had drawn up the plans for the new federal capital to be built on the bank of the Potomac. His vast and orderly project provided for a capitol where Congress would meet, a beautiful house for the President, avenues, squares, monuments. But in 1800 the site of Washington was a lake of mud, the Capitol was unfinished, and the city consisted of nothing but a few Negro cabins. Nevertheless, it had been decided to hold the ceremony of inauguration there, and a few days before March 4, with his customary simplicity, Jefferson had come to stay in the Conrad Boarding House.

In his inaugural address at the Capitol in Washington, the President proclaimed tolerance for all, even for those who were hostile to the Union; equal justice for all; liberty of the press; liberty of thought; support for the states in defense of all their rights; commercial peace and honest friendship with all nations; a lasting alliance with none. 'Sometimes it is said,' he went on, 'that Man cannot be trusted with the government of himself. Can he then be trusted with the government of others? Or have we found angels in the form of kings to govern him?' Jefferson thought that a good government was one that allowed men to perform their work freely. He hoped to repay the debt, and to this end wished to reduce expenses, eliminate unnecessary personnel, and avoid war. When the ceremony was over Jefferson returned to the Conrad Boarding House, and that is where he formed his cabinet. For Secretary of State he chose Madison.

The two men came from Virginia, and Jefferson had a father's protective love for Madison. Not that the difference in their ages was great: Jefferson was fifty-eight, Madison, fifty. But the President was tall and vigorous, the Secretary of State small and frail. In the Treasury Jefferson placed Albert Gallatin, a recently naturalized Genevan and a friend of Madame de Staël and of Baring, the English banker. Gallatin, after being elected to Congress, had revealed a true genius for finance. His incorrigible French accent made this transoceanic Necker a hard orator to understand, but the clarity of his ideas far outweighed this defect.

At the end of a few weeks Jefferson went to live in the presidential mansion, which had been ironically named 'the Palace,' and which Abigail Adams had inaugurated in the midst of plasterers. 'The Palace' was not finished, and in particular had no stairway. At his receptions Jefferson decided to do away with all right of precedence. Guests went in to the table *pêle-mêle* (it was a word he had brought back with him from France). He believed 'all human beings are perfectly equal, be they fellow countrymen or strangers, great lords or simple mortals, and should be treated as such.' This resulted in angry ambassadors seeing their chairs snatched away from them by more vigorous congressmen. But the food was worthy of Virginia, the hospitality that of the South, generous and inexhaustible, and the conversation was brilliant. Since Jefferson was a widower, the charming Dolly Madison, wife of the Secretary of State, played the part of First Lady.

The most important act of Jefferson's Administration was the acquisition of Louisiana. This immense territory, much more extensive than the state which today bears that name and comprising a large part of the valley of the Mississippi, had been ceded by France to Spain in 1763. The latter had granted Americans the right of navigation on the Mississippi and the right to store merchandise at New Orleans. These two rights were indispensable to the Americans of the Ohio River Valley, that is to say, the farmers of the West for whom the river highway was the only possible commercial outlet. And so their anxiety was aroused when they learned in 1802 that Spain by secret treaty had returned Louisiana to France in exchange for Tuscany. Bonaparte, then at the zenith of his glory, seemed a much more dangerous neighbor than feeble Spain, and the Americans were alarmed. They had reason to be. Talleyrand, who knew America, was urging the First Consul to rebuild a French empire, to unite by way of the valley of the Mississippi the bonds between Louisiana and Canada, perhaps even to reconquer the latter and wipe out the Treaty of 1763. As preparation for this enterprise, and to assure a base, General Leclerc had been sent to Santo Domingo, where the Negro Toussaint l'Ouverture had established a dictatorship in defiance of France. Leclerc vanquished the black Bonaparte, but subsequently died himself of the yellow fever that ravaged his army.

Jefferson, the friend and admirer of France, was nevertheless the first to understand that if France occupied the mouth of the Mississippi the United States would have no choice but to throw herself into the arms of England. He instructed James Monroe and Robert R. Livingston, his minister to France, to open negotiations with France and to offer fifty million francs for New Orleans and Florida; if France refused, they were to offer three-quarters of that sum for the island of New Orleans; failing that, the negotiators were to ask for a territory on the left bank of the Mississippi; if that also failed, perpetual right of navigation and storage. Finally, if all failed, Monroe and Livingston were immediately to start conversations with England.

The American envoys were astounded when Talleyrand answered them by saying: 'Buy New Orleans? Why New Orleans? Would you not prefer all Louisiana?' The fact was that the expedition

THOMAS JEFFERSON. By Caleb Boyle. *Lafayette College, Easton, Pennsylvania.* ▶

MERIWETHER LEWIS. By Charles
Willson Peale. Thomas Jefferson put
Lewis in charge of a reconnaissance
mission starting at the mouth of the
Mississippi-Missouri and going all the
way to the Pacific Ocean. William Clark
joined Lewis and both men successfully,
if not without some difficulty, carried out
their dangerous task. This ensured
America's claim on the West. *Independence
Hall, Philadelphia.*

to Santo Domingo had disgusted the French with
that climate; the First Consul needed money,
and at the moment when he was beginning a war
with England he had no wish to make himself
vulnerable by dispersing his armies, especially on a
distant continent where England, mistress of the
seas, would have all the advantages. There was a
brief period of bargaining, and the Americans
purchased an empire for the sum of sixty million
francs. The acquisition of Louisiana more than
doubled the area of the United States. It assured
Americans of free navigation on the Mississippi,
that is, of the economic future of the West. It
enormously increased military security. To the
westward the frontier was so vague that the entire
continent 'might well become American. Jefferson
would have liked to see an amendment made to the
Constitution, giving him the legal power to sign.

But Livingston and Monroe were pressing him.
Talleyrand and Bonaparte might change their
minds. He signed, and the Senate ratified his
decision.

One might say it was Thomas Jefferson who made
the United States a continental power. Not only
did he give the country Louisiana, he was also the
first to send an American expedition by land toward
the Pacific. The west coast had been reached on
many occasions by Spanish, English, and Russian
navigators. It was known that a great river, the
Western River, flowed down from the high mountains to the ocean. An explorer had recorded the
name *Oregon*. Since 1783 Jefferson had been dreaming
of occupying the territory 'from one ocean to the
other' granted to the first colonists by the royal
charters, and of dispatching an expedition from the
Mississippi to the Pacific. At that time the necessary

money could not be found. But in 1803, when he was
President, he obtained from Congress two thousand
five hundred dollars 'for a literary project.' This
strange description was intended to avert the
suspicion of England, who also had designs on
that region. The exploration was entrusted to two
young men, Meriwether Lewis and William Clark.
Lewis had been Jefferson's secretary, and the latter
had recognized his courage, perseverance, knowledge
of the Indians, and honesty. The journey was as
romantic as any that could be imagined. Lewis and
Clark proceeded up the Missouri, crossed the
Rocky Mountains, descended the Western River,
and finally heard the waves of the Pacific breaking
at the mouth of the Columbia. This trip was to be
of inestimable importance later on in establishing
America's claim to this region.

The Louisiana affair was not yet settled. The
Creoles of New Orleans thought it had been
agreed that Louisiana should become a state, and
indeed it would seem that Jefferson's ideas would
not permit him to impose external authority upon
another people. But Congress refused to admit
Louisiana and made it a territory.

Meanwhile Napoleon and Great Britain were
vying for the domination of the world, and to
recruit their sailors the English had recourse to
force, or 'impressment.' Some Americans were
among those forcibly recruited. Jefferson thought
that he could secure respect for America by means of
what he called 'peaceable coercion.' By this strange
and paradoxical formula, he meant the old method
of breaking off trade relations. 'Our commerce is so
valuable to them,' he said innocently of the French
and English, 'that they will be glad to purchase it
when the only price we ask is to do us justice.' A

member of Jefferson's own party, John Randolph, protested against this 'milk and water bill.' 'It is too contemptible,' he added, 'to be the subject of consideration . . . of the pettiest state in Europe.' It must be admitted that facts bore Randolph out. Monroe, sent to London to negotiate, achieved nothing. An American embargo on all foreign commerce (December 22, 1807) did much more harm to America than to France and England. Moreover, American shipowners disregarded it. Freight rates were so high that they were willing to run any risks. The result was that in 1808, by a decree from Bayonne, Napoleon ordered the seizure of all American vessels found in French ports. 'For,' he said ironically, 'these vessels cannot be American; if they were, they would respect the embargo; they are, therefore, camouflaged English ships.'

The Federalist shipowners began to ask if their interests were to be sacrificed indefinitely to the agrarian pacifism of the 'charlatan' in Washington. 'I will lift the embargo,' Jefferson told Paris and London, 'if the Orders in Council and Decrees are abrogated.' Foreign Secretary Canning replied with courteous mockery that 'His Majesty would be happy to see the lifting of the embargo which caused the American people such hardships,' but he retained the Orders in Council. In New England anger rose to the point of sedition, and in certain town meetings there was even talk of secession. Three days before the inauguration of his successor, James Madison (March 1809), Jefferson had to capitulate. He lifted the embargo. As the first four years of his Administration, including the purchase of Louisiana, had been brilliant, so the last four years had been undistinguished. John Randolph compared them to the lean kine in the Bible who came after the fat kine. Toward the end Jefferson himself was beginning to wonder whether the country could avoid war. 'Perhaps,' he wrote to a friend, 'perhaps the whale of the ocean may be tired of the solitude it has made on that element, and may return to honest principles; and his brother robber on the land may see that, as to us, the grapes are sour. . . . I think one war enough for the life of one man; and you and I have gone through one which at least may lessen our impatience to embark in another. Still, if it becomes necessary we must meet it like men, old men indeed, but yet good for something.' He was happy to hand on the office to Madison, whom he had chosen as his successor and imposed upon the party. Never did prisoner delivered from his chains, he said, feel relief equal to his when he was freed from the manacles of power.

War's Labor Lost

A great expert in constitutional law, of subtle and honest mind, far better informed than Jefferson, Madison had shone from youth onward as a second-magnitude star of singular brilliance. But his frail constitution, which had prevented him from fighting in the War of Independence, made him timid. From childhood he had believed himself destined to an early grave; he was to live to the age of eighty-five. A small blond man with blue eyes, always clad in black, with powdered hair gathered at the nape of his neck, he spent his life reading and writing. His friends loved him; he was unknown to the masses. Although witty and sometimes Rabelaisian in private, he seemed so insipid to those who did not know him well that they thought it impossible even to invent a scandal about him. Without his wife and without Jefferson he would never have been President—and would have found that easily bearable. At forty-three he had married a young widow, the pretty, plump Dolly Todd, who was as skilled in politics as her husband was the reverse. On the day of his inauguration Madison trembled so much that it was hard to hear what he said. Moreover, he did not say much. Jefferson, on the contrary seemed radiant. As for Dolly Madison, at the reception that followed the ceremony, she had the air of a queen in her white gown with a long train, her rope of pearls, her turban imported from France, and her bird-of-paradise plumes. Madison, for his part, looked exhausted. The Republican party at that time was so divided by foreign policy and the embargo that Madison had great difficulty in forming a cabinet. He kept Gallatin in the Treasury, but as Secretary of State he had to accept Robert Smith, whom he did not like and who began the Administration with a diplomatic disaster. It was agreed between the State Department and David Erskine, the British minister, that the United States should authorize commerce with England, but the

A CORNER OF GREENWICH STREET, NEW YORK CITY. *New York Public Library.*

agreement was not carried out. Meanwhile the ships were once more tied up at the harbor quays, and the Yankee sailors were protesting. Congress tried a new policy: it authorized the reopening of *all* commerce but decided in advance that if either France or England abandoned the offensive measures, then commerce with the other would be suspended. The American navy had violently resented the humiliation of the *Chesapeake* affair, when an English frigate had attacked that vessel in peacetime, and was hoping for revenge. It was granted when Commodore Rogers, who was on patrol in his frigate *President* in the neighborhood of New York, encountered an English ship, tried to stop her in order to search for an 'impressed' sailor, fired,

killed nine men and wounded twenty-three. The score was now even. The English, suddenly less uncompromising, agreed to return the sailors taken from the *Chesapeake*, or at least the two still living, and to indemnify the families of the dead.

Since the promulgation of the Northwest Ordinance, three new western states—Kentucky, Tennessee, and Ohio—had been admitted to the Union. Others were in the process of formation. The movement of migration toward the West was uninterrupted. New cities—Cincinnati, Cleveland, Pittsburgh—were developing. Countless rafts floated down the Ohio loaded with the meager possessions of families on their way to settle lands sold to them by real-estate companies whose advertising had

NAVAL BATTLE AT LAKE ERIE. ▶
Perry, a young American officer,
won a decisive victory here over
the British fleet in September 1813.
*The Mariners Museum, Newport
News.*

DUPONT DE NEMOURS HOUSE, IN
ANGELICA. Watercolor by Baron-
ess Hyde de Neuville. *Blérancourt
Museum. Hachette photo.*

attracted them. By 1810 Kentucky, Tennessee, and Ohio were inhabited by established citizens who were building houses instead of cabins, laying out cities, endowing colleges, and founding churches. And so in the West there arose the elements of two new political parties. On the fringe was born the democracy of Ohio, more equalitarian, ruder, more picturesque than that of Jefferson, dominated by men who wore coonskin caps and short hair instead of powdered wigs. In the new cities a self-reliant and individualistic middle class arose with unlimited hopes and ambitions. The two groups had one desire in common; they wanted land, always more land; the pioneers in order to push forward and clear it, the middle classes for purposes of sale and speculation. But in their rush toward land they encountered the Indian, and they believed that behind him, arming him and exciting him to resistance, were the British in Canada. And so all these men of the West, impatient of obstacles, declared in favor of a rapid expansion in the country, even at the cost of a conflict.

Young Henry Clay, congressman from Kentucky and, at thirty, Speaker of the House of Representatives, an eloquent man with charming manners, and an aggressive nationalist, was one of the most vigorous champions of this warlike policy. In southerners like John C. Calhoun, the brilliant orator who represented South Carolina in Congress, he found allies who responded by crying 'Florida!' when Clay shouted 'Canada!' But if the war hawks of the South and West were fiery, the Federalists, and the Yankees in general, for the most part condemned this agitation. What, they asked, were the United States' grievances against England? She was arming the Indians? That had not been proved. She 'impressed' sailors? She had made apologies, the offenses were mutual, and there had been British deserters on American ships. As to the conquest of Canada, it was a large enterprise, and the Yankees, having tried it several times, retained an unpleasant memory.

It is only fair to remember that for the men of the frontier the Indians represented a real and terrifying danger. As formerly in Pontiac's time, a powerful chief, Tecumseh, and his brother, the Prophet, had succeeded in uniting a number of tribes. On November 7, 1811, General William Henry Harrison crushed them at Tippecanoe and found that they had been armed with English muskets. At this news the warmongers exulted. A member of Congress who had seen his three brothers killed by Indians talked sternly of 'the power that seizes every occasion to intrigue with the savages and encourages them to mutilate our women and children.' President Madison hesitated a long time. Finally he gave in. His enemies lost no time in pointing out that this was the year when the question of his re-election was to be decided, and he knew that he had no chance without the support of the young partisans of war led by Clay and Calhoun. However that may be, on June 1, 1812, he sent Congress a message that was nothing but a long list of British offenses, at the head of which, in the place of honor, stood the 'impressment' of sailors. Although all these grievances were old stories, war was declared on June 4. Five days later, the British prime minister who of course knew nothing about these discussions in Washington, withdrew the Orders in Council. Most reasons for fighting were gone, but the battle had begun.

America went to war without army or navy. She had about seven thousand men, badly commanded and without a general staff, and sixteen ships against the immense British fleet. New England thought it wrong to attack England at the moment when she was defending the liberty of the world against Napoleon. New England could not understand why war should be declared in 1812 when the principal pretext was the *Chesapeake* affair, which had taken place in 1807 and which, moreover, had been satisfactorily settled. The truth was that the real motives were quite different from the ostensible ones. When Henry Clay discoursed about the rights of sailors, he was thinking of the wishes of the pioneers. The war was a sectional one, and when election came it was by a sectional majority of the West and South that Madison was re-elected.

The invasion of Canada was a lamentable fiasco, although Canada had no troops, barely four regiments plus militia and Indian auxiliaries, and numbered only a half-million inhabitants, against over seven million in the United States. On the other hand, the United States covered itself with glory at sea. In London there had been talk of 'a few fir-built frigates manned by a handful of bastards and freebooters.' But the frigates *Constitution*, *United States*, and *President* each had a firepower superior to any other frigate in the world, and they inflicted terrific blows on the British fleet. Naturally, these successes, however brilliant they might be, could not decide the issue of the war. But on the northern lakes other and more decisive naval engagements were being fought. The control of the lakes was necessary to assure the service of communications and supplies in those uninhabited regions. Oliver Hazard Perry, a young American officer, built a flotilla on Lake Erie and in September 1813 gained a naval victory there so complete that it enabled General Harrison to retake Detroit, destroy Tecumseh's Indians, and make safe the northern frontier. In 1814, when Napoleon had been defeated, England became stronger and more active in America. She devised a plan for invading the United States from three sides: by way of Niagara, Lake Champlain, and New Orleans. In the north, at the battle of Lundy's Lane, the now well-trained American army put up a good fight. On Lake Champlain Commodore MacDonough scored a decisive victory over the British fleet, putting an immediate end to an invasion that might have been dangerous, for it was threatening New York by the classic corridor of the Hudson. But on the Atlantic coast the English succeeded in a most effective raid against the American capital. The city of Washington was defended by no more than a few gunboats. A small expeditionary force of four thousand five hundred men arrived from Bordeaux, landed on the shores of Chesapeake Bay, and advanced overland on Washington without firing a shot. Madison called out the militia; less than one-tenth of the men summoned appeared; they were hastily assembled at Bladensburg, five miles from the Capitol. Few of these militiamen had ever tasted fire; after a few shots they fled in disorder toward Washington. Their excuse was that the British, lacking bullets, had launched rockets at the American positions; these did little damage but were startling and most effective. This rout was called not the Battle of Bladensburg, but the 'Bladensburg Races.' Only four hundred sailors were left to delay the enemy and save the militia from massacre, but they could not save the city. Madison, his wife, and his cabinet had to cross the Potomac in haste, Dolly

Madison carrying the silver spoons and the portrait of George Washington by Gilbert Stuart. Admiral Cockburn found the presidential dinner still hot and ate it. The next day he burned the public buildings in the city in reprisal, he said, for the burning by the Americans of the Parliament of York (Toronto). In the Virginia fields Madison was received with insults by the people, who believed him responsible for this disaster, but he remained unmoved. When, later on, the President returned to Washington, it was necessary to repair and entirely repaint 'the Palace', which had been ravaged by fire; after that it was called the White House.

It was the unique characteristic of this conflict that the peace negotiations were begun almost on the day of the declaration of war and were never interrupted. In 1814 the American negotiators met the British negotiators at Ghent. All the American delegates were at one in demanding the abandonment of 'impressment'; all the English delegates were at one in refusing this. They, for their part, demanded an end to the American fishing rights in Newfoundland, a vast Indian reservation in the Northwest, and a rectification of the frontier on the basis of the territory they then held. The negotiations seemed hopelessly involved. But Wellington, whom the British government proposed to send out to win this war in America, replied very wisely that without control of the lakes he could do nothing. The general's prudence was a useful lesson for the British government, which decided to give up the idea of territorial acquisitions. And the Indians? They would not be used again. And the fishermen? They were to be passed over in silence. The rights of neutrals at sea? Too dangerous a subject. The Mississippi? Not a word. The treaty contained nothing more. And so there was no reason at all for not signing it, which was done on Christmas Day 1814.

The reactions of nations are as unpredictable as those of individuals. It is hard to imagine a more absurd and fruitless conflict than the War of 1812. The pretext for it was a determination to assure the freedom of the seas; it was concluded by a peace in which this was not even mentioned. It had so completely divided the country that President Madison was afraid of secession. It ended with such a spirit of unity that the famous Hartford Convention,

which met to consider the problems of New England, dissolved without making any demands.

Monroe to Jackson

In the eighteenth century Americans were sharply divided into pro-English and pro-French. After 1815 they were all exclusively pro-American. More than ever the United States felt itself independent and autonomous. During the war the East had given birth to industries; the South had regained her wealth through the growing of cotton; in the West, a whole continent awaited development. The unity of the country was assured by its common prosperity. It was manifested in striking fashion in the two elections of Madison's successor, James Monroe, who had been his Secretary of State. In 1816 Monroe had all the states for him except three: Massachusetts,

Connecticut, and Delaware. In 1820 he was elected unanimously, except for one vote, and that single ballot was withheld only as a matter of principle—in order that Washington should remain the only President to have been elected unanimously. Was an era of national union to follow that of partisan and sectional strife? For several months one might have thought so.

Monroe deserved to be the beneficiary of this national unity. Like Jefferson and Madison he was a Virginian, but neither the East nor the North held it against him. Jefferson said of him that he was so honest you could search his soul and not find a single blot. He was conscientious and modest; he dressed in the old fashion. The Republicans substituted for the ancient colonial system of England something that they called the American system. The idea was simple. America could and should

NAVAL BATTLE AT LAKE CHAM-
PLAIN. Engraving by B. Tanner.
MacDonough inflicted a severe defeat
on the British fleet and on the same
day, September 11, 1814, the English
troops suffered a setback at the hand of
General Macomb. *Library of Congress,
Washington.*

THE STEAMBOAT 'HURON' ON THE
MISSISSIPPI. *Museum of Natural
History, Le Havre. Photographic Archives.*

be henceforth sufficient unto herself. New England
would produce the manufactured products needed
by the South and West, and the agriculturists would
find markets for their products in the industrial
states. The American system was accepted for the
time being by the whole country. Monroe made a
trip to the former Federalist sections; the warmth of
his reception proved that grievances had been
forgotten. A Boston newspaper said that this trip
inaugurated 'the era of good feeling.' The phrase
pleased the President, and he made frequent use of it.

Naturally the idea that the American system
would satisfy all America was nothing but a beautiful
dream. Sectional interests continued to be in disagreement on many points. The South and the
East both sought the commerce of the new western
states and vied with each other for it. The natural
access to this region was the Mississippi. Around the
beginning of the century a new invention, the
steamboat, had greatly increased the usefulness of
the river. As soon as the steamboats were powerful
enough to proceed against the current, the price of
passage fell to thirty dollars. By 1825 there were on
the Mississippi one hundred twenty-five steamboats,
picturesque floating palaces. To compete with New
Orleans, the ports of the East had only one resource:
to open a direct means of communication with the
Great Lakes. Then they would be able to drain off
the commerce of the northern part of the new states.
In answer to this need the Erie Canal was constructed from Buffalo on Lake Erie to Albany on the
Hudson River. It was built by the State of New
York and inaugurated in 1825.

A message to Congress on December 2, 1823,
enunciated what was called the Monroe Doctrine.
This message said: (*a*) that the American continents

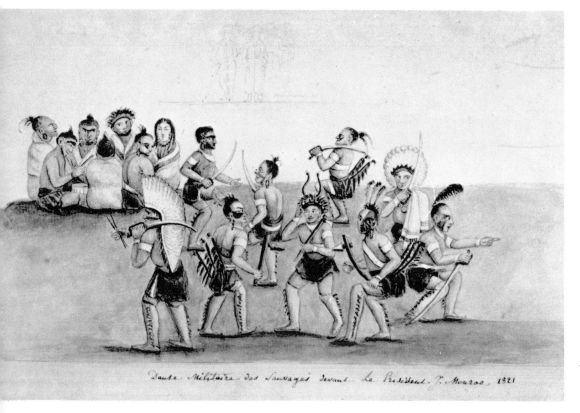

Daute Militaire des Sauvages devant Le President T. Monroe 1821

henceforth were not to be considered grounds for future colonization by European powers; (*b*) that the United States would not take part in any war between the European powers; (*c*) that, on the other hand, it could not view with indifference what happened in America, and that any attempt on the part of monarchic powers to establish their political systems on this continent would be regarded as dangerous; (*d*) that it would not intervene to deprive the European powers of colonies they already possessed; (*e*) that any intervention against the independence of the republics of South America would be considered by the United States as unfriendly. The Monroe Doctrine was one of the aspects of the nationalism that at that time welded a constellation of states into a nation.

In this era of good feeling, nationalism, and unity, one subject threatened a profound division of the nation; that was slavery. About the time of the Revolution, this institution had seemed doomed. The products hitherto grown for export in the South—tobacco and indigo—could no longer be

sold at a reasonable profit. The climate of the South was favorable to cotton, but the work necessary to separate the fibres from the seeds was so prolonged and costly that it made the price prohibitive. A slave could barely clean one pound a day. In 1793 a young student, Eli Whitney, heard talk about these difficulties and conceived the idea of a machine. When the machine he built was tried out, it became evident that with its aid a single man could gin as much cotton as fifty by hand. Through this very simple device, cotton growing became profitable, and it developed with prodigious rapidity. In 1791 the United States exported less than two hundred thousand pounds of cotton; in 1809–1810, ninety-three *million* pounds, while retaining sixteen million for American manufactures. Now this form of agriculture lent itself to the employment of slaves. From that time the number of slaves mounted rapidly (seven hundred fifty-seven thousand in 1790, about four million in 1860). Their price increased. For the southern planters slaves became not only a property of immense value but a necessary

condition of their own wealth. In South Carolina and in Georgia, King Cotton reigned and controlled politics as well as economics.

The northern states, which had condemned slavery and prohibited it within their boundaries, looked on with disapproval when the South obtained, at the very beginning of the Republic, twenty supplementary seats in Congress thanks to a black population that did not vote. Great care had been taken in admitting new states so as to maintain an equal balance between slave states and free states.

At the time of the Louisiana Purchase planters had transported their slaves there. New states had been created, some slave, others free. But always the balance had been maintained. Good will had triumphed; but one could prophesy that ill will was to have its turn. When the time of the presidential election of 1824 approached, John Quincy Adams began to glance longingly at the White House. Did he not have every right to it? He was awkward and arrogant in public, a mediocre orator, but by no means displeasing in private. He prided himself on his ability to write, kept a private diary, and learned by heart the *Fables* of La Fontaine in French, which he recited while riding horseback. Dazzled by the brilliance of his own culture he was, like his father before him, annoyed to find himself confronted by rivals whom he considered unworthy. The East was proud of having the most eloquent of Americans, the inspired orator, Daniel Webster. The West had made an idol of Henry Clay, a Virginian who had come at an early age to Kentucky, had grown up with his state, and represented it in Washington.

The dark horse in this presidential race was General Jackson, hero of New Orleans and other places; his state, Tennessee, had proposed his candidacy two years earlier. That Jackson was a remarkable man, no one doubted, but some said he was a great democrat, others 'a despot and a demagogue.' Despite his duels, his picturesque oaths, his rages, he read the Bible and possessed the dignity and courtly manners of the South. Although he recognized him as a possible and dangerous rival, John Quincy Adams had a fondness for Jackson. Before the election he gave a ball in his honor. Between the tall and cadaverous general and the short, stout Secretary of State, Mrs. Adams

looked as though she were receiving between Don Quixote and Sancho Panza. Came the vote: ninety-nine for Andrew Jackson of Tennessee, eighty-four for John Quincy Adams of Massachusetts, forty-one for Crawford of Georgia, and thirty-seven for Henry Clay of Kentucky. No candidate had obtained an absolute majority, and so it became the duty of the House of Representatives to make the choice. When the House voted, John Quincy Adams had thirteen states for him; Jackson seven; Crawford, four.

At first Jackson took his defeat in good part, and on the evening of the election, meeting Adams, he graciously congratulated him. The General's friends maintained that he had been beaten by fraud and that a disgraceful deal had been arranged between Adams and Clay. Jackson refused to believe it. But when Adams very tactlessly offered to make Clay Secretary of State, a unanimous outcry arose. Here was proof of 'the bargain of corruption,' said the Jacksonians. In reality there had been neither corruption nor a bargain. Jackson broke with Adams on that very day and thenceforth pursued him with an inexorable hatred. The country came to detest the President.

To direct the policies of a country when one possesses neither a majority nor popularity and has against one a rival whom the masses adore is a hopeless task. It was rendered more difficult still by Adams's ineptitude at all measures of compromise. Consequences were easy to foresee; the President soon had Congress against him, and all his measures were defeated. He wished to carry out a nationalist policy, give a liberal interpretation to the Constitution, have the Federal Government build the roads and canals desired by the West, establish a national university and observatories, encourage the development of the continent, maintain a Bank of the United States, protect industry by import duties, and make America a closed system. This 'American System' had hitherto been favored by the country, but Adams's support was enough to make it unpopular, and moreover resurgent sectional antagonisms were undermining the national program. The Northeast, where a powerful industry was developing, would perhaps have supported Adams, but the South abandoned him and soon was opposing him. Clay thought he could bring him

JOHN QUINCY ADAMS. By G.P.A. Healy. The rivalry between the short plump Secretary of State Adams and the tall gaunt General Jackson, the hero of New Orleans, was a re-enactment of the Jefferson-Hamilton quarrel, i.e., the classic dispute between Federalists and anti-Federalists. Adams's election as President in 1824 was for a long time mistakenly regarded as fraudulent, and all his legislative measures were defeated by Congress. *Blérancourt Museum. Photographic Archives.*

the support of the West; Jackson offered this support to the South and many former Jeffersonians rallied to Jackson. Thus was re-established under new names and with the new addition of the West the ancient division of the United States into Federalists and Antifederalists. Hamilton and Jefferson were reborn in Clay and Jackson—because Hamilton and Jefferson are eternal.

Jackson's campaign for election in 1828 began the year after Adams's election. Admirably organized, it was promoted for three years throughout the whole country by committees, newspapers, and banquets. Everywhere Jackson found allies. In the Ohio Valley he had for him all those who were still animated by the spirit of the frontier, all those who were irritated by the aristocracy of the coast, all those who thought that 'America begins on the other side

of the Alleghenies.' In the South, Georgia was furious at Adams because he had supported the Indians in their territorial claims, and the South in general accused the President of sacrificing states' rights.

This powerful combination of enemies determined to keep Adams from winning a second term made his political life more difficult than that of any of his predecessors. Congress was debating an amendment to the Constitution providing for the direct election of the President by the nation, and in the course of the discussion the case of John Quincy Adams, President *against* the will of the American people, was cited many times in painful fashion. The most innocent actions of the President became crimes in the eyes of his tormentors. Had he bought a billiard table for the White House? The purchase proved his futility—a curious epithet for an Adams. Did he speak French with Lafayette, who, in 1825, was revisiting the country he so greatly loved? Immediately his European, un-American education was recalled. In 1826, on July 4, the fiftieth anniversary of the Declaration of Independence, John Adams, the father of the President, died, and on the same day Thomas Jefferson also died. The loss of his father earned the President no respite. It seemed easy to foresee the results of the presidential election. Theoretically there was only one party: the Republican party. The campaign was violent nevertheless. Jackson denounced the politicians and proved himself the most skillful of them. Adams complained of the cruel malice of the Jacksonians, but his friends treated Jackson with at least equal cruelty. They recalled his quarrels, his duels, and handed out little coffins bearing the names of his victims.

The intention of these respectable blackmailers was to provoke Jackson, the violence of whose character they well knew, to an outburst that would destroy him. But Jackson was too astute for them and controlled himself. As for the crowds, they shouted 'Hurrah for Jackson!' They had chosen their hero; they would listen to no arguments. And even in Kentucky, his own state, Clay felt that he was beaten. The result was crushing: Jackson had one hundred seventy-eight votes; Adams, eighty-three votes. New England alone had remained true to the President. Calhoun, in return for his support of Jackson, became vice-president.

The Transformation

Andrew Jackson was not a cause but an effect. He did not in his Administration, transform American democracy; he became President because American democracy, between 1790 and 1830, had undergone a profound transformation. In those forty years, the population of the United States had tripled, growing from four million to twelve million, and its area had doubled. 'We are large and we continue to grow rapidly. I had almost said *terribly*,' wrote Calhoun in 1817. There was indeed something terrifying for any American government in the tide that submerged the West under successive waves of immigrants and in the continuous creation of new states which effectively altered the political equilibrium of the country every ten years.

For the immigrant, the first weeks were hard, very hard. In the Mississippi Valley, for example, the lot sold the immigrant was almost always deep in the forest. The family had to sleep on the boat while the men cut down the trees. All the arms and all the axes of the neighborhood seemed to be at the service of the newcomer. It was the custom to send one man from each family to help. The kindness and good will of the neighbors seemed to be the dominant characteristics of this society. No sooner had a plot of land been cleared than the wife started a kitchen garden. At the end of six weeks she was cooking her own vegetables. As for the house, made of rough-hewn logs between which came light and wind and smoke, it went up even faster.

The American frontier was not what Europeans call a frontier, the line of demarcation between two countries. The word 'frontier' in America meant 'the fringe of foam that marked the extreme advance of the human waves,' the zone where the density of the population was less than two or three inhabitants per square mile and where the whites adopted the Indians' way of life. There the pioneer type established itself with its virtues and defects. The man of the West was rugged, optimistic, and independent. Daily life with its struggles against the Indians and the forest became an adventure novel. Equality in the West was not a principle; it was a fact. Many immigrants had commenced with little besides their wives, a few benches and chairs, a Bible, and a gun. They saw their village grow, cities arise, states come to birth. On lands that yesterday had been jungles civilization spread with the rapidity of a forest fire. It was a prodigious spectacle such as the world had never seen before. A French traveler who had been a witness of this soaring flight wrote mournfully: 'America is rising, Europe sinking.'

The other two sections also changed very markedly. For the East, the essential problems were to develop its own industries and to attract to itself as large a part as possible of the commerce of the new states. England had been the first to have steam-driven machines for spinning and weaving. She had hoped to maintain a monopoly and for a long time forbade the emigration of technicians and workmen. But such secrets cannot be kept. Francis Cabot Lowell of Boston, after a long tour of

[121]

inspection abroad, built a factory in Massachusetts where for the first time all the operations of spinning and weaving cloth were united under one roof. The War of 1812 gave an immense impetus to American industries by severing the connections with England and by directing into the channels of industry funds that could no longer find a place in commerce. It was 'the industrial war of independence.' With his brother-in-law, Patrick Tracy Jackson, Lowell created the textile capital that bears his name. And a short time later, in order to connect the city of Lowell with Boston, he built one of the first rail-roads in America. In 1817 the Frenchman Merle d'Aubigné was filled with admiration for a firm that manufactured beautiful blue and black cloth and that had been given by its founders the name of Nouveau-Louviers. In 1840 the textile industry employed more than one hundred thousand work-

men. At this time the discovery of coal and iron in localities close to each other was leading to the development of the iron industry. This produced stoves and nails in great quantities. Tanneries and shoe factories grew. In Colonial times the South had been richer than the North; now the cities of the North prospered, those of the South declined. The southern planters had to seek capital from the nor-thern bankers and blamed the protective tariff, instituted by the North, for their poverty.

The development of industry raised a labor problem. Hitherto the only labor problem had been to find workmen. After 1825 labor unions, then called trade associations, multiplied. In 1827 for the first time the workmen's associations of a whole city, Philadelphia, joined a union. In 1834 there appeared a proposal for national federation. The political influence of the workmen's unions certainly

THE TEXTILE INDUSTRY IN
AMERICA. The invention of the
power loom provided the impulse for
the rapid expansion of the textile
market in the United States. *U.S.I.S.*

contributed to Jackson's election. A movement to
obtain a ten-hour day was started, and Jackson
limited the working day in state-owned factories.

As to the South, its new problems were to
dominate the history of America from 1830 to
1865. For a long time it had received its intellectual
directives from Virginia. Since the prodigious
development of cotton growing, which had become
the great source of wealth in the black belt, the
generous, courtly, and humanitarian spirit of
Virginia had been succeeded by the vigorous, harsh
realism of the slaveowners of South Carolina. In
ten years slavery, which had been on the point of
disappearing at the end of the eighteenth century,
had become indispensable to the planters. And, as
always happens, they had found reasons to justify
in theory what was necessary to them in practice.

The American System was not simply an essay
in economic autonomy; education and literature
as well assumed, little by little, a purely American
character. On the frontier schools were scarce;
many children, like Andrew Jackson, educated
themselves. A future President of the United States,
Andrew Johnson, did not know how to read or
write at the time of his marriage; from this resulted
a certain contempt for the old culture and a wish
for intellectual independence. The War of 1812 had
stirred up resentment against England, while the
Napoleonic wars had spoiled the friendship between
the United States and France. The West was not,
like Virginia or New England, sentimentally a child
of the old continent. The sense of humor of the
Mississippi Valley exercised itself at the expense of
European taboos. America was becoming conscious
of an intellectual emancipation. 'I ask,' said Everett
in 1826, 'whether more has not been done to

THE REAL ESTATE SPECULATOR. By ▶
James H. Beard. *Edward Eberstadt and
Sons Collection. Francis G. Mayer photo.*

FENIMORE COOPER. Portrait by
Bailly. His daring, colorful heroes,
such as Leatherstocking and Hawkeye,
became familiar to readers of all ages
the world over. *The Last of the Mohicans*
gave rise to an entire literature, both
popular (in its directness and accessi-
bility) and truly epic (in its tone, scope,
simplicity of setting, primitive rugged-
ness, and the almost mythological
grandeur of the characters). The
present-day 'Western' is only a
watered-down, colorless version of
his works. *Hachette photo.*

extend the domain of civilization, in fifty years,
since the Declaration of Independence, than would
have been done in five centuries of continued colonial
subjection?' Certain European visitors, Alexis de
Tocqueville, for instance, accepted this judgment
and came to America in search of lessons in government. Others protested. 'During the thirty or forty
years of their independence,' said Sidney Smith,
'they have done absolutely nothing for the sciences,
for the arts, for literature. In the four quarters of the
globe, who reads an American book or looks at an
American statue?' But Sidney Smith, like all witty
men, had a tendency to mistake an epigram for a
statement of fact. Actually in 'the four quarters of
the globe' men were reading *The Last of the Mohicans.*
James Fenimore Cooper appealed to the readers of

the whole world because his work and his heroes,
Leatherstocking and Hawkeye, were of an epic and
romantic character. The place taken at that time
in the intellectual life of the country by the aggressive
financial city of New York was in itself an indication
of the birth of a new America. 'The bewilderment
of old Rip Van Winkle, on his return from the hills,
was the bewilderment of the colonial mind in the
presence of a new order.' America was becoming
American.

Since the ratification of the Constitution one of
the most controversial questions had been that of
the respective rights of the states and the Federal
Government. Could a state refuse to enforce a law
passed by Congress? Could it, if it disapproved of
the policy of the Federal Government, detach itself

from the Union? The argument that secession was legitimate had been supported by the northern states. Calhoun himself, the Vice-President of the United States, subscribed to a doctrine called 'nullification': since the Union was an agreement entered into by sovereign states, each of these states had the right to decide whether an act of Congress was constitutional—an infinitely dangerous doctrine. Jackson, patriot and nationalist, condemned it. But Calhoun and his friends had taken up positions from which retreat was difficult. When in 1832 Jackson signed a new protective tariff, a South Carolina convention declared that the law was null and void and did not bind either the state, its officers, or its citizens. If the Federal Government attempted enforcement by violence, said the con-

vention, then South Carolina would consider herself released from all ties to the Union and free to act as a sovereign state. Medals with the inscription: 'J. C. Calhoun, first President of the Southern Confederate States' were already being minted.

Jackson was not the man to leave such a threat unanswered. He issued orders to the navy to be in readiness to dispatch a squadron to Charleston. He armed the forts and declared 'by the Eternal' he would defend the laws. A strong proclamation by the President answered the Statute of Nullification: 'I consider, then, the power to annul a law of the United States, assumed by one State, incompatible with the existence of the Union, contradicted expressly by the letter of the Constitution . . . and destructive of the great object for which it was formed.'

From this time the country would have drifted toward civil war if the astute Van Buren had not realized that this controversy, by dividing the Democrats, would be damaging to his future political career. Henry Clay, who was not displeased at depriving Jackson of a brilliant and easy success, Calhoun, who had no wish for an armed rebellion, and Van Buren naturally worked together to achieve a compromise. Henry Clay, a master in this field, secured the passage of a new law that provided for the next ten years a progressively descending scale of tariffs. The South agreed. Both sides considered it a victory. That is always a proof of the excellence of an agreement. But Jackson, who did not have the same tender feelings for compromise measures as did Henry Clay, believed that the reckoning had only been postponed. He wrote to a friend that the tariff had been no more than a pretext; the real objective was a Confederacy of the South. 'The next pretext will be the question of slavery.'

Jackson's second Administration was marked by extraordinary prosperity. Jackson completed his term in the false glow of the inflation. In the election of 1836 the country was once more divided into two parties: the Jacksonian Democrats, who had Van Buren as their candidate, and the National Republicans, often called the Whigs. Van Buren was Jackson's choice. This was enough for him to be elected. It had been expected that Van Buren's Administration would be that of the Little Magician —a nickname given him owing to his skillful use of the spoils system; instead it was that of the Sorcerer's Apprentice. Jackson had bequeathed to his friend a country pregnant with crisis. Bank notes without security, lands without purchasers, cities without inhabitants, canals without traffic, mortgages without value, artificially inflated prices, and the exorbitant cost of necessities had raised a fragile house of cards that would collapse at the first breath. A bad harvest, a deficit in the foreign-trade balance, Jackson's *Specie Circular*—enjoining government agents from further sales of land except for hard cash—and bankruptcies in England finally brought on, in 1837, a panic of the first magnitude. Van Buren, who had never been loved by the crowds, was now hated. The panic was to cost him his second term.

It is always the ruin of a party to be in power during a depression. The President's policy of temporizing may have been wise, but the Whigs had succeeded in making it appear foolish. Jackson's picturesque popular appeal had been the reason for his success. The Whigs must find another Jackson. Since old soldiers were at a premium, they went looking for an old soldier: they discovered General William Henry Harrison. He was not a great general, far from it; but he had once defeated the Indians at Tippecanoe. . . . *Tippecanoe*. . . . The word was sonorous and bizarre. Why not *Tippecanoe?* President Harrison was inaugurated on March 4, 1841. 'He was not a great man but he had lived a long time and he had been associated with great undertakings.' Clay and Webster, the leaders of the Whig party, believed they would have no trouble handling this old soldier, who seemed less crusty than Jackson. A month later the President died. He had caught pneumonia, thus playing a wretched trick on the Whigs. In the shadow of Tippecanoe, Clay had planned to become Mayor of the Palace and to reverse Jackson's policy completely by re-establishing a federal bank, a program of public works, and tariffs. His discomfiture and that of the party were great when Harrison's death brought to power Tyler, a Democrat who was hostile to the whole Whig program. At once there was a rain of vetoes—a veto on the bank, a veto on the public works program—resulting in the resignation of the whole cabinet, with the exception of Daniel Webster, who stayed on to complete his negotiations with Lord Ashburton, the representative of the British government.

JACKSON SLAYING THE MANY-HEADED MONSTER. General Jackson, now President Andrew Jackson, is no longer the romantic hero portrayed by Thomas Sully (see p. 121). His temples are balding, his eyes glint viciously behind his glasses, and he is brandishing his weapon, the veto. A scroll is coming out of his mouth (this is the traditional device of popular imagery, now seen as the comic-strip balloon). Here are Jackson's words in part: '. . . thou Monster Avaunt!! Avaunt I say! Or by the Great Eternal I'll cleave thee to the earth, aye thou and thy four and twenty hideous satellites!' *New York Historical Society.*

GENERAL JACKSON SLAYING THE MANY HEADED MONSTER.

IV
Growing Pains

The South and its Problems

One of the characteristics of the American pioneer was his apparent need to press on constantly toward virgin territories. In Europe a similar need was felt by certain individuals, and it resulted in the conquest of colonies and the founding of empires. In America the words 'conquest' and 'empire' were unpopular. It was considered preferable to say that the 'manifest destiny' of the people of the United States was to occupy and civilize the entire continent. The western farmers wanted lands; King Cotton demanded lands; where were they to be had? There was nothing to be done about Canada, for experience had shown that it was useless and dangerous to attack England. To the south and west, on the other hand, stretched the ancient Spanish empire whose weakness seemed to invite invasion.

Texas, Mexico's vast and fertile province, was a fine prey, coveted by the pioneers of Tennessee, Mississippi, and Louisiana. The country was almost uninhabited. At the beginning of the century a few American farmers settled there without asking permission from the Spanish authorities. The Mexican law allowed to each immigrant, who had to be a Catholic, one hundred seventy-seven acres of tillable land, four thousand and four hundred and twenty-five acres of pasture, no taxes, abundant game, and as much corn as he cared to raise. A farm in Texas was surely worth a mass. By 1830 more than twenty thousand Americans were living in Texas, and some of them had transported their slaves there. The Mexicans, who had abolished slavery in their own country, were sorry to see it re-established on one of their provinces.

In 1834 a soldier named Antonio Lopez de Santa Anna gained control of the Mexican government. He was shocked at the condition of Texas, where the Mexican laws on Catholicism and slavery were being violated with impunity. He wished to make Texas a military province and enforce respect for the Mexican authorities. Mexicans and Texans knew that complete secession was bound to follow sooner or later. It came in 1836. Santa Anna at the head of a small army marched on San Antonio. He very cruelly massacred a detachment of Texans. In San Antonio the inhabitants and soldiers had fortified the Alamo, a mission consisting of a chapel, a cloister, and a convent, the whole surrounded by thick walls. There about a hundred and eighty Texans defended themselves heroically for thirteen days against some four thousand Mexicans. The position was taken only after the death of almost all its defenders. 'Remember the Alamo,' became the rallying cry of the Texans. One of them, General Sam Houston, raised an army and scored a complete victory over Santa Anna at San Jacinto (1836). Santa Anna, taken prisoner, granted Texas its independence. The Texans chose Sam Houston president, an excellent choice. Houston was an old friend of Andrew Jackson, and he had a fine presence that awakened spontaneous and enthusiastic loyalty. The Texans' flag bore a single star. It was their way of proclaiming their desire of taking a place in the American constellation. They called themselves Americans and hoped to be annexed by the United States. English policy, on the other hand, was to try to prevent this annexation. The English, inconvenienced by American tariffs, saw the possibility of making Texas a vassal state and buying cotton there as well as gaining a market independent of the United States. Why not turn the Texans to England, who would finance the cultivation of cotton in Texas? Houston sent word to his old friend Andrew Jackson that Texas loved the United States tenderly and approached it like a bride arrayed for the wedding night; but that if the bridegroom showed too little enterprise there were other lovers on the list.

Webster's successor, Secretary of State Calhoun, immediately asked the Mexican minister whether a peaceful annexation or purchase would be acceptable to his country. The reply was once more that annexation would mean war. Despite this, Calhoun, who did not fear the risks and saw in the acquisition of Texas a means of strengthening the South, concluded a treaty of annexation in April 1844. The Senate refused to confirm it. It was the year of a presidential election. Annexation became a campaign weapon. It was possible to use it as a bait both for the South and for the West by demanding simultaneously 'the reoccupation of Oregon,' the object of a border dispute with England, and 'the re-

annexation of Texas.' This was intended to imply that Texas and Oregon already belonged by right to the United States. The candidate of the Whig party was the perennial and charming Henry Clay, the compromise expert. Clay tried not to raise either the question of annexation or that of slavery; he succeeded brilliantly in alienating both sides. The Democratic convention had to choose between Van Buren, an anti-annexationist because of his eastern friends, and James K. Polk, of Tennessee, who was a much less famous statesman but an ardent expansionist. Polk was honest, and he despised the vanities of the world. His wife, an energetic Presbyterian, would forbid dancing at the White House; he had no sense of humor. But perhaps, from time to time, there has to be a President who is more solid than brilliant. As a candidate, Polk said to George Bancroft, a member of the Massachusetts delegation: 'Four great measures will occupy my administration: reduction of tariffs; an independent treasury; settlement of the Oregon question; and the acquisition of California.' Polk was nominated and elected. Tyler, the retiring President, accepted the verdict and obtained from Congress a vote of annexation in February 1845. The news was received in Texas with unprecedented enthusiasm, and toward the end of the year that country became one of the states in the Union.

After he became President, Polk, in order to fulfill his program, had to annex Oregon. After long negotiations a treaty with Great Britain was signed. The forty-ninth parallel was agreed upon as the frontier. It was an equitable solution. There remained the question of the Mexican provinces. If no American wanted a war with England, many entertained without dismay the idea of a war with Mexico. The latter did not recognize the annexation of Texas, at least in theory, for in practice Mexico had never attempted to reconquer the province since it had claimed its independence. Polk sent John Slidell as minister to Mexico. The Mexican government refused to receive Slidell, and General Taylor received orders to take up a position on the Rio Grande. There was a cavalry skirmish, men were killed, and Polk sent the following message to Congress: 'The cup of forbearance has been exhausted . . . Mexico . . . has invaded our territory, and shed American blood upon the American soil.'

Congress declared 'that by the act of the Republic of Mexico a state of war existed' (May 13, 1846). The real object of this war was the conquest of California. President Polk made no mystery of it, and his cynicism was pardonable. Only ten to twelve thousand inhabitants, more Spaniards than Mexicans, lived in this immense territory. Attracted by the mildness of the climate and the richness of the soil, Americans in small numbers had settled there.

In January 1846 Polk sent General Kearny and eighteen hundred men, of whom five hundred were Mormons, to conquer California. When Kearny arrived he found the conquest completed. The American navy had landed at Monterey. An American officer and explorer, John C. Frémont, happened at that time to be in the Rocky Mountains. A few comic-opera battles, without dead or wounded, had given him the whole country. General Kearny, arriving on the scene, came into conflict with the Mexicans and with Frémont. The latter, a spoiled child, who had thus far always had his own way, tried to resist. Kearny had him court-

martialed for mutiny. Frémont was found guilty, refused the pardon Polk offered him, and resigned his commission. This little adventure had political consequences: it made enemies of the old friends Benton, the Democratic leader, and Polk, and made Frémont a victim, a senator from California, and, later on, in 1856, a candidate for the presidency.

Meanwhile General Zachary Taylor was invading Mexico so successfully that he alarmed the Democrats; he belonged to a breed of which the Whigs all too easily made president. Polk prudently ordered another general to land at Vera Cruz, this time Winfield Scott, a Whig like General Taylor, but haughty and elegant and thus with small popular appeal. Scott was to take possession of Mexico City before Taylor won any dangerous successes. As bad luck would have it, they were both victorious, Taylor at Buena Vista, Scott at the gates of Mexico City. By the Treaty of Guadalupe Hidalgo (1848) Mexico recognized the Rio Grande as its boundary and ceded New Mexico and Upper California in exchange for fifteen million dollars. Polk had given

his country a million square miles and the Whig party two candidates. The problem was now to assimilate these conquests without destroying the balance of power among the different sections of the country.

That the human wave which had in a few decades peopled the immense valley of the Mississippi would gradually overrun the whole continent seemed likely. At the end of the eighteenth century there had occurred the very minor event, already mentioned, that transformed both the interests and the ideas of the South—the invention of the cotton gin by Eli Whitney.

The gin made cotton the principal and almost the only product of the South. It made possible and necessary the employment of an immense amount of slave labor. The economic weakness of slavery hitherto had been the necessity of supervision, the ineptness of the slave, and his lack of adaptability. But cotton growing was easy, mechanical work, and it extended most of the year; supervision was simple because of the low height of the cotton plants. The slave, whose support cost an average of twenty dollars a year, was cheaper than the free worker. Therefore, since 1800 the number of slaves had doubled every twenty years; in 1850 it was to reach three million nine hundred thousand. The price of human flesh had risen as well. In 1780 a young male Negro sold for two hundred dollars; in 1818 for one thousand; in 1860 for thirteen hundred to two thousand. Slaves had become the South's greatest and almost only asset, for the land, impoverished by one-crop farming, was rapidly decreasing in value. Since the importation of slaves had been prohibited after 1808, they had become all the more valuable. On some Virginia estates, human beings were raised for export to other states, although their owners denied this. Thus, little by little, the inhabitants of the South had rallied in perfect good faith to the heated defense of an institution that seemed to them one of the conditions of their existence.

Men have always found it only too easy to discover moral justification for profitable conduct.

THE OLD PLANTATION. Watercolor. The setting is an unidentified ►
estate in South Carolina. A group of black slaves are dancing in front of
their cabins to the accompaniment of an old long-necked banjo and a
primitive drum. *Abby Aldrich Rockefeller Folk Art Collection, Williamsburg.*

Custom blunts sensibilities. The planters no longer saw the odious aspects of slavery any more than the northern manufacturers were moved by the ills resulting from child labor.

In the North slavery was becoming more and more unpopular. There self-interest and morality were in the same camp. On the little New England farm, with its diversified tasks, slave labor could not be used. The representation accorded to the South on the basis of a slave population that was disfranchised appeared a monstrous and shocking injustice. The owner of fifty slaves had thirty-one votes for himself alone. It was absurd. The Irish, Scottish, and German immigrants, newly arrived from Europe, considered slavery an archaic and barbarous institution. The North was determined not to let a majority of slave states dominate the country. Each time a new state was admitted, the North and South clashed. If Missouri asked to be admitted to the Union as a slave state, the North demanded first the admission of Maine as a free state to maintain the balance of power. Little by

little the tone of the controversy became more strident. Until 1820 it had been possible for one living in the South to admit opposition to slavery. There were even southern societies that collected money to buy slaves and send them back to Africa. After 1820 the pressure exercised by the cotton growers, economic necessity, and above all the exasperation caused by northern criticism made it dangerous to voice antislavery sentiments in the South.

Among the northern opponents of slavery two groups must be distinguished—the antislavery men and the abolitionists. The antislavery people were only opposed to the principle and to the extension of slavery; the abolitionists went farther and demanded the liberation of all slaves. In the 1820s a New Jersey Quaker named Benjamin Lundy began an ardent campaign in favor of gradual emancipation. He traveled on foot through a large number of states. Almost everywhere he went, women joined him in founding antislavery societies, which were prudently called 'reading circles,'

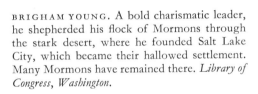

PHILADELPHIA NEGROES SINGING IN THE STREET. By Paul Svinin. African slaves had no qualms about converting to Christianity, their white masters' religion. The denominations varied according to the regions. Here, under the leadership of a gray-haired minister, Methodist Negroes are singing in the street. Some of them are prostrated, their foreheads on the ground, others are dancing and leaping in a state of religious ecstasy reminiscent of pagan rites. *U.S.I.S.*

BRIGHAM YOUNG. A bold charismatic leader, he shepherded his flock of Mormons through the stark desert, where he founded Salt Lake City, which became their hallowed settlement. Many Mormons have remained there. *Library of Congress, Washington.*

'women's clubs' or 'lecture societies.' Men such as Daniel Webster, opposed to slavery but reasonable in their opposition, recognized that the South had an economic and political problem that could not be solved by a few brutal phrases like those Lundy used in his newspaper, *The Liberator*. It was certainly unfortunate that some millions of blacks had been introduced into the midst of a white society, but now there they were. Regrets and accusations are not solutions. The cotton crop had to be planted and picked. Webster considered that slavery, so far as the South was concerned, was 'a calamity, not a crime.' He thought that if the Negroes were to be emancipated, some means would have to be found to indemnify the planters. This prudence exasperated the virtuous abolitionists.

To add to the territory of the United States might have been and should have been everybody's wish. But would the new domains be slave or free? Would their acquisition alter the majority in the Senate? Partisan spirit for a time triumphed over national spirit.

From the Compromise to Lincoln's Election

The immense territories the United States had just acquired supported a very few white settlers, either American or Spanish. Difficulty of access explains this fact. Nevertheless, more and more numerous caravans adventurously set out on the different trails leading toward the Pacific. One of the strangest episodes had been the founding by a religious sect called the Mormons of a prosperous commonwealth in the midst of the desert.

The founder and prophet of the group was a young man named Joseph Smith, who had been born in Vermont and at the age of about fifteen, while he was at his prayers, had seen, so he said, the apparition of an angel who had revealed to him the existence of sacred books engraved on tablets of gold that constituted the revelation of Christ to the ancient inhabitants of America. Guided by the angel, Smith had found the gold tablets and with the aid of magic spectacles had deciphered them. The book, called the Book of Mormon after the name of

SALT LAKE CITY IN 1853. A town created in the heart of the desert. In the early years of the city's existence, housing generally consisted of wooden barracks. Its roads were no more than rutted tracks, flecked with mud puddles. It is now the capital of Utah, and its population is 190,000. *Utah State Historical Society.*

the prophet who had written it, was published and became the holy book of the Mormon Church, or the Church of Jesus Christ of Latter-day Saints. Disciples gathered around Smith, and about 1830 the Church numbered more than three thousand loyal members. Brigham Young, who succeeded him, and who was a bold and energetic organizer, led his persecuted people into the desert and founded Salt Lake City. The beginnings were hard. The apparently sterile soil was entirely dependent on irrigation. But the Mormons had great qualities. Their Apostles organized the state with the same thoroughness as the Church. Soon the tide of emigration toward the Pacific brought them prosperity.

Oregon, California, New Mexico, Utah—it was inevitable that the acquisition of this great domain, which once more doubled the area of the country, should give rise to new controversies between the advocates and the opponents of slavery. In 1846, on the very day when news came of the peace with Mexico, David Wilmot, a northern Republican, proposed that slavery be forever banished from all territories acquired by conquest or purchase from

Mexico. The House voted for the Wilmot resolution, but it was defeated in the Senate.

Meanwhile, in the course of the year 1848, a new event had modified the California problem. When the Americans had occupied California it was a Spanish country, tranquil, majestic, voluptuous. But one day an American named Marshall, employed by a Swiss colonist, Captain Sutter, discovered gold in the spillway of Sutter's mill. He sent nuggets to San Francisco to be assayed. There was no question; it was gold. Quickly the news spread that the valley of the Sacramento was the richest gold region in the world. A true rumor, since in fifty years two billion dollars was to come from the mines of California. When Congress met in 1849 the recognition of California as a free state immediately aroused fierce controversy. In the case of California the proponents of slavery realized with horror that if California was admitted the free states would have a majority in the Senate. What was to be done? Some thought of annexing Cuba, others of organizing slave states in the territories of Utah and New Mexico. But as a matter of fact no palliative could satisfy the aroused proponents of slavery.

ONE OF SUTTER'S MILLS IN CALIFORNIA. On January 24, 1848, James Wilson Marshall discovered gold in the water feeding the mills of the Swiss landowner Sutter. In less than half a century two billion dollars were produced by the California gold mines. *U.S.I.S.*

Henry Clay proposed a compromise: (*a*) California should be admitted as a free state; (*b*) territorial governments should be organized in New Mexico and Utah with the inhabitants free to decide the question of slavery for themselves; (*c*) a more effective law regarding fugitive slaves should be passed, making it easier for the South to recover them; and (*d*) slave trade should be prohibited in the District of Columbia. This compromise was inspired by the sentiments Clay had always had: pity for the infirmity of human nature and a desire to find an equitable and honorable solution. The wise men of both parties hoped that the Great Compromise of 1850 would reconcile the fraternal enemies. Actually, after three years' respite, it was destined to cause the break. The most dangerous element in it was the Fugitive Slave Law, the enforcement of which was to show the northerners the wrongs of slavery in

their worst aspects and to transform a political agitation into an emotional revolt. The law charged federal officers with the apprehension of runaway slaves. It required everyone to assist in tracking down these unfortunates. It provided punishments for citizens who aided escaped slaves even though they might be ignorant that those in question were fleeing slaves. No proof was demanded for arrest; the testimony of Negroes was not admitted; the right of trial by jury was refused them. Such stark injustice could not but arouse the indignation of even the most moderate. *Uncle Tom's Cabin*, a novel that contained an emotional description of the fate of fugitive slaves, increased the indignation of the North. Although the author, Harriet Beecher Stowe, had tried to be fair, the South considered the picture false and incomplete. But the world at large accepted it as true, and the novel was translated into

twenty-two languages. It contributed, perhaps more than the author would have wished, to the formation of public opinion.

In 1852 the Democrats had elected Franklin Pierce by an immense majority. Pierce was totally lacking in distinction, but he represented a coalition of the southern planters and the eastern business-men. The Whigs had once more sent into the fray a military hero, General Winfield Scott; he failed to repeat Harrison's success. Pierce's election showed that the nation, despite all antislavery propaganda, remained faithful to the Compromise of 1850. It was a time of economic prosperity, and the voters, who were making money, were desirous of domestic peace. The discovery of gold and silver mines was producing a rise in prices; the lands of the Middle West were astonishing everyone by their fertility, and in the South cotton-growing was prospering. America was receiving many immigrants that the Revolution of 1848 in Germany and the famine in Ireland had driven from their homes. The flourishing country absorbed this new influx effortlessly. But the slaveholders had not laid down their arms. They now demanded the annexation of Cuba. The business had been dragging on for some time. President Polk had offered to buy the island from Spain and had received the reply that Spain would prefer to see Cuba sunk to the bottom of the ocean than transferred to another power. If one believed the abolitionist newspapers, southern planters took a sadistic joy in beating their Negroes, which was false. If one believed the slaveowners, Kansas could not live without slaves, which was absurd. Confusion was increasing in men's minds. The Whigs had been divided into northern Whigs and southern Whigs by the abolitionists' campaign. The Democratic party supported slavery, but liberal Democrats (and there were many of them in the West and North) did not approve this stand. To unite the malcontents, small new groups were formed. Thus was born a united party called Republican. It had taken the ancient name of Jefferson's supporters and as platform had adopted the resolution that, suspending all differences on the subject of political economy, its members would act in cordial union against the extension of slavery until the end of the conflict.

The extreme proslavery doctrine could lead only to civil war. If it were set aside, there remained two more reasonable points of view. They were embodied in striking fashion in the course of a senatorial campaign in Illinois by the rival candidates, Stephen Douglas and Abraham Lincoln. The two men were far from equal in point of prestige. Douglas had been a senator, a leader of his party, and a presidential possibility. Lincoln, although he was already forty-nine years old, had been nothing more than a congressman, but in Illinois, where he practiced law, he was famous for his honesty, common sense, humor, for the vigor of his logic, and also for his physical strength. Lincoln's prudent realism kept him from being a fanatical abolitionist. He did not preach hatred toward the slaveowners; he recognized the difficulty of their position. But in the speech delivered in Springfield (July 1858), in which he agreed to be a candidate for the Senate against Douglas, he courageously indicated the conclusions to which his long solitary meditations had led him. The ideological positions of the two men were simple: in the matter of slavery, Douglas pronounced himself in favor of popular sovereignty for the states and territories; Lincoln, for the authority of Congress. The voters of Illinois elected Douglas by a small majority. It is important to understand just what this election meant to the South. The latter now felt itself completely different from the North. Not only was it defending a civilization founded on different principles, but it resented tariffs, whereas the North wanted them; it remained rural and agricultural, whereas the North was becoming urban and industrial; it was hostile to bankers, whereas the North favored them. Most of the new railroads were built in the North and for the North. The immigrants, attracted by the factories and repelled by slavery, went to the North. Thus, the population of the North was growing faster than that of the South, and the difference in strength was increasing. Now what legal means did the South possess of defending its customs and its way of life? Congress? But the South had lost its majority in both Houses. The Supreme Court? But the President named the justices, and a series of Presidents hostile to the South could, in time, make a Supreme Court completely favorable to the North. And so the presidency remained the last protection of the southerners. It is easy to understand their

HARRIET BEECHER STOWE. Daguerreotype. Her novel, *Uncle Tom's Cabin*, placed the problem of the Negroes in America before world public opinion and may have unwittingly contributed to the discord between the liberal North and the southern slave states. *The Metropolitan Museum of Art, New York. Ph. Stokes, A. Hawes, and M. A. Hawes Collection.*

JEFFERSON DAVIS, PRESIDENT OF THE CONFEDERATE STATES OF AMERICA, IN A BALCONY APPEARANCE. Jefferson Davis, a planter, son of southern pioneers, was elected by the convention of the first seven southern Confederate States in Montgomery. *Louisiana State Department. Francis G. Mayer photo.*

ABRAHAM LINCOLN EARLY IN 1861. Standing under the Star Spangled Banner (then bearing thirty-four stars), during his speaking tour, Lincoln is vainly trying to calm the people: 'Blood will not flow unless the government's hand is forced.' The bombardment of Fort Sumter started the hostilities. *Lincoln National Life Foundation, Fort Wayne, Indiana.*

anxiety. There were now in the Union eighteen free states and fifteen slave states. Lincoln carried all the free states and was elected President; he had a minority of the popular vote but a majority in the electoral college. In the South he received only twenty-four thousand votes. Nine southern states had voted against him unanimously without a single dissenting voice. The nation was literally split in two by the ax of Abraham Lincoln. Every mail brought death threats to the President.

Civil War

In place of the three traditional sections, East, South, and West, there were now two blocs, the North and the South—blocs of opposed passions and loyalties far more than of opposed interests. On each side there was implicit faith in the worth of the ideas that had been espoused. The people of the South sought to maintain an ancient and honorable society. They considered the emancipation of the slaves impossible and the condemnation of slavery base hypocrisy. The election of 1860 had finally crystallized resentment. To the people of the South, Lincoln, that strange man with the great awkward body, the long arms, the provincial frock coat with sleeves that were too short, seemed a grotesque

and unacceptable leader. The planters of the Carolinas dreamed of restoring a republic of gentlemen, such as their fathers had known in the first days of independence. 'Resistance to Lincoln is obedience to God,' they said.

Henceforth an attempt at secession seemed certain. From moment to moment frightening events impended. Southern extremists maintained that secession would bring them great advantages. They would be free to arrange the life of the commonwealth to suit themselves; they would be free from tariffs designed and enacted to serve interests that were not theirs; their trade with Europe would therefore be facilitated; they could import more slaves from Africa, which would put an end to the rise in the cost of labor. To the southern moderates who feared a war, the extremists said that this war would never occur; that secession could be arranged on a friendly basis; that since the North needed the cotton and the markets of the South, it would accept the *fait accompli;* and finally that England for identical reasons would support the South. Even in the North there were those who had resigned themselves to the inevitable. They agreed that the Union was simply a confederation that the states had voted to join and that they could likewise vote to leave. At the beginning of

1861 Mississippi, Florida, Alabama, Georgia, and Louisiana had rallied to the support of South Carolina, which had declared that the Union was dissolved. Texas followed them. Virginia, North Carolina, Arkansas, and Tennessee hesitated.

In February a convention of the first seven states met in Montgomery, Alabama, and founded the Confederate States of America. The South needed a president. Jefferson Davis was chosen. He was a planter, a retired colonel who had served in the Mexican War, and for a long time he had been one of the most ardent defenders of states' rights. He was by no means a southern aristocrat, but the son of a farmer, born in a log cabin in Kentucky. In Montgomery he delivered a grave and measured speech: 'Placing our confidence in God, in the purity of our hearts and in the strength of our rights, we shall defend the Right to our utmost.'

Meanwhile Lincoln was traveling toward Washington and, along the way, making optimistic speeches that irritated his followers. There is no crisis, he said, except an artificial one. He did not disguise the fact that he hoped to avoid war: 'Blood will not flow unless the government's hand is forced.' The inauguration took place on March 4. The occasion was lacking in brilliance. A plot to assassinate Lincoln had been discovered by the police, and the President was strictly guarded. He seemed ill at ease and so embarrassed by his cane and high hat that his rival, Douglas, who was near him on the platform, relieved him of them at the moment when he stood up to speak. What then was the secret of his strength? Motley said he was the great American *demos*: honest, skillful, rustic, wise, gay, brave, sometimes making mistakes but progressing through those mistakes toward what he believed to be right. He was proud of being a man of the people: 'As I would not be a slave, so I would not be a master. This expresses my idea of democracy.' Unlike many Yankees, he felt no hatred for the people of the South. He called them 'our late friends and adversaries.' He understood the difficulty of their position and sympathized with them. His policy toward them was at once firm and moderate. He

wished to limit the extension of slavery, perhaps progressively to liberate the slaves with an indemnity to their owners, but above all to save the Union.

In order to do this, it was first of all necessary to prevent the secession of more states. Those that formed the frontier between slave and free territories had not yet declared themselves. Lincoln took into his cabinet representatives of Missouri and Maryland with a view to binding those states more closely to the Union. His hesitation about whether to reinforce Fort Sumter, where all the federal government's troops at the entrance to Charleston Harbor were assembled, also is to be explained by his fear of offending the wavering states, including Kentucky. 'Lincoln,' sneered the southerners, 'would like to have God on his side, but he needs Kentucky as well.' What was to be done? Evacuate Fort Sumter and cover up this retreat by blaming the preceding Administration for its negligence? That was to accept defeat. Wait? That meant endangering Major Robert Anderson and his men at the fort. Lincoln, against the advice of his cabinet, decided to send supplies. But on April 12 the Confederate authorities took the initiative and bombarded the fort. Next day the fort was in flames and Anderson had to surrender. The flag of the Confederacy, the Stars and Bars, replaced the Stars and Stripes above the fort. On the fourteenth Anderson marched out proudly with colors flying and his band playing 'Yankee Doodle.'

On the fifteenth Lincoln issued a proclamation summoning seventy-five thousand militiamen for three months' service. In Washington the atmosphere around him grew stormy; the city was Virginian, southern at heart, and the offices were full of his enemies. But the bombardment of Fort Sumter rallied the whole North behind the President. The Confederates had fired on the flag of the Union. This offense united the parties. Pierce and Buchanan, the Democratic ex-Presidents announced their support of Lincoln. Virginia, Tennessee, Arkansas, and North Carolina joined in secession, and the city of Richmond, Virginia, became the capital of the Confederate States. The Negroes expected

LINCOLN. By Alexander Hesler. 'As I would not be a slave,' wrote ▶ Lincoln, 'so I would not be a master. This expresses my idea of democracy.' *U.S.I.S.*

SLAVES BEING SOLD AT AN AUCTION IN A SOUTHERN STATE. ▶ Drawing published in *Harper's Weekly* in 1861. *Library of Congress, Washington. U.S.I.S.*

RECRUITMENT POSTER IN THE BEGINNING OF THE WAR OF SECESSION. *New York Historical Society.*

great things, but in the beginning nothing in their attitude revealed this. They remained respectful and assumed an indifferent manner. Four slave states— Delaware, Maryland, Kentucky, and Missouri— stayed in the Union after internal struggles. Although the geographical division was a division into North and South, there were northerners in the southern army and southerners in the northern army. Many families were divided. Three brothers of Mrs. Lincoln were to die for the South. The general on whom Lincoln was counting to command the Union armies, Robert E. Lee, became instead the best of the southern leaders. Lee was a noble character, and he was so little in favor of slavery that he had freed his own slaves; he did not believe in the right of secession, but he was a Virginian.

Since the secession of Virginia, the Stars and Bars had been floating on the other side of the Potomac, and Lincoln expected to see Confederate gunboats on the river. Many inhabitants of Washington fled from the city. The President, striding up and down his office called with anguish for the northern troops. 'Why don't they come?' he repeated. 'Why don't they come?' Finally they did come. A Massachusetts regiment was attacked while passing through Baltimore, a city that was southern in sympathy, and a bloody skirmish ensued. But other regiments from Boston and New York arrived by sea, and on April 25 a small army marched up Pennsylvania Avenue singing 'John Brown's Body.' The capital had been saved.

How did the opposing sides compare with each other? The North had about twenty-two million inhabitants; the South, five million whites and close

BATTLE OF ANTIETAM. By James Hope. The artist was a Vermont ▶
Second Infantry Regiment captain; hence the lifelike character of the drawing. *Century House, Watkins Glen. U.S. Army.*

to four million slaves. Historians disagree about the total number of soldiers engaged in combat. In the matter of supplies, railroads, and bank deposits, the North had an advantage of three to one. Its industry was greatly superior to that of the South. The local production of arms and munitions at the beginning of the war was inadequate on both sides. In fourteen months the Union government bought 30,000 rifles in America and 726,000 in Europe. Thus all material factors favored the Union. On the other hand, the southern soldiers had more experience in sports than the northern ones, and this is good training for military life. The planters were good riders and good shots. Some of the best officers that had been graduated from West Point (Lee, Johnston, Jackson) came from the South and were destined to become the competent leaders of the Confederate armies. The militiamen of the North, who formed the nucleus of the army, had had no training. The commander of the Union armies was Winfield Scott, an able general but worn out by age and illness. Thus in the beginning the South had certain temporary advantages, but the North possessed a superior war potential. The question was how long the resources of the South would last, how long the North would take to utilize its own.

What were the strategic objectives of the North? The really vulnerable points of the Confederacy were those controlling its lines of communication. The cotton-producing states, which were one-crop regions, could live only by importing their food, either by sea or from the western Confederate States. Now there were only three railroads that provided communication with the West. They crossed the Mississippi at Memphis, Vicksburg, and New Orleans. The capture of these three cities, an expedition through the valley of the Ohio and the Mississippi, would cut the new nation in two, and supplemented by a blockade, the operation would assure victory. But this was not understood by the North till later on.

There were already thirty thousand volunteers fidgeting in Washington and shouting: 'On to Richmond!' It was hard to restrain their eagerness. The army set out for battle as though for a picnic.

No one doubted victory. Senators and congressmen followed the troops in the expectation of 'seeing the Lord deliver the Philistines into their hands.' The rebels were about to be crushed. One lady armed with opera glasses said gaily: 'Tomorrow we'll be in Richmond!' Many farmers had come in spring wagons bringing their wives, and hampers of provisions, to see the battle. But of two poorly trained armies the one that is on the defensive has the advantage. When the reinforcements from the Shenandoah Valley came to the support of the Confederates, the northern army gave way and its retreat quickly became a rout (Battle of Bull Run).

At the time of the declaration of war the unity of the North was admirable, but defeat breeds discord. After Bull Run, Congress blamed the President. Lincoln summoned General George B. McClellan, a young man of thirty-four who had been very successful in Virginia and in the West, and gave him command of the Army of the Potomac. Five months later he appointed him to the chief command of the military forces of the United States. The choice seemed bold and promising. McClellan, an engineering officer, had gone through West Point, had been nourished on the classic works of strategy, and had been sent to Europe to follow the course of the Crimean War; and so he had had some experience of modern warfare. The general in command in the West was Frémont, the former presidential candidate, the hero of the Californian adventure, the son-in-law of the powerful Senator Benton, and the extremely wealthy owner of gold mines—and for all these reasons an unruly fellow. In Saint Louis, where he established his headquarters, he created a scandal by his princely way of life, the foreign officers he had around him, and most of all by the violence of his proclamations. After Bull Run all was quiet on the Potomac front. Both sides were raising large armies. Volunteers came in crowds. To equip them, both sides turned to Europe. The North made its purchases in England. All the Belgian factories worked for the South. To receive shipments it was necessary to keep the ports open. In this respect the North, the traditional home of shipowners, was in a better position and possessed

a fleet superior to that of the South in the ratio of ten to one. But the South showed more daring and ingenuity. At the beginning of the war it had occupied the navy yard at Norfolk and there found the hull of the frigate *Merrimac*: the southerners covered this hull with iron plate and armed it with cannon.

General McClellan was a strange man. He had a large army, the largest that had ever been assembled on this continent. The government gave him all the arms, uniforms, and means of transport he could wish. But he made no move. He always believed that the enemy was stronger and better armed. Lincoln was worried. The country's anger at McClellan burst out when the Confederate General Joseph E. Johnston suddenly, without any interference at all, abandoned the position at

Bull Run that McClellan had been preparing for months to attack. There was a violent change in public opinion, and the demand was made that the enemy should at least be pursued. But McClellan declared he could not take Richmond by frontal attack, and that he would proceed up the Yorktown peninsula, sending his army there by sea. The campaign in the peninsula is a classic example of a battle lost through lack of character in a general. When McClellan arrived before the entrenchments at Yorktown, he found them held by a force of only five hundred men. Did he attack? Not at all. He entrenched himself. He had facing him General Lee, who with great audacity detached his best lieutenant, Thomas J. Jackson (nicknamed Stonewall Jackson), and sent him into the Shenandoah

Valley to immobilize the federal troops by this feint. Jackson swept everything before him, captured three thousand prisoners and twenty-five thousand dollars' worth of provisions, then joined Lee at Richmond. From this raid McClellan deduced that Lee had at least two hundred thousand men. Finally, a series of bloody engagements called the Seven Days' Battles took place before Richmond, in which Lee lost twenty thousand men; McClellan, sixteen thousand. Again at that time McClellan could have taken Richmond. He gave the order to retreat and withdrew toward his base, losing a great number of arms and wagons, which were seized by the Confederates. When this temporizing Napoleon brought his Grand Army back to the Potomac, he was relieved of his command. Then, as his successors fared no better and indeed met defeat in a second battle of Bull Run, which opened the way for an invasion of Maryland, he was recalled and finally stopped Lee at Antietam. By stopping the invasion, the Battle of Antietam put an end to a period that had been disastrous to the North. It was time, for Lincoln's position was becoming difficult.

After Antietam, in September 1862, Lincoln called together the members of his cabinet and said that he was going to act without consulting them. He had vowed to free the slaves as soon as Maryland was saved. God had done his part; he would do his. He did not intend to ask Congress or to apply the measure to those states that had remained in the Union, but rather to act in virtue of his powers as commander in chief, which was his right in enemy country. A preliminary proclamation declared that after January 1, 1863, all slaves in the rebellious states should be free forever and that the Federal Government recognized their liberty. On January 1 Lincoln signed the definitive proclamation. The results of the proclamation were surprising. That the South, threatened by the loss of its possessions and its form of society, should be more determined than ever to fight to the death is natural enough. But one might have supposed that the North would acquire renewed fervor through this act. This was not the case. The abolitionists saw in the gesture a belated adherence to their doctrines. The

northern Democrats denounced it as a political maneuver. Only the slaves felt the stirring of the first breath of freedom.

The objective of the war in the East was Richmond; the objective of the war in the West was the conquest of the Mississippi. It was there that the great northern generals, Grant, Sheridan, and Sherman, proved their worth. Ulysses S. Grant was one of those eccentric military figures whom armies discard in time of peace and whose value is suddenly realized by war. When the Civil War began, he volunteered and was made colonel of an Illinois regiment. A few successful engagements brought him the rank of brigadier general. In February 1862 he captured Fort Donelson, thus assuring the Union the possession of Kentucky; and when the enemy asked for terms, he replied 'Unconditional surrender!'

Of the three crossing points on the Mississippi that had assured the transport of reinforcements and supplies between the Southeast and the Southwest, two, Memphis and New Orleans, were in the hands of the northerners by 1863. New Orleans had been very courageously captured by the gunboats of Captain David G. Farragut, who commanded the flotilla of the Mississippi. After this the Union troops had ascended the river, burning and destroying everything on their way. The South justifiably complained of the brutality of the Yankees. Many soldiers pillaged the homes of the Confederates, slashed the paintings, burned the documents, and ended by setting fire to the house. Civil wars always excite fierce emotions, and the northern officers refused to feel sympathy for 'those damn Secesh women.' After the loss of New Orleans there remained only one artery through which the South could obtain nourishment—Vicksburg. If Grant took Vicksburg, the southern government would find itself cut off from its western states. Taking advantage of interior lines, Grant with great skill first defeated the Confederates at Jackson, Mississippi; then with his rear secure undertook the siege of Vicksburg. What could the Confederates do? Nothing, for their means of transportation did not allow them to send a new army to attack from

◀ ROBERT E. LEE. Hero of the campaign of Virginia, he was long regarded as invincible. The Gettysburg rout was the first flaw in the legend. *National Archives, Brady Collection. U.S. Signal Corps.*

THE BATTLE OF GETTYSBURG.
By M. de Thulstrup. Union
General Meade had the advantage
in numbers and a hill-top position.
This enabled him to decimate
General Lee's attackers. But being
almost as timorous as his predecessor, McClellan, he did not
take full advantage of the Confederates' retreat. *Chicago Historical
Society*.

the rear. Thereupon a siege in the classic manner was begun, with mines, countermines, breaches, and forays, and ended on July 4 with the surrender of the city. Grant captured thirty-one thousand prisoners, and one hundred seventy-two cannon. He generously gave orders to his men not to make any slighting remarks to the vanquished. Soldiers in blue and in grey fraternized. The besieged welcomed the victors to their trenches; the besiegers studied the effects of their gunfire. On both sides courtesy and magnanimity gave rise to friendly conversation. Grant paroled and sent home all the prisoners who came from the Southwest. The capture of Vicksburg was an important victory inasmuch as it gave the North control of the Mississippi.

On the preceding day, July 3, 1863, the southern

armies had suffered another grave defeat. General Robert E. Lee, hero of the campaign in Virginia, had invaded Pennsylvania with the intention of reducing the pressure on Vicksburg. Lincoln sent General Gordon Meade against Lee, and the two armies met near Gettysburg. Lee had about seventy-five thousand men; Meade, eighty thousand. Lee was in a position to accept or decline battle. He accepted. 'And this time,' he said to his officers, 'we are going to show Yankees how we can fight.' His army had been victorious so often that he thought it could do anything, and as a matter of fact men have never attacked more bravely than did Pickett's Virginians, advancing behind their blue flag. But before they reached the crest of the hill three-quarters of the division fell before the northern

◀ GENERAL GRANT'S CHARGE DURING
THE BATTLE OF SHILOH, APRIL 6–7, 1862.
Illinois State Historical Society.

GENERAL WILLIAM TECUMSEH SHER-
MAN. This daguerreotype reflects Sherman's
energy, not to say his brutality. His men were
free to destroy, loot, and set fire to anything
on their path. Georgia and the Carolinas
remembered his passage for a long time.
U.S.I.S.

fire. The losses were so great that Lee was compelled to order a retreat toward the Potomac. Meade could have pursued and destroyed him. But he was a hesitant and prudent general of the same type as McClellan. Despite Lincoln's insistence, he let the enemy escape. Lincoln said: 'Our army held the war in the hollow of their hand, and they would not close it. . . . We had gone all through the labor of tilling and planting an enormous crop, and when it was ripe we did not harvest it!'

It was on the battlefield of Gettysburg, when the many dead had been buried, that Lincoln delivered the famous speech that remains a classic of English prose worthy of a Pericles or a Demosthenes: 'Fourscore and seven years ago our fathers brought forth on this continent a new nation, conceived in liberty and dedicated to the proposition that all men are created equal. Now we are engaged in a great civil war, testing whether that nation or any nation so conceived and so dedicated can long endure. . . .'

Although Lee had saved his army after Gettysburg, the position of the South was becoming critical. The only hope that remained to the South was weariness on the part of the North. There was some reason to anticipate it. Lincoln and the war seemed unpopular. In the beginning volunteers in the North had rushed to the colors. But toward 1863 they had become so few in numbers that many states had to offer bounties to attract them. During the autumn of 1863 Grant's successes continued. Lincoln revived the rank of lieutenant general for him, and he was

[161]

placed in supreme command. On March 8, 1864, Grant went to Washington for the first time in his life. Lincoln wanted him to take Richmond, which hitherto had resisted all assaults. Grant thought the operation possible. The northern armies were now armies of veterans; the service of supply was well organized; Generals Sherman, Sheridan, and Thomas were animated by the same offensive spirit as Grant himself. The method of frontal attack would be costly, but the North had a vast reservoir of men and could make good its losses. Finally Grant besieged Richmond. At the same time General Sherman was to make his way across Georgia and sever Richmond's communications with the South. If Sherman and Grant could close this vise on Lee the war would be over.

In his march to the sea Sherman laid waste everything he found on his way, destroying railroads, enveloping cities in the smoke of the fires he had set, and leaving behind him dreadful memories that took years to efface. Lincoln was a candidate for re-election in 1864. He had changed a great deal in four years, and his character had further developed. The masses had become fond of him, of his humor, of his strangeness, of his love for the people. Honest people realized that he had done his duty without hesitation in dreadfully difficult circumstances. But a peace party was opposed to Lincoln. He was accused of having misused his powers as commander in chief, of having suspended *habeas corpus* without an act of Congress, of having authorized illegal judgments by military tribunals.

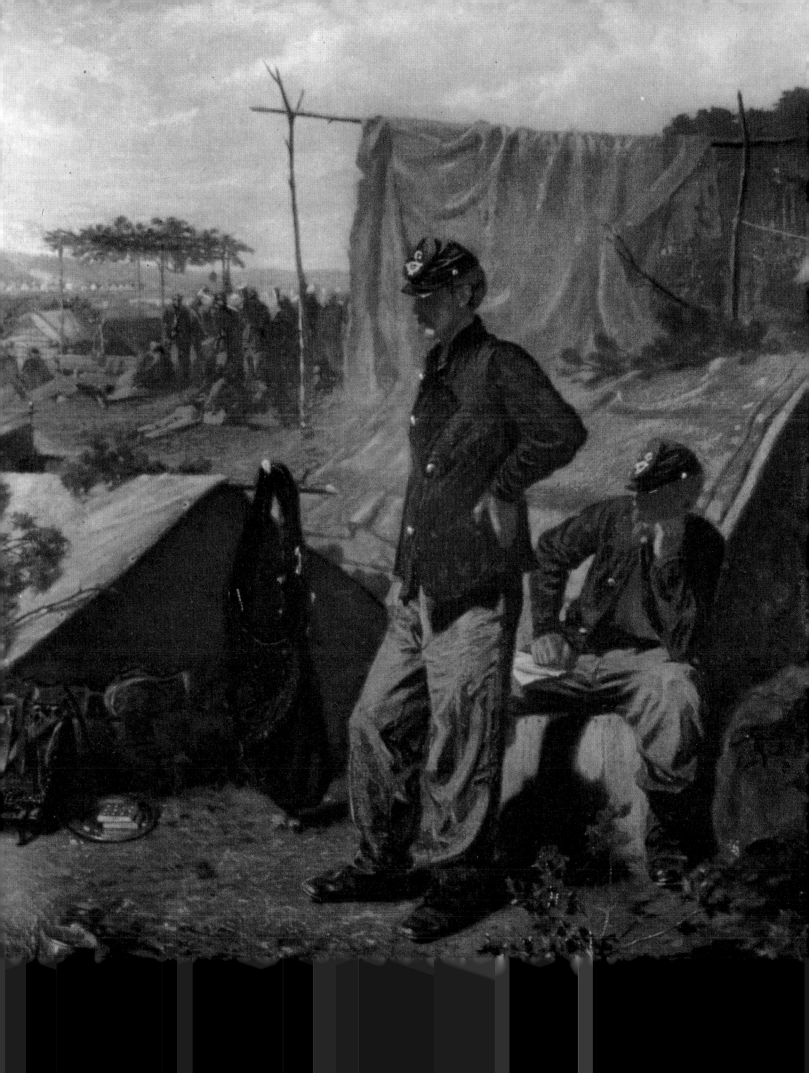

SHERMAN'S MARCH THROUGH ▶
GEORGIA. Painting by Carlin. This
naïve work gives an idyllic view of
General Sherman's passage. The soldiers
are peacefully marching without disturbing the fieldwork, while some of the
inhabitants are bringing a fat goose to the
liberators. Actually, Sherman and his
men tore down everything on their path,
destroyed cities and railroads, looted
houses, burned books. Some, with a
practical turn of mind, even sent their
wives the Georgia and Carolina women's
linens. *Mrs. McCook Knox Collection.
Francis G. Mayer photo.*

DEAD SOLDIERS ON THE GETTYSBURG
BATTLEFIELD. *National Archives. U.S.
Signal Corps photo, Brady Collection.*

ABRAHAM LINCOLN'S SECOND IN-
AUGURAL SPEECH OF MARCH 4, 1865.
The President is at the peak of his career
and of his glory. The War of Secession is
nearing its end, bringing victory to the
Federal Government. One month later,
on April 14, an assassin's bullet killed
Lincoln. *Library of Congress, Washington.*

[168]

Within his own party he was assailed by the radicals, who demanded the immediate abolition of slavery in all states. The Democratic convention of 1864 met in Chicago, called to order by August Belmont, agent of the House of Rothschild in New York. It was hard to agree upon a platform because the party was divided half-and-half between pacifists and supporters of the war. The Democrats finally declared in favor of the cessation of hostilities and chose a general for their candidate, the renowned McClellan. He accepted the nomination, but wrote a letter to the national committee saying he could not endorse the platform. The confusion resulting from this misunderstanding, combined with the victories of the summer, gave the election to Lincoln by an electoral vote of two hundred and twelve to twenty-one. Andrew Johnson, a Demo-crat and a supporter of the war, became Vice-President. Lincoln's election did as much good as a victory. Only the North could make the North lose the war. Since the North had decided to fight, it was sure to win.

Sherman marched through the Carolinas, wreak-ing even more havoc than in Georgia. His soldiers had become experts in pillaging. They emptied closets, sent their wives the linen belonging to the women of the South, smashed pianos, and burned books. It was a strange orgy of hatred, owing perhaps to the length of the war. From a military point of view, the objective was to join forces with

[170]

Grant, but the latter did not wait for Sherman, and in March 1865 pressed the attack against Richmond. Lee, greatly outnumbered, abandoned the capital and advised Jefferson Davis to leave. The Confederate government fled. On April 3, 1865, Lincoln came to Richmond, the conquered capital, said a few kindly words, and was received by the Negroes, who alone had remained and who greeted him as the Messiah come to deliver them; they awaited some miracle, though they did not know what. Lee beat a retreat, followed and enveloped by the North's cavalry. On April 7 Grant sent a note to Lee: 'General, the result of last week should convince you of the vanity of all further resistance.' Lee replied that in order to avoid useless bloodshed

he wished to know the conditions of surrender. At this time Lee had neither ammunition nor food. On April 9 the two generals met at the village of Appomattox. This conference is one of the famous episodes of history. The contrast between the two men was striking—Lee so handsome, so correctly dressed in a new gray uniform and wearing the beautiful sword that had been presented to him by Virginia; Grant untidily turned out in the uniform of a common soldier. Neither of the two was especially interested in the political aspects of the struggle. The conditions of the armistice were generous. The soldiers of the Confederacy were to return home on parole and take their horses with them. 'They will have need of them for their spring plowing,' Grant

LINCOLN'S ASSASSINATION. On
April 14, 1865, John Wilkes Booth, an
actor without fame or talent, stole into
President Lincoln's box at the Ford
Theater and killed him with a bullet in
the back of the head. General Grant
said when he heard the news, 'Reconstruction has been set back, no telling
how far.' *Viollet Collection.*

said. Lee, who was very religious, believed that
God governs the affairs of men to his own inscru-
table ends, and he accepted defeat with resignation.
It was over. The South was disarmed and at the
mercy of the North.

What sort of peace would the North dictate? So
far as Lincoln was concerned there could be no
question. He hoped to reconstruct without humi-
liating. Provided the conditions of peace contained
two things—the maintenance of the Union and the
abolition of slavery—he was ready to sign. It was
natural to pity the South. It had suffered so much.
Its gracious women had sacrificed everything for
victory that had not come. Their houses were in
ashes, their plantations ruined, their sons dead.

On April 14, 1865, as the President and Mrs.
Lincoln sat in Ford's Theater, the bullet of an
assassin put an end to Lincoln's life. John Wilkes
Booth, a half-mad actor and fanatical secessionist,
had killed the President. It was Good Friday. That
morning Lincoln had said to the members of
his cabinet: 'I had a strange dream. . . . I seemed
to be in a singular and indescribable vessel, that
was moving with great rapidity toward a dark
and indefinite shore. I have had this extraordinary
dream before great events, before victories. I had
it preceding Antietam, Stone River, Gettysburg,
Vicksburg. . . .' A victory? No, Lincoln's death was
not a victory; for all Americans it was a dreadful
defeat. 'It would be impossible for me,' said Grant,

STROLL ON THE BANKS OF THE HUDSON
AROUND 1870. The name of the artist is not
known and neither is the date of the painting.
In all likelihood it was not too close to the
time mentioned in the title, unless the anony-
mous painter was a genuine double and
genial forerunner by about twenty years of
Henri Rousseau, the *Douanier* (especially in
his rendering of the tree trunks, leaves, and
the landscape generally). *Abby Aldrich
Rockefeller Folk Art Collection, Williamsburg.*

[175]

'to describe the feeling that overcame me at the news. I knew his goodness of heart, and above all his desire to see all the people of the United States enter again upon the full privileges of citizenship with equality among all. I felt that reconstruction had been set back, no telling how far.'

Toward a Modern Nation

Andrew Johnson was not Lincoln's equal, and he seemed much less capable of liquidating the war without useless suffering. Nevertheless, he was far from being an unworthy executive. His political position was complicated. Offspring of poor whites, he hated the rich planters who constituted the slavocracy. He was sincere, law-abiding and devoted to his country; he had few ideas but was faithful to them. He could not be, as his enemies claimed, a traitor to the Republican party, for he had never belonged to that party.

The situation that Lincoln had bequeathed to him was dangerous, in spite of the victory. Two questions seemed settled: the Negroes were no longer slaves, and the Union was no longer threatened. But these negative solutions were clearly not enough. The Negroes had no clear understanding of what had happened to them and thought that the government was going to give each of them a farm and livestock. In the North hysterical radicals, maddened by hatred, were demanding punishment for the rebels, confiscation of their property, and the death penalty for their leaders. The desire of the radicals was not to bind up the wounds of the country and restore its unity but to humiliate that proud oligarchy and to see that it was governed by the blacks it had oppressed. This had certainly not been Lincoln's postwar plan.

As soon as he was in power Johnson felt the danger of a policy of revenge. In May 1865 he granted an amnesty to the rebels. Lee, who had intended to seek refuge in some home in the woods, became president of Washington College (now Washington and Lee) and taught young Virginians their duty as good Americans. The Negro problem was far from being settled by emancipation. There were over four million blacks in the South. Emancipation had set them loose, naked, hungry, and miserable without a roof over their heads. At first many stayed on the plantations. The master would call them together in front of his handsome house and tell them that they were free. They would reply: 'Massa, we stay here with you.' Left to themselves, the planters and the freedmen would probably have reached a compromise. Most of the Negroes were kindly and easygoing by nature. But agitators circulated among these unhappy masses, telling them that they must prove their independence by leaving their masters, refusing to work, maltreating the whites, and taking over their churches. The planters could not deny the equality of all men before God. Nevertheless, the first time a black man in Richmond knelt among the whites for communion, those near him drew back. On this occasion it was General Lee, with his customary dignity, who took his place beside the Negro, thus setting an example that was followed. Immediately, the Negroes, eager for learning, filled the few inadequate schools that were open to them. For the rest they waited for the Federal Government to become a Santa Claus and give each of them 'forty acres and a mule.' As a matter of fact, the agitators from the North were making use of the Negroes for their own purposes; what they wanted was the black vote, and they were trying to make sure of it in advance. During the summer of 1865, taking advantage of the fact that Congress was not in session, Johnson tried to put Lincoln's plan into operation. In a number of states he appointed military governors under whose protection conventions met to abolish the ordinances of secession, ratify the Thirteenth Amendment ('Neither slavery nor involuntary servitude . . . shall exist in the United States . . .') and vote new constitutions. But when in December 1865 the senators and representatives of the states of this reformed Confederacy presented themselves in Washington, Congress refused to recognize 'Johnson governments,' which was its right, since each House has the privilege of passing

◀ NEGRO CHILDREN IN THE RUINS OF CHARLESTON, SOUTH CAROLINA. *Library of Congress, Washington.*

upon the credentials of its members. These 'Johnson governments' had tried, in their southern fashion, to solve the Negro problem. The South accepted its defeat and the emancipation. It did not believe in the immediate equality of two races, one of which had been more anciently civilized and had acquired its privileges by slow degreès. It agreed to recognize equal rights for the Negroes with respect to the protection of property, life, and liberty, but it maintained the social barriers. The 'black codes' forbade mixed marriages and maintained the principle of the segregation of races in the schools.

The temporary solution adopted by Congress was to create the Freedmen's Bureau, a joint administration made up of military and civilian personnel, charged with the duty of settling all questions of aid for the Negroes, regulation of their work, their schools and tribunals, as well as the operation of those properties confiscated from the rebels. The Freedmen's Bureau became the Negroes' guardian, and the latter were thought of as wards of the nation. This attitude was hardly more liberal than that of the black codes. Nevertheless, the institution might have given good results if it had been in competent hands. The radicals in Congress who had put all their hopes in Johnson were now exasperated by his mildness. Thaddeus Stevens with his bitter eloquence proposed to treat the southern states as conquered territories that by their secession had lost all civil rights. This thesis was absurd, since the reason for the war had been the proposition that a state could not separate itself from the Union.

CHICAGO IN 1866: COURTHOUSE SQUARE. *Chicago Historical Society.*

Stevens and his friends wanted to proscribe the Confederates and strip them of their goods to the profit of the Negroes. They spoke of the Constitution of the United States as 'a scrap of worthless paper.'

On February 24, 1868, the House impeached Johnson by a vote of one hundred twenty-eight to forty-seven. It was the first time that this provision had been applied. The Senate transformed itself into a high court and before it were laid eleven principal accusations, of which the only serious one was the violation of the Tenure of Office Act. This recently passed Act would have deprived the President of the right to change the members of his cabinet without the consent of the Senate. The trial was carried on with such evident prejudice that public opinion began to veer in favor of Johnson. But Chief Justice Salmon P. Chase, who presided, conducted himself as a magistrate and not as a partisan. The twelve Democratic senators would naturally vote for acquittal. Five Republican senators joined them, some because they were honest men (Ross was one of these), others because they did not want Wade, who was president of the Senate, to become President of the United States. With these Republican votes acquittal was assured. Thaddeus Stevens cried: 'The country is going to the devil!' The vote of the Senate was an important event, not because of Johnson, who was coming to the end of his term and had lost all chance of re-election, but for the safety of the Constitution and the independence of the executive.

SAN FRANCISCO IN 1877. *California Historical Society, San Francisco.*

An effort was made to give colored men an education. The desire for learning among the Negroes was sincere and touching. Unfortunately, too many of the schools organized by northern radicals became new hotbeds of racial hatred. In 1865 Lincoln could hope that the wounds would be quickly healed and that the best of the Negroes would be, little by little, with the consent of the whites, admitted to all rights of citizens. In 1868 the effects of the 'Reconstruction' had been such that the southern whites were firmly determined to prevent, as long as they could, all Negroes from voting. As often happens, the Negroes had been the victims of too zealous friends. The attitude of the Republican party in this matter resulted in the suspension for a long time of all political life in the South and in making fidelity to the Democratic party there an article of faith.

Between 1868 and 1870 the 'reconstructed' states of the South ratified the Fifteenth Amendment, which forbade any state to refuse suffrage to a man because of race, color, or previous condition of servitude. This enabled them to return to the Union, but they immediately set to work to destroy in secret the conditions they had accepted publicly. When a people or a group sees itself deprived of all legal means of defense, it loses confidence in law and starts to fend for itself. Throughout the South secret societies were formed. The two best known were the Ku-Klux Klan and the Knights of the White Camellia. The Ku-Klux Klan was born in Pulaski, a small town in Tennessee. There some young Confederates for purposes of entertainment had founded a *kyklos* (the Greek word for circle). At night they would disguise themselves as ghosts by wrapping themselves in shrouds and seek amusement by frightening the Negroes. The effect was so great that other towns thought this might be a means of effective action. Little by little the Invisible Empire extended all over the South. The supreme chief was the Grand Wizard. For a long time violence was unnecessary; terror sufficed to keep a large number of blacks away from the polls. The White Camellia, which had its headquarters in New Orleans, also claimed that its object was the maintenance of white supremacy 'while at the same time respecting all the legitimate rights of the blacks.' The Ku-Klux Act of 1871 authorized the Federal Government to make use of the army to suppress the activities of the Klan. But in the South the whites had already won the game, and the radical majority was rapidly diminishing. In 1872 an amnesty act restored political rights to most of the former rebels. The Negroes were prevented from voting, not by violence, which would have been denounced, but by secret threats. Little by little the Democrats reconquered all the southern states. In 1875 only South Carolina, Louisiana, and Florida remained under radical control.

Congress's mistake had been to devote its energies to the hasty and premature solution of a political problem when the most urgent problem was an economic one. The planters were ruined; as completely or more completely than the French nobility after the Revolution. Between planters and slaves the ancient bond had been broken. How were the plantations to be cultivated, and how were the freedmen to live? The method generally adopted was that of sharing the crops. The great plantations were broken up into small lots on each of which lived a family. The proprietor had to advance the farmer everything he needed, build him a house out of wood, give him tools, fertilizers, and seed. In return the proprietor had a right to two-thirds of the crop. Unfortunately, most of the proprietors had to borrow the necessary capital from the banks. Heavy mortgages weighed upon agriculture. The lenders, needing a security that could easily be liquidated, insisted upon a single crop, tobacco or cotton, and farther to the South, rice or sugar cane. It was not until 1880 that corn and wheat secured an important place in the production of the South. At the time of the Reconstruction instead of small farms or tenant properties developing as had happened in France, where a variety of things were grown and there was cattle breeding to boot, an agricultural proletariat was formed in the South in which the whites were no better off than the blacks. Bankers and real-estate dealers for a long time were the only ones to profit by this agrarian revolution. A whole new army of ruined planters came to swell the ranks of the 'poor whites.' In the sandy hills of Alabama and the sterile pine forests of Georgia lived people who had been reduced to the miserable verge of existence. They were called 'crackers' or 'hillbillies.' They still exist, and

THE COTTON BROKERS (1873). By Edgar Degas. *Fogg Art Museum,*
Cambridge, Massachusetts. Francis G. Mayer photo.

POWER THRESHER NEAR GRANGEVILLE, IDAHO. This primitive machine powered by horse-gear was already obsolete at the time (1890) and almost everywhere had been replaced by the steam-powered thresher. Here the flails are rotated (middle ground) by a shaft that the horses must step over at each turn. *Idaho Historical Society.*

Erskine Caldwell has described them in *Tobacco Road* and in *God's Little Acre*.

Defeat had not destroyed in the hearts of the men and women of the South their love of their civilization or their intention of maintaining it. Quite the contrary. Persecution had strengthened local patriotism. It had also enlarged it. Before the Civil War many would have called themselves citizens of Virginia, South Carolina, Tennessee. It was the Civil War that gave a precise meaning to the adjective 'southern.' After Appomattox the best people prided themselves on being 'men of the South,' unreconstructed and unreconstructible. For thirty years their secret goal was to re-establish the old southern independent way of life. They maintained a united and jealously guarded society. A man who came from the North, if he wanted to be on good terms with his southern neighbors, had to take care to refrain from expressing northern sentiments. One result of this state of mind was unfortunately to accentuate race feeling. The Negroes were less well treated between 1880 and 1900 than they had been between 1840 and 1880.

Another result of postwar southern patriotism was the birth of industry in the South. To struggle against the North even peacefully there was need to make use of northern arms. To save the 'poor whites' from destitution, which was turning them into agricultural workers in competition with Negroes, it was necessary to open factories. The existence in the South of great deposits of coal, iron, and copper attracted a metal industry.

THE OVERLAND MAIL COMPANY MAIL TRUNK. Mount Shasta, rising in the background, resembles ▶ Fujiyama as it appears in Japanese prints. *Wells Fargo Bank, San Francisco. Cal Pictures photo.*

Cotton-growing suggested a textile industry. At Durham the tobacco industry became extremely important. It is true that the industrial life of the South was handicapped by the climate, by the habits of an old agrarian civilization, and by the railroad rates and customs duties that even today are the tariffs of northerners made by northerners for northerners. On the other hand, the southern factories benefited by the low cost of labor and by the strange paternalism that was a survival of the plantation system. It is to this active industrial South that American historians have often given the name of the New South. In reality the New South was conceived and created for the sole purpose of preserving the essence of the Old South. It was one way of expressing the passionate feelings that for a period of thirty years turned the South into an army of loyal veterans drawn up behind its leaders and that even today struggles to safeguard what it has loved so much.

After the war the North was 'reconstructed'—or transformed—just as completely as the South. The America of Johnson still resembled in many ways that of Jackson. The sources of great fortunes still were, as they had been in the eighteenth century, commerce and navigation. The new aristocracy of the North—the Astors, the Goelets, the Beekmans, the Rhinelanders—still invested their capital in land and owned vast estates like those of the Van Rensselaers and the Schuylers. Industry remained at the stage of a family enterprise created by an individual who ran it in a paternal fashion and bequeathed it to his son. Corporations had existed since 1860 but they played no great role. One of the most important was the Western Union Telegraph Company, which had combined fifty small enterprises. A part of industry had remained in the handicraft stage; contractors distributed piecework to country women who did the sewing in their own homes. Most of the deposits of minerals

PONY EXPRESS RIDER. The mail on horseback, started by the Pony Express service in 1860, won great public admiration. As soon as the rider came to a relay station he changed horses. *Western Union photo. U.S.I.S.*

THE DAILY TIMES.

MONDAY MORNING, JANUARY 30, 1860.

LOCAL AND TERRITORIAL.

GREAT EXPRESS ENTERPRISE!

From Leavenworth to Sacramento in Ten Days!

Clear the Track and let the Pony Come Through?

NEWS!!

In our telegraphic columns a few days ago,

ADVERTISEMENT FOR PONY EXPRESS. The text of the poster is strewn with exclamation marks, which faithfully reflect the people's enthusiasm for the riders. *Kansas State Historical Society, Topeka.*

remained untouched. In 1859 petroleum had been found in Pennsylvania, but its exploitation had hardly been begun. Horse-drawn carriages were still the sole means of transportation in the big cities. In 1860 Americans had admired as a remarkable novelty the organization of the pony express, a system for carrying the mails by fast riders from Saint Joseph, Missouri, to Sacramento, California. The regular time was ten days. The riders leaped from one horse to the next at the relay stations. It was a fine sporting spectacle. But this enterprise, which had always operated at a loss, soon gave place to the railroad and the telegraph. The world had changed more between 1865 and 1900 than from the time of Caesar to that of Washington.

The war had upset and stimulated the economy of the North. To arm, clothe, and shoe the soldiers it had been necessary to increase production and expand factories. Bankers and manufacturers had learned to make better use of credit. Adequate food supplies for the army had been procured only through the use of farm machinery and by the creation of the meat-packing industry. When peace came machinery made possible the exploitation of the immense regions that were still available in Missouri, Iowa, Nebraska, and Kansas. The demobilization of the armies provided daring and hardened emigrants to clear this new frontier. But first of all it had to be made accessible.

This was the task of another type of pioneer—the railroad builder. At first animals had supplied the motive power. The only reason for building a track had been to reduce friction and permit horses to haul heavier loads. The first steam-powered locomotives had had small success. They covered the travelers with soot; they frightened the animals along the way; they irritated the farmers, who accused them of setting fire to their hayricks. Around 1825 the canal seemed to have won an easy victory over the railroad. The public praised the comfort of

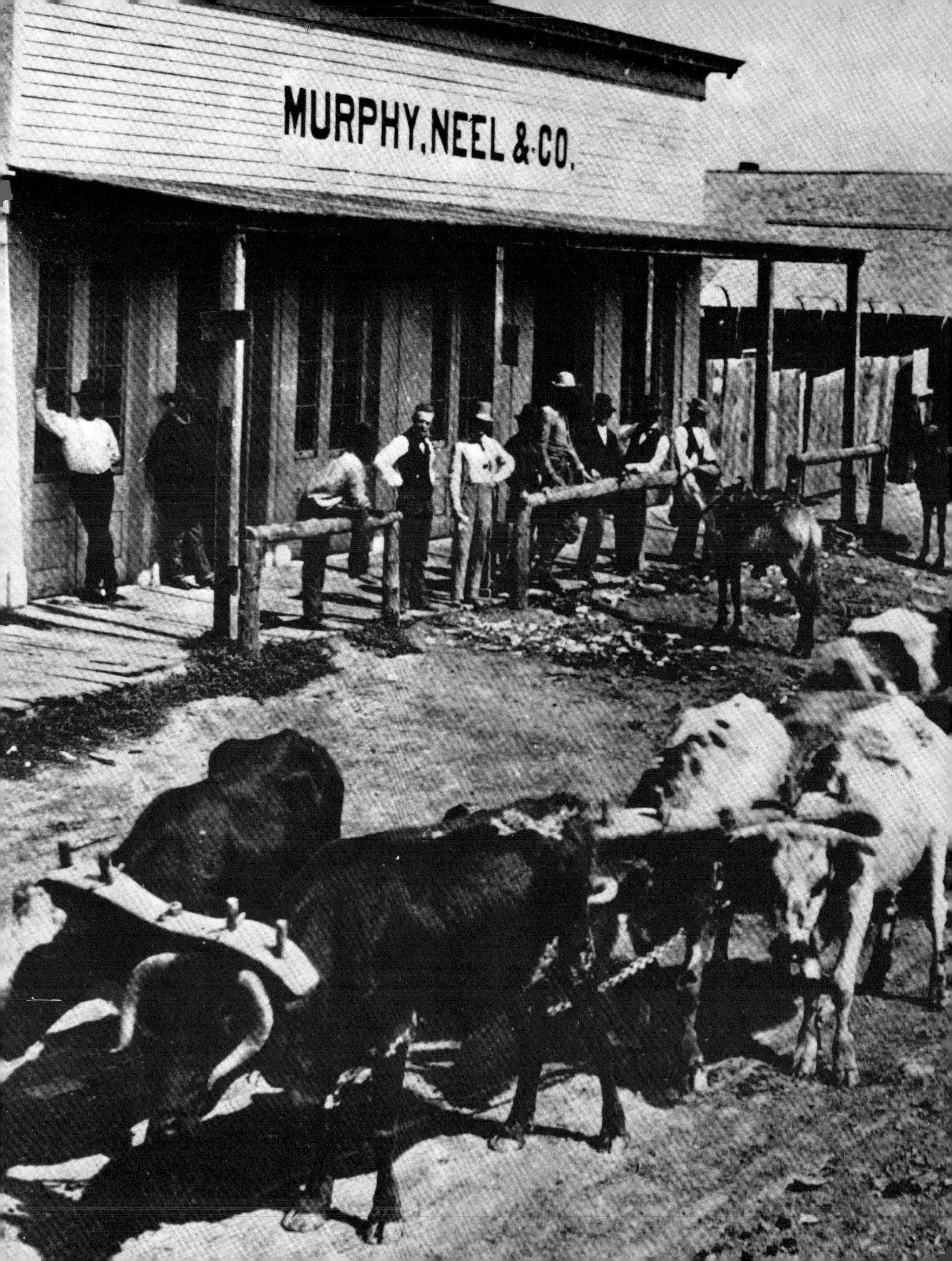
MURPHY, NEEL & CO.

YOKE OF OXEN IN BENTON, MON-
TANA. In the West oxen were used
much more than horses by most
enterprises to carry goods and even
people. The convoys were escorted by
a cowboy, and the name itself was
indicative of his main occupation.
This setting has been made famous by
the western films: wood houses with
porches, planked footpaths, and rough
fences made of three logs nailed at
right angles for the cowboys to hitch
their horses. *Denver Public Library,
Western Collection.*

[189]

the barges. Nevertheless, small companies built lines between neighboring cities: Hartford and New Haven; Baltimore and Washington. Because of the absence of any organized system, it was necessary to change trains several times even for short trips and often to cover part of the distance on foot, on horseback, by carriage, or by boat. About 1860 there existed in the United States approximately thirty thousand miles of railroads divided among a number of companies. The great arterial river, the Father of Waters, retained its pre-eminence. It was by way of the Mississippi that the whole commerce of the West moved.

The Civil War closed the river. Suddenly the importance of all the railroads that connected the West with the East was augmented. Chicago and Saint Louis became commercial centers of the first magnitude. The branch lines were united into systems. After the war five important lines vied for the east-west traffic—the New York Central, the Pennsylvania, the Erie, the Baltimore and Ohio, and (in Canada) the Grand Trunk Line. In 1867 Pullman conceived the idea of the sleeping car that bears his name. The diner made it possible to eliminate long stops at station restaurants. Steel rails replaced iron rails. The development was so rapid that in 1880 there were ninety-three thousand miles of tracks; in 1890, one hundred sixty-seven thousand miles.

Philip Guedalla has said that the true history of the United States between 1865 and 1890 is the history of transportation, in which the names of railroad presidents are more important than those of the Presidents of the United States. It was the time of Homeric struggles between Commodore Vanderbilt, Jay Gould, Daniel Drew, Edward Harriman, James Hill, and the bankers J. P. Morgan and

THE 'DENVER' DOCKING AT SAINT JOSEPH. Ferry of the type used on the Mississippi-Missouri around 1860. Some of them could carry considerable loads, for instance a locomotive or even an entire train, hence the name of ferryboat. *Saint Joseph Museum photo.*

TWO LOCOMOTIVES MEET, COMING FROM OPPOSITE DIRECTIONS. Two railroad lines, the Central Pacific, or C.P., from the West, and the Union Pacific, or U.P., from the East, completed their junction in 1869, seven years after work had started. *Union Pacific Railroad photo.*

August Belmont for the control of the great 'systems'; the time of the tariff wars; the time of the battle between Philadelphia and New York for trade with Chicago. Cornelius Vanderbilt was the first of these pirates of genius who unified the railroads of the United States with great profit to themselves and indisputable advantage to the country.

The most remunerative enterprises of this time were the transcontinental railroads. In 1862 Lincoln had authorized the construction of the Union Pacific, running west from Omaha, Nebraska, and of the Central Pacific, running east from San Francisco. In 1869 the two lines met near Ogden, Utah. It was amazing that they had succeeded in crossing the wilderness in spite of the Indians, the nature of the terrain, and the labor problems. It had been necessary to arm the workmen and

to have them escorted by troops of soldiers.

At the time of Lincoln's death the immense territory extending from the Rocky Mountains on the west to Missouri and Kansas on the east was still in the nature of a 'frontier.' Scattered cities—Salt Lake City, Denver, and beyond the Rockies, Sacramento, San Francisco, Portland, and Seattle—were, like the early English and French forts, hardly more than advance outposts. As soon as you left them, you found the open prairie where the buffalo roamed. In 1865 millions of these enormous beasts lived in huge herds. Hunters undertook the methodical destruction of these animals and in a few years annihilated them almost completely. It was here that Colonel William F. Cody, called Buffalo Bill, won fame. During the construction of the Union Pacific he became the great purveyor for the gangs of workmen, supplying them with buffalo

THE BUFFALO HUNT. A picturesque and decorative, rather than truly documentary work. Three half-naked Indians on horseback, wearing feathers from waist to heels, are shooting arrows at a herd of huge buffaloes. The beasts are fleeing their formidable enemies. *Smithsonian Institution.*

meat. Later he organized the first Wild West Show and toured the whole of Europe with his wild horses and his Indians in feather headdresses.

This problem of the Indians was a difficult one. At the end of the Civil War there remained about two hundred twenty-five thousand aborigines between the Mississippi and the Rockies. Many of the tribes were civilized. In all good faith they signed treaties with the United States, granting them ownership of certain lands. Then the whites requested right of passage. They agreed. After that came the cattlemen and the farmers, who undertook to force the Indians to sell their lands. If they refused, the pale faces massacred them. In Oregon in 1871 the whites, with the aid of dogs, hunted down a group of Indians, cornered them in a cave and slaughtered them all, men, women, and children. Naturally the Indians sought revenge.

Before the terrifying strength of the whites, the Indians finally resigned themselves. The last act of war between whites and Indians occurred in 1890. By 1887 the Dawes Act had pretty well settled the administration of Indian affairs. In 1901 the members of five civilized tribes acquired American

THE LAST WAGON TRAIN ARRIVING IN DENVER. The completion of the Kansas Pacific Railroad in 1869 put an end to the use of horses to transport passengers and goods. *State Historical Society of Colorado.*

citizenship. Finally in 1924 an act of Congress decreed that henceforth every Indian born on American soil should be a citizen.

The settling of the prairies was at first the work of the cowboys, who came from the South, bringing their cattle. Since time immemorial Texas and Mexico had bred stock for their local needs. When the great territories to the north were opened, the ranchers discovered that the grass was better there than it was at home, and moreover there was a market. Their goal became the railroad, which enabled them to sell their cattle to the large meat-packing houses in Chicago, Saint Louis, Kansas City, and Omaha. The long trails that ran from Texas to Illinois were soon trodden into deep furrows by the hoofs of cattle. The whole Middle West soon came to recognize the cowboy by his leather clothes, his

high boots, his large hat that served both as umbrella and raincoat, the red scarf around his neck, his pistol, and his rope. Large cities grew up along the railroad. About 1880 cattle-raising was transformed by the invention of barbed wire, which made it possible to enclose pastures at small cost. Rich cattlemen seized lands that had formerly been public property. Queen Grass became as powerful in the West as King Cotton had once been in the South. When the farmers completed the conquest of the great plains it was the end of the 'frontier.' With it disappeared one of the great forces that had molded America.

The miners had been among the first to settle the new West. They were the ones who had caused the meteoric development of California. In Colorado, Idaho, Montana, Nevada, and Wyoming small

communities grew up around copper mines, silver
mines, lead mines, or gold mines. In Nevada the
Comstock lode produced in twenty years three
hundred million dollars' worth of silver. The
desert was peopled with millionaires. As soon as a
new deposit began to be exploited, a camp consisting
of hundreds of tents immediately sprang up.
Saloons, bars, and gambling houses were opened.
Streetwalkers flocked there. An entire mushroom
city arose.

Around it farmers cleared the ground, thinking
that they would find an easy market by selling their
produce to the miners. Then the deposit would
peter out, the city would die, the miners depart, and
the farmers would remain alone. Near Denver one
could see a ghost town, Central City; it had its time
of prosperity, and even a charming little theater;
later it was deserted. During the time of the mining
fever new states were born: Nevada was admitted in
1864; Nebraska in 1867; Colorado in 1876. The
territories of Idaho, Dakota, and Washington were
growing with the construction of the railroads and
were asking for admission. Montana was admitted
in 1889, and Wyoming in 1890. Thus the West's
power in the Senate was assured. This state of
affairs was not without danger, for it gave a
minority the power to control the foreign policy of
the country.

◀ A DOG TEAM SETTING OFF FOR ALASKA. In a Dawson street, a crowd of onlookers standing in front of the main building in the center of town, the Stock Exchange, watches the last preparations being made for a dog-pulled supply column going to the famous Valdez camp in Alaska. *National Film Office, Canadian Government.*

THE OFFICE OF JUDGE ROY BEAN. The justice of the peace is also a notary public and drink-stand owner. The open-air waiting room is guarded by office clerks armed with carbines. *Culver Pictures.*

The Difficult Presidencies

The presidential election of 1868 was an event of capital importance to all the citizens of the United States. For the Republicans it meant a chance of securing their party's hold on the national government by confirming the Negroes' right to vote; for the bankers and manufacturers, of making the most of a handsomely subsidized program to 'open the continent'; for the Democrats, of winning the peace after having lost the war, of restoring to the states a part of their rights, and of combating the tariffs. The candidate of the Democrats was Horatio Seymour, a former governor of New York and a man unhampered by prestige or talent. The Republican convention chose by acclamation Ulysses S. Grant, the famous general who had a glorious military past but so little political experience that he was not even sure he was a Republican.

Grant possessed charming simplicity, kindness, and a naïve confidence in his friends. His military victories had made him conscious of his country's debt to him. He considered the Presidency not as a responsibility but as a reward. Of the Constitution and the duties of the President he was completely ignorant, and he made no effort to inform himself. Moreover, the war had worn him out. That the United States should make him the gift of the Presidency seemed quite natural to him. The northern voters felt about it as he did. They voted in 1868, not for a program but, as Allan Nevins has said, 'for an indestructible legend, for a national hero. . . .'

Since the President was incompetent, the selection of a Secretary of State assumed special importance. Hamilton Fish was given the post and acquitted himself well, even though the President caused him anguish. Without consulting his cabinet, Grant negotiated a treaty annexing the Republic of Santo Domingo. Colonel Babcock, the President's secretary, had arranged the affair for a million and a half dollars with a revolutionary government of doubtful authority. When Grant proudly announced this news to his stupefied cabinet, Hamilton Fish tendered his resignation. Grant begged him, in his disarming fashion, to remain: 'I need you and Mrs. Grant needs your wife.' For Mrs. Hamilton Fish, an experienced woman of the world, acted as Mrs.

Grant's adviser in diplomatic etiquette. The treaty was rejected by the Senate; but the episode showed that under the influence of skillful and selfish men Grant was capable of making dangerous moves. Within the Republican party many good citizens were growing uneasy both at the latent corruption and at the brutal turn the policy of reconstruction was taking. A group of reformers grew up inside and outside the party. A large part of the country approved the reformers, and they would have had a chance in 1872 to keep Grant from winning a second term if they had chosen a strong Democratic candidate. After prolonged quarrels they nominated Horace Greeley, editor of the *Tribune*, a New York newspaper. But Grant was re-elected by an immense majority. Greeley died a month after the election. Justice is not of this world.

Grant's second term, like his first, was tarnished by scandals. Economic crises were becoming periodical. It seemed impossible to adjust buying power and production. As a matter of fact, no one tried to do so. When business was going well, enterprises multiplied; prices and salaries rose; credits expanded. A moment came when the credits exceeded real values and when the market, in disequilibrium, was at the mercy of the slightest jar. That was what happened in 1873. Europe ceased to buy American securities. Jay Cooke's bank, famous for having financed the Civil War in the North, suspended payments. The event turned the business world upside down. The public believed that Jay Cooke was as solid as the Bank of England. On the day following this bankruptcy the market went to pieces within a few hours. Soon factories were closing. In the great cities pitiful crowds of unemployed stood in line for bread. In 1874 there were six thousand bankruptcies; in 1875, eight thousand; in 1876, nine thousand. The whole country, not without cause, was demanding reform. It was the end of easy elections scored against the South by waving 'the bloody shirt'.

Among those who were angered by the panic of 1873, the bitterest were the farmers. In 1867 one man reached the conclusion that it was necessary for the farmers to unite in their own defense. This was a federal employee named Oliver H. Kelley, who had been in charge of an investigation in the South and had observed the distress of the farmers and their intellectual isolation. He founded a secret order, a kind of freemasonry that he called the Grange. Theoretically, there were to have been farmers' granges in all the states, but Kelley had so little money to launch his project that he could hardly afford to buy stamps. If an organization was ever founded on 'the rock of poverty,' it was this one. Nevertheless it succeeded in getting a number of its candidates elected to local legislatures in several states. It carried on a struggle against the railroads, successfully in many respects, and imposed more reasonable rates upon the companies.

The election of 1876 was one of the strangest in the history of the country. It seemed likely that the Republican candidate would be James G. Blaine, a politician celebrated for his graciousness, magnetism, and irresistible charm of manner. Blaine arrived at the convention with so many delegates pledged to him that he believed he was certain of the nomination. But Rutherford B. Hayes, a retired general and governor of Ohio, was nominated instead.

In the South the election was carried on amid great disorders; there was violence, fraud, and confusion. One hundred eighty-five votes were required for election. When it became known that Tilden, the Democrat, had one hundred eighty-four votes to his credit, it was thought he had been elected. But the returns from four states, Florida, Louisiana, South Carolina, and Oregon, were contested. A long debate began in Congress.

The election officials in Louisiana and Florida

GENERAL ULYSSES S. GRANT, eighteenth President of the United ▶ States. *Library of Congress, Washington.*

[204]

were Republicans. They received tempting promises from their party and, under pretexts as ingenious as they were fallacious, threw out a sufficient number of ballots to give those two states to Hayes. The Democrats protested violently. Law and common sense would have proclaimed Tilden President. But the Republicans had had long acquaintance with the machinery of government. They exhibited an energy and an absence of scruple that added to the confusion, and turned their defeat into victory. Hayes accepted this artificial victory but not without scruples of conscience. He wondered whether he had really been elected.

President Hayes was an excellent executive and as impartial as possible, but nevertheless he had a difficult Administration. The Republicans themselves were not fond of the President they had elected with so much difficulty. They found him too fair-minded, too moderate, and they referred to him as 'Granny Hayes.' They accused him of making former Confederates postmasters, a heinous crime. 'He has no idea,' members of the party said, 'of what is popular.' However, he had a very clear idea of what was wise. He found excellent solutions for several thorny questions. The importation of Chinese labor at low wages was irritating the workmen of California. Hayes reached an agreement with the Chinese government to limit this immigration. Strikes of great violence, accompanied by incendiarism and bloodshed, broke out in Pittsburgh and Chicago in 1877; the President summoned the militia of several states and re-established order. But he noted in his journal: 'The strikes have been put down by force; but now for the real remedy. Can't something be done by education of the strikers, by judicious control of the capitalists, by wise general policy to end or diminish the evil?' And in fact these were the problems that America now had to solve.

Hayes should have had a second term. His honesty brought him into conflict with his party 'machine,' a powerful combination of politicians, great and small, whose purpose was to influence the voters. Politics became for many adventurers a high road to wealth. In the name of one or the other of the two great parties one man would seek a well-paid position; another a streetcar concession; a third, a contract for paving or for the construction of some municipal building. Too often the electoral machine was made the agent of private interests. These manipulations were rendered easier by the two great parties' lack of principles. In theory, the Republican party was supposed to be nationalist and favorable to industry, while the Democratic party was the defender of states' rights and of agriculture. But the Civil War had altered loyalties. The farmers of the West voted the Republican ticket in memory of Lincoln. Because of its struggle against slavery, the Republican party had also enlisted a certain number of liberal intellectuals.

In 1880 the Republican party was cut in two. The Stalwarts, or, in other words, 'The Toughs,' were for the spoils system, for compulsory contributions by officeholders to the party funds, for high tariffs, for votes for Negroes, for the machine. The Half Breeds were 'The Softies,' the reformers who had the effrontery to think that all was not for the best in the best of all possible parties. 'The Toughs' had had the idea of advocating another term for Grant, who had just returned from a triumphal world tour and was still playing to a good house. 'The Softies' were thinking of Blaine or John Sherman, Hayes's Secretary of the Treasury. But the convention had one of those sudden impulses to which assemblies are subject, and crying, 'Anything to beat Grant!' it nominated the obscure General James A. Garfield of Ohio. To appease the great tumult of the Stalwarts, one of their own men, Chester Arthur, the customs collector who had been dismissed by Hayes for multiplying useless offices to give to friends, was chosen as Vice-President. The election of Garfield exasperated the masters of the machine, Roscoe Conkling and 'Me Too' Platt, who went to the length of handing in their resignations as senators.

Then a half-demented fanatic, Charles Guiteau, fired on the President, saying: 'I am a Stalwart of Stalwarts. Arthur is President now!' Garfield languished for several months, then died, which did indeed put Chester Arthur into the White House. Once more events showed to what extent the law that makes the Vice-President heir presumptive of the President exposed the country to surprises. In this case, however, the surprise was a happy one, for Chester Arthur, whom everyone thought completely partisan, proved reasonable and moderate.

V
World Power

Entry into the World

For almost twenty-five years the Republican party had been master of the country, and no one could say that the use it had made of its power had been either happy or adroit. By its policy of reprisal it had earned the hatred of the South. Because of the corruption of some of those whom it had put in office it had lost the confidence of the public. It retained the favor of the business world and of the veterans of the Civil War, but its majority was narrow and precarious. Within the party itself many respectable citizens were hoping for reform. These were surprised and irritated when in 1884 the magnetic James G. Blaine was chosen as candidate by the Republican convention. Blaine was the most loved and the most hated man of his time. His wife, who adored him, wrote during his absence: 'I miss his constant attention and his no less constant neglect.' He was the avowed and willing champion of government of the politicians, by the politicians, for the politicians. A certain number of party leaders decided in disgust to vote for the Democratic candidate provided only that he was an honest man.

These eminent turncoats were ironically called Mugwumps, an Indian name meaning great chieftains. The nomination by the Democrats of Grover Cleveland satisfied the Mugwumps.

Grover Cleveland, a brave and energetic man, had little genius, but he did have solid intelligence, common sense, and character. His enemies tried to make capital of his private life: he had had an illegitimate child in Buffalo. His friends asked him what they should say in reply. 'Whatever you say, tell the truth,' he answered. The Republicans chanted, 'Ma! Ma! Where's my Pa? Gone to the White House. Ha! Ha! Ha!' to which the Democrats replied, 'Burn this letter, James G. Blaine. Burn this letter, James G. Blaine,' a reminder of a letter from Blaine that allegedly contained that postscript. The contest was close, and the result depended on New York State. There, Irish Catholics were powerful. A Republican supporter, the Reverend Dr. Burchard, committed the incredible blunder of describing the Democratic party, which was antiprohibitionist, Catholic, and sympathetic to the South, as standing

PRESIDENT CLEVELAND'S INAUGURAL ADDRESS IN WASHINGTON.
A skilled politician, but without great presence, Grover Cleveland might
not have been elected if the Republican party, which supported Blaine, a
powerful, likeable candidate, had not been so ruthless during the campaign. *Library of Congress, Washington.*

UNVEILING OF THE STATUE OF LIBERTY. By Edward Moran. On ▶
October 28, 1886, the giant statue by the French sculptor Bartholdi,
Liberty Lighting the World, was unveiled in an atmosphere of popular
rejoicing. *Mrs. Seton Henry Collection. Francis G. Mayer photo.*

THE OPENING OF AN EARLY TELE-
PHONE LINE. Alexander Graham Bell
himself, the inventor of the telephone, is
the first to call Chicago from New York.
American Telephone and Telegraph.

THOMAS ALVA EDISON. The American
inventor Edison (1847–1931) was also an
astute businessman and industrialist,
something fairly frequent in America.
He invented and manufactured the
incandescent light bulb, built the first
phonograph (the principle having been
discovered by the poet Charles Cros). He
also took part in the race for the exploitation and improvement of the first movie
camera. *Library of Congress, Washington.*

for 'rum, Romanism, and rebellion.' This unfortunate and offensive phrase, sedulously exploited by
the Democrats, gave New York to Grover Cleveland,
who was elected President, breaking his party's
jinx and defeating the magnetic Blaine.

After his inauguration, Cleveland had asked:
'What is the most important question of the day?'
'The tariff,' he was told. 'I am ashamed,' Cleveland
said, 'but I know nothing about the tariff.' He
studied the question. The high tariffs that had been
enforced during the Civil War no longer seemed
necessary. It was no longer possible to justify them
as protection for the growing industries, since the
'war babies' had grown up and were fending quite
well for themselves. The financial state of the
country was so fine that the budget showed a
surplus, and it was easily possible to get along without customs duties. Cleveland adopted the principle:
'Duties for revenue only.' To put it another way:
no protective tariffs. This aroused the anger of the
manufacturers and the resentment of Congress,
which looked upon the surplus as a reservoir upon

which to draw for local favors and pensions. All
these resentments resulted in Cleveland's defeat in
1888 by an obscure Republican, Benjamin Harrison,
a cultured man whose chief qualifications were the
fact that his father had been a congressman, his
grandfather President (Tippecanoe), and his great-
grandfather a signer of the Declaration of Independence. The second General Harrison had been a
good soldier in the Civil War, during which he had
commanded a brigade. When he learned of his
election he cried: 'Providence has given us the
victory!' This exclamation shocked John Wana-
maker of Philadelphia, who as treasurer of the
Republican party had collected the funds for the
campaign. Harrison, as President, was reserved,
modest, cold, and therefore unpopular. He sincerely
intended to refuse all compromises. But he was
forced to give in, like so many others, and to expend
the surplus in favors and pensions. The most
important law of this period was the Sherman Anti-
Trust Act of 1890. Its object was to impose regula-
tions upon manufacturers and bankers whose

unchecked individualism was becoming dangerous. American industry in the course of thirty or forty years had developed in prodigious fashion. Jefferson had thought at the beginning of the century that America would be a rural and agricultural country; it was becoming an industrial and urban one. In 1890 one could foresee that it would outstrip all the old European nations combined. Why this triumph? The reason was that America had every advantage: she possessed the finest deposits of coal, iron, and petroleum and of many other secondary metals; she had immense reserves of water power; she offered industry a vast market without trade barriers; she produced talented inventors—Fulton of the steamboat; Morse of the telegraph; Bell of the telephone; Edison of the electric light; Sholes and Glidden of the typewriter; McCormick of agricultural machines; later Ford of the automobile; Orville and Wilbur Wright of the airplane—finally she produced daring business leaders who were not handicapped by the weight of tradition and who showed themselves ready to run great risks because

they were playing for huge stakes. In a few decades America had become dotted with factories.

In the metals industries in particular, concentration had been rapid. Andrew Carnegie, who had started as a workman, showed such intelligence and ability that at thirty he had made a great fortune. In 1865 he decided to devote himself exclusively to iron: rails, bridges, locomotives. When Kelly in America and Bessemer in England discovered that a blast of air could be used to convert iron into steel, Carnegie perceived the possibilities in this discovery. With the financial support of the Pennsylvania Railroad he became the great master of the steel mills of the country. Associated with Frick, the coke king, he acquired great fleets of steamers on the Great Lakes, mines, ports, and railroad companies. Thanks to him, by 1890 the production of iron and steel in the United States exceeded that of Great Britain. Nevertheless, Carnegie did not have a monopoly. His rivals were numerous and powerful, and in his old age he found himself menaced by a price war. Tired out and

TEN-MINUTE STOP FOR RE-
FRESHMENTS. These harried-
looking people are not drinking
strong liquor or even beer—the
usual beverage in those days—but
merely tea. True, this is a poster of
The Great American Tea Co.
Chicago, Historical Society.

ready to retire, he decided to mobilize his fortune for the foundations that would survive him. In 1901 he agreed to sell all his business interests to a company organized by the banker J.P. Morgan, which brought together most of the steel mills of the country: United States Steel, with a capital of one billion four hundred million dollars.

Thus the steel trust came into being. At first the word 'trust' was used for a group of companies whose stock was placed in the hands of trustees, charged with the duty of running them; then for any combination of interests brought together to reduce competition. Many such combinations had been formed before United States Steel. John D. Rockefeller had organized Standard Oil and little by little had eliminated competitors. The great packing interests (Swift, Armour) had come to an understanding. Guggenheim had created the copper trust; Mellon the aluminum trust. There had been a sugar trust, a whisky trust, a nickel trust. But public opinion was very suspicious of the trusts. How could they be controlled?

In 1887 Congress had voted a law governing interstate commerce, and an Interstate Commerce Commission had been created to control the commerce of the nation, but a long time was to elapse before these measures became effective. The Sherman Anti-Trust Act of 1890 ruled: (*a*) that every contract, combination, or conspiracy in restraint of trade between the states or with foreign nations was illegal; (*b*) that any person who attempted to monopolize any part of this commerce was guilty of a crime. The obvious intent of the law was to allow federal courts to intervene, for by virtue of the Constitution, the Federal Government had the right to legislate on commerce between the states. But the Sherman Act did not clearly define what constituted a crime, and it was hard to enforce. Nevertheless some measure was necessary. The active and greedy individualism that had dominated industry since the Civil War had served its purpose. To its aggressiveness was due the commercial development of the country. But if all businesses ended by being concentrated in a few hands, if all competition became an illusion, if a single trust dominated each industry, what would become of the spirit of initiative and daring that had made the new America?

ANDREW CARNEGIE. The model career of the American man. By the time he was thirty this former telegraph operator had made an immense fortune, owing only to his intelligence and know-how. The Iron and Steel King went into partnership with Henry Clay Frick, the Coal King, to gain control of steamship and railroad transportation. At the end of his life he decided to use his wealth and his time for philanthropic foundations, and he partially succeeded in his idealistic endeavor. *Underwood and Underwood, New York.*

JOHN D. ROCKEFELLER. Another model figure: the Petroleum King and founder of Standard Oil. Rockefeller willed part of his fortune to France for the restoration of Versailles and Fontainebleau after World War I. *Keystone.*

If, of all the working classes in the world, that in the United States was at that time the one most in need of protection by a powerful trade union, it was also the one in which such an organization seemed hardest to promote. The obstacles were, on the one hand, a constant influx of immigrants who did not speak English, whom no propaganda could reach, and who had an urgent need of work; and on the other hand, the federal character of the country. Nevertheless, labor unions slowly developed. In 1886 Samuel Gompers, a tobacco worker who had undertaken a study of European trade unionism, organized the American Federation of Labor. His policy was like that of the British trade unions. It was cautious, adroit, nonviolent, and little by little it gained the confidence of a public that had at first been hostile. As for the syndicalist and revolutionary groups, they remained sporadic and unimportant.

More discontented even than the workmen were the farmers in the West, for they were suffering from a deflation of agricultural prices that made it impossible for them to pay the interest on their borrowings. The grievances of the western pioneers were comprehensible. They had crossed prairies and

deserts; they had wrung harvests from a hitherto sterile land; and their reward was poverty. Toward 1890 they worked with the American Federation of Labor to form a new party—the People's Party, or the Populists. In 1891 they held a convention in Cincinnati and wrote a platform that included free coinage of silver, abolition of national banks, an income tax, nationalization of the railroads, and election of United States senators by popular suffrage. As presidential candidate in the election of 1892 they nominated James B. Weaver, who received a million votes and carried several states. The two old parties had nominated proved candidates: Cleveland and Harrison. Cleveland was elected.

A commercial crisis of the first order was looming. All the premonitory signs could be detected. The building of railroads and of cities had stopped. Goods no longer found a market. Unemployment was increasing. The Democratic party, under the strong influence of Populism, believed the only remedy to be silver currency. Bimetallism had become one of those strange mental diseases that afflict nations from time to time. Fanatical advocates of silver currency appeared. Miners, farmers, and

SAMUEL GOMPERS. One of the founders of the trade-union movement in the United States. In 1886 he created the American Federation of Labor, or A.F. of L. *U.S. Signal Corps.*

workmen looked to silver as their salvation. But economic reality was exactly the reverse. Since the real value of silver currency was lower than its face value, silver put gold to flight. Gold currency was hiding. The fear that the United States would pay in silver prevented foreigners from buying American securities. Cleveland sensed the danger and was intractable on the gold issue. Dividing his party, he took a position for hard currency. He knew that if the United States stopped paying in gold, its credit would fall to the level of some small discredited country. He asked Congress to repeal the Sherman Silver Purchase Act, which made it obligatory for the Government to purchase silver at the expense of the gold reserve. Despite the senators from the seven silver states, the President had his way.

From this time on, Cleveland was hated by his party and the country as no President had been since Johnson. But beneath the storm of insults he remained stoic and immovable.

His difficulties became even greater when labor troubles broke out. At the end of 1893 the crisis was in full swing with the usual accompaniments of reduced wages, bankruptcies, and discharged workmen. An army of unemployed, led by Jacob Coxey, marched on Washington. Coxey demanded that Congress raise five hundred million dollars in bonds, the money to be devoted to making work for the unemployed. The march on Washington ended in the arrest of Coxey's men by police for walking on the grass at the Capitol. In addition to being blamed for having defended gold and order, Cleveland was also assailed for having offered to return the Hawaiian Islands to the native queen who was their legitimate ruler. The latter had been deposed in the time of President Harrison by a provisional white government that had had the support of the United States. Cleveland proposed to restore her to the throne if she would abandon her plans for vengeance against the Americans. She proved unreasonable, and the islands were later annexed (July 1898). But Cleveland had energetically maintained the United States' traditional doctrine: respect for small nations and the supremacy of right over might. This earned him new insults.

When his term ended in 1897, Cleveland had earned lasting hatreds. But public hatreds are phenomena and not judgments. Cleveland had been a statesman, an energetic leader, a rock in the midst of the tempest. He was to die saying: 'I have tried so hard to act well. . . .' And he had the right to say it. His enemies had nicknamed him 'His Obstinacy.' His Democratic friends, to replace him, looked about for a man more responsive to the will of the people. They found William Jennings Bryan.

Many farmers, most of whom did not understand anything about bimetallism, believed that if Bryan was elected, they would have sixteen times more money. But a retired officer, Major William McKinley, of Ohio, was elected.

President McKinley was a perfect man, almost too perfect. He was honest, scrupulous, kindly, indulgent, responsive to popular desires. At his side watched the Warwick who had made this king, Senator Marcus Hanna of Ohio, ambassador to Washington of 'a triumphant plutocracy.' Neither Senator Hanna nor President McKinley had any desire to become involved in discussions of international policy. What interested them was the business world, its prosperity, the maintenance of the tariff, and the victory of the gold standard. But these questions, which had stirred up such violent emotions, quickly fell into second place. In 1896 thousands of Americans had been ready to fight for silver money. Then came the discovery of gold mines in the Klondike and in South Africa; this had led to a drop in the real value of gold and a rise in prices; in the Middle West an abundant harvest had been sold at a good price; and the searchlight of public opinion had swung in another direction.

The question of Cuba had concerned more than one administration. The island lay close to the continent; Americans had large commercial interests there; they bought its sugar and tobacco; Spanish domination in Cuba had been accepted reluctantly. But the United States had not officially intervened in any of the numerous Cuban revolutions. As long as the controversy between the North and the South continued, the Cuban affair had been judged, not on its own merits, but for its possible repercussions on the politics of the United States. Later the Cuban Revolution of 1868 had aroused warm sympathy in North America; the Cuban flag had been flown in New York. But the North, which had

just defended a government's right to stamp out rebellion, could hardly refuse this same right to the Spanish government.

By 1897 the anarchy in Cuba had begun to disturb Americans who had plantations there. In February 1898 the Spanish ambassador in Washington, Señor Dupuy de Lôme, wrote a letter to one of his friends in which he described McKinley as a hesitant and opportunistic politician. The letter fell into the hands of Hearst's *New York Journal*, which published it. Dupuy de Lôme was forced to resign. The battleship *Maine* was sent to Havana to protect American citizens. On February 15, 1898, the *Maine* blew up, and a large part of the crew were killed. On April 20 Congress declared that a state of war existed between the United States and Spain. A small American expeditionary force of fifteen thousand men was able to capture Cuba, thanks to the support of the fleet, which destroyed a Spanish squadron in the Bay of Santiago. In the Pacific Commodore Dewey with a small squadron appeared in Manila Bay and destroyed the Spanish fleet. As for the Spanish island of Puerto Rico, resistance there

was so brief that one humorist spoke of the campaign as a large-scale picnic or a moonlight excursion.

Spain signed a treaty in Paris, though the conditions were bitter. She gave up Cuba and Puerto Rico and agreed to the occupation of Manila until the Philippines question was settled. It was the end of the Spanish empire. In February 1899 an anti-imperialist league had been organized in Boston by Charles Francis Adams and Carl Schurz; its program was to oppose the acquisition of colonies. So far as Cuba was concerned, this doctrine triumphed. In Puerto Rico a compromise solution was adopted.

The Philippine question was more complex. If America retained these distant possessions, she would become a colonial power. Many Americans disliked this idea. For governing such conquered but not yet assimilated territories, the Constitution of the United States provided no machinery. The President sent a civil governor, Judge William Howard Taft, an amiable giant whose good sense and moderation accomplished wonders. The Americans succeeded in making the Filipinos like them, and at the time when war broke out in 1941, they

THEODORE ROOSEVELT WITH HIS MEN AFTER THE CAPTURE OF SAN JUAN HILL IN CUBA. Before he became one of the wise Presidents, Theodore Roosevelt served as a colonel in Cuba. He was the impetuous commander of the Rough Riders. Upon his return he was elected governor of New York State. *Library of Congress, Washington.*

THE ROUGH RIDERS IN ACTION DURING THE SPANISH-AMERICAN WAR. *Underwood and Underwood.*

had the honorable and generous intention of giving the Philippines complete independence in 1944.

But in 1900 the controversies on the subject of imperialism were violent. McKinley knew his people. He knew that at this time the country approved his foreign policy. He had a popular plurality of over nine hundred thousand, and to mark all the more clearly the national character of the election, Theodore Roosevelt, the colonel of Rough Riders who had become Governor of New York, was made Vice-President. But on September 6, 1901, in the first year of his second term, McKinley was assassinated by an anarchist and died as he had lived, saying exactly the right thing. He had been, said John Hay, 'one of the sweetest and quietest natures I have ever known among public men.' The dynamic and fiery Colonel Roosevelt became President.

The Wise Presidencies

Theodore Roosevelt had been born in 1858, of one of the oldest and most respectable New York families. In him Dutch blood was mixed with that of the French Huguenots, the Scots, the Welsh, and the Quakers of Pennsylvania. His ancestors had occupied various local administrative posts, but he, in his childhood, seemed too frail for public life. He had a narrow chest and suffered from asthma. On his father's advice he undertook to build up a strong body through will power and persistence. Daily gymnastics made him not only a normal man but an athlete with muscles of iron. In reaction against his own preferences, which were those of a historian and a man of letters, he acquired an enthusiastic taste for boxing, hunting, life in the open air, and all forms of energetic and violent action. Upon leaving Harvard, he decided to embark upon a political career. His friends said that a young man of good family would find this a rough and disagreeable life and in general 'dirty business.' He replied that the true ruling classes had to be found in political committee meetings and not in fashionable drawing rooms. Then with energy and courage he plunged into the municipal life of New York. At the time of the Spanish war

[219]

McKinley appointed him Assistant Secretary of the Navy. His enthusiastic activity at first alarmed the members of the department. His superior, John Davis Long, said that this new assistant threatened to cause more dangerous explosions in the navy than that of the *Maine*. Happily, Roosevelt himself resigned in order to go to Cuba as colonel of the Rough Riders. He believed that a man who loves his country and hopes one day to govern it should be willing to fight for it. 'It was not a big war,' he said almost regretfully, 'but we didn't have any other.' His courage made him popular, and on his return he was elected Governor of New York. In this important post he so annoyed Senator Platt by his independence that in 1900 Platt, in order to get rid of him, had Roosevelt, to his disgust, nominated as candidate for the vice-presidency. 'Vice-President?' said Roosevelt. 'I don't see what I could do. I should be simply president of the Senate and that would bore me to death.' Certain of the party elders did not wish any more than he did to see him nominated. Senator Marcus Hanna, the boss of bosses, asked McKinley if he had taken into consideration what would happen if by mischance 'this damned cowboy' should become President of the United States. When McKinley was assassinated and the damned cowboy became President, Senator Hanna had to accept the situation. He did so with good grace. Very soon the President was calling the senator 'old boy' and Senator Hanna was calling the President 'Teddy.' Although he was a vigorous reformer, Roosevelt knew how to make concessions to persons when superior interests demanded it. He planned to fight certain abuses; he knew that he could not do so without the support of the party, and he was determined to retain that support.

Roosevelt administered the country justly, 'without fear or favor.' On his initiative laws were passed for the protection of public health, thanks to which even today the food of the American people is the most carefully safeguarded in the world.

Thereafter it was illegal to pass off a product as anything except what it actually was. This was a great and laudable novelty.

Because the President was an outdoor man and had an inquiring mind, he was well acquainted with the geology and geography of his country. He knew that one of the grave dangers that threatened the America of the future was the mad prodigality with which the America of the past had squandered her natural resources. Coal mines and oil wells had seemed so inexhaustible to the Americans of the nineteenth century that they made no effort to conserve them. If a region became deforested, if the land was exhausted, what did it matter? There were other lands farther on. Little by little this optimism ceased to be justified. By the beginning of the twentieth century the forest trees felled each year were three times the number of the new trees. The disappearance of wooded areas altered the rainfall of the country, removed the protection against wind, and became the cause of disastrous erosion over immense areas. The public grazing lands were subjected to ruinous treatment by the great cattle raisers. Roosevelt undertook to conserve the existing resources and to create new ones. To save the forests, he annexed many of them to the national domain. To protect the grazing lands, he exacted payments from those who had hitherto used them free of charge. Naturally these measures aroused fierce opposition and lasting resentment. To create new resources, the President undertook to irrigate arid lands and constructed most successfully the Roosevelt Dam in Arizona, which opened seven hundred fifty thousand acres to agriculture. Theodore Roosevelt's foreign policy was a happy combination of firmness and moderation. He made frequent use of the familiar adage: 'Speak softly and carry a big stick; you will go far.' Throughout his Administration Roosevelt carried a big stick.

The Panama Canal is one of the monuments of the Roosevelt Administration. In 1888 an attempt to pierce the Isthmus had been made by a French

HAMMERSTEIN'S ROOF GARDEN. By William J. Glackens. An example of American art at the end of the nineteenth century. A strange and daring work in treatment as well as in subject. It is interesting to note the very fashionable upper-middle-class audience, and the hall with its period décor reminiscent of a Paris or London concert hall, contrasting with the unsophisticated, minstrel-like show. *Whitney Museum of American Art*.

THE WORLD'S CONSTABLE.

company under the direction of Ferdinand de Lesseps, the builder of the Suez Canal. It had failed for technical, political, and financial reasons. The canal remained uncompleted. This project was of great importance to the United States, not only from a commercial point of view but from a strategic one as well. The United States' new interests in the Pacific made it desirable that the fleet should be able to move easily from one ocean to the other. During the Spanish War, the battleship *Oregon* had been forced to make its way around Cape Horn, and the length of the voyage had emphasized the need for a canal. But the treaty of 1850 between England and the United States constituted a serious obstacle, for the two nations had agreed not to exercise exclusive control over any such canal. John Hay, formerly United States Ambassador to the Court of

St. James and then Secretary of State, determined to secure a friendly annulment of this treaty, and in the end he succeeded. In America itself there were two opposed schools of thought on the subject of the canal: one advocated buying the French concession in Panama, the other wanted to dig the canal through Nicaragua. The first proposal (Panama) was the easier to carry out, but the French company was asking one hundred ten million dollars, and the American company was willing to pay only forty million. Moreover, the country of Panama was theoretically a part of the Republic of Colombia, although it was separated from it by high mountains. Now Colombia was making very heavy demands on its own account. When in 1903 the French company agreed to accept forty million, the Nicaraguan proposal lost ground. It lost even more when

THE DIGGING OF THE PANAMA CANAL. The site in December 1907. *Doc.X*.

William Nelson Cromwell, the sponsor of the New Panama Company, had the generous idea of donating sixty thousand dollars to the Republican campaign fund.

Philippe Bunau-Varilla, a French engineer who had worked with Lesseps, came to New York and proposed a simple means of dealing with the growing demands of Colombia. If a revolution were to break out in Panama, if the Panamanian nation were to declare itself independent and grant the United States the land necessary to build the canal, there would be no further problem. The government of the United States had to admit that this solution would indeed be very fine, but it declared through the mouth of Secretary of State John Hay that it could not take part in negotiations as unorthodox as these.

In November 1903 the Panamanians revolted; the revolution was carried out without loss of life; a new state was born; the American fleet gave it protection; Bunau-Varilla was named minister from Panama to the United States and signed a treaty leasing the Canal Zone to the government in Washington. Since a treaty with England (the Hay-Pauncefote Treaty of 1901) had prepared the way, there were no protests from abroad except those of Colombia, and she ended by settling for twenty-five million dollars.

Teddy was elected in 1904 for a second term by a large majority. In the course of this second term his prestige was further enhanced by the authority he was able to exert in world affairs.

It was through his good offices in 1905 that peace was concluded between Russia and Japan. At the

[223]

Conference of Algeciras in 1906 he helped, by his forceful action, to prevent a European war. His policy was not always strictly constitutional, for he sometimes undertook commitments that threatened to lead his country into war without the consent of Congress, but he taught the European world to take account of the strength of the United States. And indeed, far from precipitating wars, he dissipated more than one menace. He could easily have obtained a third term in 1908, but he had always said he would not ask for it, and he worked to secure the election of his Secretary of War, William Howard Taft. Taft's most obvious claim to the White House was his friendship with Roosevelt. The latter made him President as Jackson had Van Buren. But Taft, amiable and easygoing, whose gentle voice issuing from his enormous body was a constant surprise, was a good candidate possessing sterling personal qualities. He had, thanks to his common sense and the contagious laughter that made him shake like a bowl of jelly, succeeded admirably in the Philippines. His friends called him Big Bill and loved him. They failed to see that he was by no means suited to govern a democracy. After the inauguration of his successor, Roosevelt planned to leave on a long trip so as not to embarrass Taft, to whom he thought he could entrust his work and his organization. Hardly had the retiring President left when Taft, not through disloyalty but by instinct, called back 'the old guard.' From the very beginning, the men Roosevelt had appointed were removed from key positions. When the ex-President returned after hunting big game in Africa, receiving the Nobel Prize and an Oxford Doctorate, and sojourning with the sovereigns of Europe, he was given a triumphal reception in New York and found his party boiling. All the liberal Republicans were up in arms against Taft. They blamed him for the weak attitude he had taken toward the trusts, for his 'dollar diplomacy'; they blamed him in short for being Taft and not Roosevelt.

Roosevelt studied the situation. 'Taft means well,' he was to say later, 'but he means well feebly.' What was to be done? Roosevelt was only fifty-two years old; he felt as strong as a bull moose; he had an ardent desire to continue to serve his country; he thought his program of reforms was far from completed. When a group of governors suggested

that he should be the candidate in 1912, he hesitated, then accepted. 'My hat is in the ring,' he said. Taft was deeply wounded. Why should his best friend try to deprive him of a second term? The Republican convention, which was dominated by the machine, nominated Taft, but Roosevelt withdrew in disgust and organized a new party, called the Progressives but named by the public the Bull Moose party (since the Republican party had an elephant for its mascot and the Democratic party a donkey). The Progressive party naturally nominated Roosevelt as its candidate. The rupture between Taft and Roosevelt was complete; it was unfortunate, for both were good men. It put an end to Teddy's public life and earned him the lasting hatred of the Republican party (G.O.P.). But the failure of the Progressive party should not obscure the importance of the work accomplished by Roosevelt from 1901 to 1909. He had helped Americans to recognize the necessity of aiding the poor, protecting the public, and maintaining peace in industry. He had made his country respected abroad; he had not involved it in any ill-fated enterprise; and he had established it in the position of a world arbiter. Eight well-filled years.

Since the Republicans were divided, the Democrats had an excellent chance of winning the presidential election of 1912. Whom should they choose as standard-bearer? As orthodox and regular candidates the machine offered Champ Clark of Missouri and Oscar W. Underwood of Alabama. Bryan, who was tired of his many defeats, no longer wished to represent the liberal elements in the party and they secured the nomination of Woodrow Wilson, governor of New Jersey. Who was Wilson? A professor who had entered political life barely two years before, and who represented a type of candidate new in presidential contests. But the choice was less surprising than it seemed. Wilson was born in 1856, the son of a southern Presbyterian minister. He had taught social science and history at Bryn Mawr, Wesleyan University, and Princeton. Everywhere he had been an immediate success. The distinction of his manners, the beauty of his diction, the precision of his language and the clarity of his expositions, all contributed to it. He had written a thesis on *Congressional Government* and *A History of the American People*. The liberals in the Democratic

HERALD SQUARE ON ELECTION NIGHT (1907). By John Sloan. The village-fair atmosphere of American elections at the turn of the century, which still pervades present-day conventions, is illustrated by this florid painting, whose style was rather revolutionary at the time. *Marion Stratton Gould Fund, Memorial Art Gallery, University of Rochester.*

party began to think of him as a possible candidate
in 1912. A gentleman from Texas, Colonel House, a
small, mysterious, and affable man, who was tempted
by the role of Grey Eminence, undertook to make
Woodrow Wilson President of the United States. At
the Baltimore convention the conservative Champ
Clark was the candidate of the machine, but Bryan
declared himself in favor of Wilson. The Bryan boys
cried: 'We want Wilson!' And on the forty-sixth
ballot he was nominated. In his campaign he was
aided by his oratorical talent and the deep split that
divided the Republicans. Wilson and Roosevelt
stood for substantially the same ideas and demanded
the same reforms, but Roosevelt did not have the

solid framework of an old traditional party to support
him. Both were eloquent: Roosevelt's eloquence
was aggressive; Wilson's, persuasive. Wilson was
elected.

Wilson had the support of the western farmers,
brought to him by Bryan; the Solid South, happy to
vote for a southerner; and, in the East, the Irish
and the liberals. Samuel Gompers, head of the
American Federation of Labor, had advised the
workmen to vote for Wilson. Taft and Roosevelt
divided the Republican votes about equally, and
Wilson won.

What would this professor do in the White
House? The politicians anxiously asked this question.

The reply was simple: he would teach. Wilson always retained the attitude of a man accustomed to speak *ex cathedra*. If he had an important question to settle, he studied the facts as one would prepare a lecture, listened attentively to opinions, made his decision, clothed it in general ideas, and thereafter resisted all opposition. He demanded from his collaborators complete obedience and submission at all times.

For the first time since Jefferson, who had given up the custom, the President addressed Congress in person. Wilson knew that eloquence was his forte, and he exercised a constant pressure on the two Houses to obtain a quick vote for those measures

which lay close to his heart. Despite the vehement protest of the industries affected, the tariff was reduced. The banking system of the country was completely reformed by the creation of twelve Federal Reserve Banks, each entrusted with a vast territory and authorized to issue banknotes against a security of commercial paper. A Federal Reserve Board unified their operations. All other banks of the country were permitted to affiliate themselves with the Federal Reserve System and to pass over their paper to it.

An antitrust law (the Clayton Act) was passed in an attempt to control the dangerous concentration of wealth and to prevent multiple interlocking

AMERICAN SOLDIERS IN MEXICO, ▶ 1914. A military chief as well as a bandit, Huerta, the Mexican dictator, had arbitrarily ordered the arrest of American seamen. Wilson, usually levelheaded and conciliatory, sent in troops which took Vera Cruz. Huerta fled and was replaced by Carranza, an elected President. *Branger-Viollet photo.*

PRESIDENT WILSON MAKING A SPEECH AT THE INAUGURATION OF THE AMERICAN UNIVERSITY IN WASHINGTON. *G. V. Buck document, Washington.*

directorates. The Federal Trade Commission was created to prevent unfair competition. The labor unions were protected; the farmers were given new credit facilities. Wilson studied all these questions, employing Colonel House as his liaison officer, and himself tapped out on his typewriter his plans and decisions. By 1914 he had become an undeniable moral force in America and even in Europe.

Until 1911 the dictator Porfirio Diaz had maintained order in Mexico in the interests of the big landowners and the foreign capitalists. When a popular revolution, inspired by Francisco Madero, overthrew Diaz, the rich raised up another dictator, Victoriano Huerta, who was a combination of bandit and military leader, with a preponderance of bandit. Most of the European states recognized Huerta in the hope of protecting their investments,

and the American capitalists demanded that Wilson follow their example. He refused. This attitude produced a certain tension between England and the United States. Wilson wanted the two countries, both of which had interests in Mexico, to pursue the same policy. Now he found that he had a bargaining point. The Panama Canal was just being completed, and Congress had decided, in 1912, that all American coastwise shipping should be exempt from tolls. Great Britain maintained that this decision was a violation of the Hay-Pauncefote Treaty. Congress replied that the phrase 'open to all nations on terms of entire equality' meant 'foreign nations' and did not apply to the United States, which had built the canal. Wilson sent Colonel House to carry on negotiations with Sir Edward Grey, then appeared himself before

[228]

Congress to demand, with unusual vigor, the abrogation of this clause. In a speech surcharged with mystery he hinted that he needed this concession to England in order to arrange a more delicate matter. Congress understood that this meant Mexico, and consented. The canal was opened, an event of great commercial and strategic importance. All the nations were treated on terms of equality, and Great Britain's policy in Mexico from that day forward became strangely similar to that of the United States.

In 1914, when Huerta arrested American sailors without reason, the President demanded an apology. It was refused. The American marines, always prepared, took Vera Cruz. A war with Mexico seemed inevitable, but Wilson was firmly resolved not to make war. Perhaps he would have failed if

the 'ABC powers' (Argentina, Brazil, and Chile) had not offered to mediate. Wilson accepted, and the powers proposed the creation of a constitutional government in Mexico. This was not what Huerta wanted and, finding no support in Europe, he fled. An elected president, Carranza, replaced him. Disorder continued in that country. The bandit Villa crossed the frontier on several occasions to raid estates in Texas and New Mexico. Anyone but Wilson would doubtless have annexed Mexico at the cost of a short war. The campaign would have been easy and profitable but morally wrong, and, despite the pressure of public opinion, the President attempted instead to stabilize the Carranza government. Events have proved that Wilson's patience was wise. Relations between the two neighbors became, and are still growing, ever more friendly.

LANDING OF THE AMERICAN TROOPS IN SAINT-NAZAIRE. *Rol photo.*

The First World War

For a century the foreign policy of the United States had been dominated by two principles: not to meddle in European affairs and not to permit Europeans to meddle in American affairs. For a decade the United States had been enjoying remarkable prosperity. The people saw their numbers and their wealth increasing. Few Americans in August 1914 thought that their country would ever take part in the war, and fewer still that it was a duty for her to take part in it.

President Wilson more than anyone leaned toward neutrality, owing to his temperament as well as to his way of thinking. Not only did he proclaim the neutrality of the United States; he demanded that his fellow citizens should be neutral in thought as well as in deed and that they should reserve their judgment on this conflict until the end of the war.

Nevertheless, Wilson himself was drawn, quickly enough though against his will, toward the Allies by the call of blood and culture. Whether he liked it or not he belonged to the British tradition, and he understood the arguments of the English better than those of the Germans. Bryan, who was Secretary of State and a thoroughgoing pacifist, thought the President was prejudiced in favor of the Allies. This was not the opinion of the Allies.

Soon America became the great purveyor of supplies and ammunition to the Allies. France and England were the principal clients of American industry because they alone, thanks to their control of the seas, could take delivery of their orders. A period of unprecedented prosperity began in the United States. Meanwhile, after purchase and transportation, payment became necessary.

[231]

In September 1915 the State Department announced that public subscriptions for a loan to the Allies were to be opened. A billion and a half dollars were subscribed before the country entered the war.

On May 7, 1915, the liner *Lusitania* was torpedoed without warning. Among the nearly twelve hundred victims were one hundred twenty-eight Americans. The anger that shook the country showed, for the first time, that sooner or later the United States would enter the war. When three days later the President said that one could quite easily conceive of a man who was 'too proud to fight,' the phrase was not well received. Roosevelt and his friends assailed Wilson for his pacifism, while Bryan and his friends criticized him for being too warlike. A number of notes were exchanged with the German government. Finally, as a result of the sinking of the *Sussex* in the Channel, the President secured a promise from Germany that in the future she would

not torpedo merchant ships without warning and that she would make an effort to save the lives of passengers. This was, for Wilson, a diplomatic victory.

Many Americans did not believe that Germany would keep her promise, and they demanded that the country should prepare for a war that they now judged to be inevitable. The standing army was increased to one hundred sixty-five thousand men; the construction of numerous warships was authorized; fifty million dollars were allotted for the merchant marine.

In the presidential election of 1916 Roosevelt, who represented the policy of intervention, might have stood a good chance against Wilson, but the Republicans could not forgive him for causing their defeat in 1912.

A Progressive convention nominated Roosevelt as candidate; he sent a telegram saying that he could not accept the nomination before he knew

the attitude of the candidate of the G.O.P. on the vital question of the day. This candidate was Charles Evans Hughes, associate justice of the Supreme Court, who had been Governor of New York. He would have been elected if the Progressives and the Republicans had all voted for him; but many Progressives, upon Roosevelt's refusal of the nomination, turned to Wilson, who, like them, stood for reform in domestic politics. 'He kept us out of the war' became Wilson's campaign slogan, which pleased the West and the Middle West. He also said that he had two duties: to maintain the peace and to safeguard the honor of the United States, and that a time might come when it would be impossible to fulfill both duties simultaneously. Meanwhile, Roosevelt was violently attacking Wilson and saying that his election would prove that America was ready to accept any insult, including the massacre of its women and children, in order 'to make money.' On the evening of election

day it was thought that Hughes was President. *The New York Times* announced it. But some returns were not yet in, and when they came in they were all favorable to Wilson. Wilson was finally elected by two hundred seventy-seven votes to two hundred fifty-four.

The decision to throw America into the war was made neither by Wilson nor by the American friends of the Allies, but by the German general staff. On March 1, 1917, there was published a note from the German foreign minister Zimmermann to the German ambassador at Washington, a note that had been handed over to the State Department by the British intelligence. In it Germany proposed to Mexico an alliance against the United States in the event of war, the reward for which was to be Texas and New Mexico. This time the measure overflowed. On April 2 Wilson appeared before Congress and read a message in which he asked the latter to proclaim the existence of a state of war,

[American Cartoon]

His Easter Egg

—*From The New York Times.*

Slow in hatching, but a healthy bird.

brought about by Germany: 'We have no quarrel with the German people but only with Germany's military despotism. . . . The world must be made safe for democracy. . . . It is a fearful thing to lead this great peaceful people into war, into the most terrible and disastrous of all wars, civilization itself seeming to be in the balance. But the right is more precious than peace, and we shall fight for the things which we have always carried nearest our hearts—for democracy, for the right of those who submit to authority to have a voice in their own Governments, for the rights and liberties of small nations, for a universal dominion of right by such a concert of free peoples as shall bring peace and safety to all nations and make the world itself at last free.'

The United States was not rushing to take part in a victory already won. In 1917 the Allies' prospects were not brilliant. Roumania had collapsed; Russia was turning tail; Italy had just met with a serious defeat; France had no more men upon whom to call; England lacked ships, and her reserve supply of provisions was barely sufficient for six weeks. Shipping losses constituted the most immediate danger; they were so great (close to a million tons a month) that if they were to continue for long they would spell disaster for the Allies. It was for this reason that Germany had not hesitated to provoke the United States rather than limit her submarine warfare. The English Admiral Jellicoe said to Admiral Sims: 'It is impossible for us to go on, if losses like this continue. . . . The Germans will win unless we can stop the losses, and stop them soon.' In regard to land warfare, General Pershing was no more optimistic: 'We must come to their relief in 1918. The year after may be too late.' And so the Allies expected from their 'associate,' first of all ships, then participation in the war against submarines—food, arms, and reinforcements. This support had to be supplied with extreme speed;

otherwise there was a chance that it would be useless.

At sea, America supplied everything the Allies had expected of her. The German ships that happened to be in American ports were seized. A merchant fleet totaling eleven million tons was built by the Emergency Fleet Corporation. More than two million American soldiers were transported to France, one million in English ships, nine hundred twenty-seven thousand in American ships, and the rest in French and Italian vessels. The American navy escorted a large part of these convoys without loss of life. At the same time American destroyers took part in the battle against the submarines, and American mine-layers cooperated with the Allies in sowing an immense barrier across the whole of the North Sea. On land an army was improvised in a very short time by conscription (as Wilson wished) and not by voluntary enlistment (as Congress desired). At the end of the war the United States had four million men under arms. Training camps were organized. The Allies sent instructors who were attached as officers to the regular American army. The commander of these armies was General Pershing, an experienced soldier, taciturn and energetic, who moved to France with his general staff in June 1917. He was received with an enthusiasm that proved French morale was still good. The greeting credited to him, 'Lafayette, we are here!' is still famous. On July 4 the Americans marched down the Rue de Rivoli amid a crowd that threw flowers and shouted, '*Vive l'Amérique!*'

By the end of 1917 only two hundred thousand American soldiers were in France, and there was one division at the front. Although military aid was not immediate, the moral support and the great hope it aroused gave the Allies strength to hold on. There are three ways of financing a war: by printing money, by borrowing, and by taxation. The first leads to inflation and a rise in prices. McAdoo, the Secretary of the Treasury, had recourse to the other two and decided to raise one-third by taxation. Some people thought he could have gone farther. Bonds totaling fourteen billion dollars were offered to the public. The people subscribed nineteen billion. There was great enthusiasm. Banks helped to the best of their ability, even though they were not on the best of terms with President Wilson. Movie stars, heroes of war and of sport were transformed into salesmen. The country was plastered with signs announcing the Liberty Loan drives. Close to ten billion dollars was loaned by the United States to the Allied governments.

There can be no enthusiasm without faith. It was necessary to inspire this faith in the average American and make him understand the meaning of the war. This was the task of the Committee on Public Information, whose chairman was George Creel. He made use of every means. Seventy-five thousand volunteers addressed audiences in the theaters and movie houses of the country. Pamphlets, translated into every language spoken in America, broadcast hatred of the enemy. Abroad the most effective propagandist was the President. He exerted a real influence on the morale of the Germans and Austro-Hungarians by repeating that the United States was not making war for any material advantage but for justice, and that the peace would be a just peace.

On January 8, 1918, he enumerated the Fourteen Points of his program. Those of the enemy who believed these Fourteen Points were acceptable resigned themselves, at the bottom of their hearts, to an Allied victory.

There is no shadow of a doubt that it was the fresh American troops that made it possible to win the war in November 1918. Germany was still scoring great successes in March, in April, and in June. Once more her armies had advanced as far as the Marne and were threatening Paris. England and France had no more troops with which to oppose her. Up to then Pershing had insisted that the American soldiers should be used as a separate army under his command. When Foch, who had been made generalissimo, told him that the war might be lost through numerical inferiority, he generously gave up his project and put all the trained men he possessed at the disposal of the commander in chief. It was then that the First and Second American Divisions distinguished themselves and that the marines retook Belleau Wood. On July 15 American troops helped to throw back the last German offensive, and on the eighteenth they took part in Foch's counterattack, which was the first clarion call of victory. Once the danger was past Pershing obtained, as he had desired, a regrouping of the American army so that he could have a sector of his own. This was the

AMERICAN MARINES DURING THE BELLEAU WOOD BATTLE. By ▶
Sergeant Tom Lovell. *Defense Department, Marine Corps.*

CONVOY OF AMERICAN RESERVE FORCES ON THEIR WAY TO SAINT-MIHIEL.
General Pershing had obtained the use of his troops as a separate army under his own
command. Actually, he took advantage of this special provision only when the danger
was over, after the last German offensive of July 1918. Foch then assigned him the
Saint-Mihiel sector. *National Archives, U.S. Signal Corps.*

sector of Saint-Mihiel south of Verdun. The Americans mopped it up and advanced rapidly. Then General Foch entrusted to a million two hundred thousand Americans the battle that was destined to free the Meuse and the Argonne and that constituted a part of his general offensive.

Germany no longer had any hope of winning the war. On October 3, 1918, Prince Max of Baden, the new German chancellor, accepted President Wilson's Fourteen Points as a basis for negotiation.

The Germans have often said that they were tricked by Wilson and that, having laid down their arms because they had faith in a generous enemy, they were compelled to sign an armistice and a peace the conditions of which were much harsher than the Fourteen Points. This is not accurate. The Germans did not ask for an armistice in 1918 because they believed in the Fourteen Points but because they had been militarily defeated and were incapable

of continuing the war. Moreover, most of the Allied military leaders were opposed to the idea of a premature armistice. They thought it desirable to invade Germany and make her feel the brunt of defeat. General Pershing belonged to this school. Marshal Foch did not wish to sacrifice human lives uselessly; he wished to cease firing as soon as victory had been won and the enemy was incapable of doing further damage; but he was not in favor of the Fourteen Points, which threatened to prevent France from insuring her future security through the terms of the peace treaty. The conditions of the armistice were what they had to be; by the very nature of an armistice they were provisional. It now remained to be seen whether the peace would be the peace of Wilson or that of Clemenceau.

Wilson had been victorious in the presidential election of 1916 but only by a narrow margin. Much hatred had accumulated against him in

America, as it must against any man who attacks long-established privileges. In 1918, before the election of the new Congress, the President had made an appeal to the voters, asking them to return a Democratic Congress to Washington so that the nation might present a united front in that time of crisis. This partisan attitude, in a war election, made a bad impression, and the country elected a Republican Senate and House. This situation should have warned the President to exercise great caution. To gain acceptance of a peace treaty he needed the support of two-thirds of the Senate. It would have been courteous, natural, and wise to invite that body to collaborate at the Paris Conference. America was to send five delegates. Should the President be one of them? Colonel House advised him against it, and with reason. At a distance the President of the United States would remain a god. If he took his place at the council table, he would become a man and vulnerable. But the President loved his ideas as others love their children and insisted on defending them himself. And so he occupied one of the seats. Naturally both Secretary of State Lansing and the faithful Colonel House deserved the right to accompany him. There remained two places, which he might have given to influential senators or to prominent Republicans, such as Hughes, Taft, or Root. He chose to give them to General Tasker H. Bliss and to Henry White, against whom there was nothing to be said except that they did not represent American public opinion. Before this delegation left for Paris, Theodore Roosevelt wrote: 'Our allies and our enemies, and Mr. Wilson himself, should all understand that Mr. Wilson has no authority whatever to speak for the American people at this time. His leadership has just been emphatically repudiated by them.'

WOODROW WILSON LEAVING THE ORSAY PALACE. The President of the United States was more concerned with establishing the League of Nations than with guaranteeing the security of the European nations against any future German aggression. Besides, the just peace he sought could not be backed by his own country, since, as Theodore Roosevelt declared, Wilson was no longer speaking for American public opinion, which had most emphatically repudiated him. *M. Branger photo, Paris.*

And so the Allies were warned. The national leader who was attempting to impose his Fourteen Points on them no longer had his country behind him. Nevertheless, the people of Europe believed in Wilson, and his journey to Paris, London, and Rome was one long ovation. The crowds expected him to redress all their wrongs. Wilson himself passionately wanted to be just, but he had a tendency to confuse justice with his own will. In his eyes the thing that mattered above everything else was the League of Nations. The words 'covenant' and 'pact' warmed his Presbyterian blood. Frontiers? Guarantees? Armaments? What mattered those details as long as the League of Nations would be there to attend to them? These were not the sentiments of the elderly realists who represented the victorious nations at the conference. Clemenceau, a disillusioned old man ablaze with a single passion, patriotism, demanded guarantees for France. She had been invaded by Germany twice in fifty years she had lost the best of her young men; she had a right to security and, whatever President Wilson, in his 'noble candor,' might think about it, a pact was neither an army nor a frontier. The subtle Welshman Lloyd George, a skillful politician and an orator of genius, was ready to talk Wilson's language but with an understanding wink at Clemenceau and an inquiring glance toward the experts of the Foreign Office. Orlando, the Italian, did not speak English and confined himself to an obstinate repetition of his country's demands. No one of these three men, any more than their seconds, Balfour, Sonnino, Pichon, could be touched by Wilson's idealism. One element in the tragedy was that Wilson was strong enough to prevent the realists from making a harsh but cautious peace, and not strong enough to force his own country to guarantee an equitable peace.

Just what was the League of Nations to be? Wilson wanted a permanent executive council, the boycotting of rebellious countries, the transfer of the German colonies to the League of Nations, which would thus immediately acquire a domain to administer. The professor of history quite rightly recalled the role that had been played in the unification of the United States by the Northwest Ordinance. In three weeks' time, with a special committee of which General Smuts, Léon Bourgeois, Eleutherios Venizelos, and Lord Robert Cecil were members, Wilson drew up a plan. The League was to be administered by a council of nine members. Its decisions had to be unanimous. An assembly of all the members was to meet each year, but it was not sustained by any executive power. Article X (which was to cause trouble) stated that 'The members of the League undertake to respect and preserve as against external aggression the territorial integrity, and existing political independence, of all members of the League.' Article XVI gave the council the right to demand of the various governments the support of their military and naval forces to enforce respect for the pact. As soon as these provisions became known, more than one-third of the United States Senate signed a protest against commitments that might compel America to make war for foreign causes without the consent of Congress. Congress demanded that the peace treaty and the pact should be two separate documents, so that it might be able to ratify one and reject the other. That was exactly what the President did not wish. For the League of Nations he had a father's love and the faith of an apostle. Through it he hoped to go down in posterity as one of the great benefactors of mankind. For it he was prepared to make the greatest sacrifices.

He had to make them. In order to get the pact incorporated in the treaty he surrendered several of the Fourteen Points. At the beginning of 1919 he made a quick trip to the United States. His reception there was not enthusiastic. To Congress he said: 'When the Treaty comes back, gentlemen on this side will find the Covenant not only in it, but so many threads of the Treaty tied to the Covenant that you cannot detach it from the Treaty without destroying the whole vital structure,' and the senators saw in this statement a threat that completely alienated them. Upon his return to France, Wilson perceived that his authority had been impaired, and he was forced to accept a program of reparations and indemnities that were inflated to astronomical proportions. Thus was elaborated a treaty 'too harsh to have any softness, too soft to have any strength,' which gave the world a much shorter time of respite than had the treaties of 1815. But on April 28, 1919, the Pact of the League of Nations was unanimously adopted, and this success was balm to Wilson's wounds. On June 20 the Germans accepted the peace terms in the Trianon Palace at Versailles, and on June 28 they signed in the Hall of Mirrors. Next day President Wilson sailed to champion his work in the United States.

This trip and the thirty speeches he delivered completed the destruction of Wilson's health. In Colorado he had a stroke and had to be brought back half-paralyzed to the White House. From that time on he was an invisible invalid, a mysterious phantom who no longer communicated with the outside world except through his doctor or through Mrs. Wilson. This isolation and illness increased the President's stubbornness. In the Senate the battle continued over Article X of the pact; it was the one on which Wilson was unwilling to accept any reservations. When a vote was taken the unmodified treaty failed to receive the necessary two-thirds vote. The treaty, with reservations, was likewise rejected. Congress tried to end the state of war by a simple resolution; the President vetoed it. It was a deplorable situation, and the peace of the world was to be the cost of this stubborn rivalry. Without the United States the League of Nations could impose respect neither for frontiers nor for the rights of man. With the United States any hope would have been permissible. The return to isolationism of the most powerful and the most disinterested country in the world was a dreadful misfortune for all the nations of the earth. Wilson had shown loftiness of conception, moral grandeur, and courage. He had been betrayed by his character and his physical strength.

Shakespeare conceived nothing more tragic than the end of Woodrow Wilson. For more than a year the specter of a President governed America. From time to time, from his impenetrable retreat in the White House, there emerged a recommendation for

SIGNING OF THE VERSAILLES TREATY IN THE HALL OF MIRRORS. Painting by the British artist Sir William Orpen. From left to right in the center of the table: Orlando, Wilson, Clemenceau, Lloyd George. *Imperial War Museum, London.*

a law or a veto signed in a trembling hand. When stories were circulated that Wilson had lost his mind, he made an appearance at a cabinet meeting, where he seemed sane enough but diminished, exhausted, and only with difficulty able to concentrate. Little by little, life returned to his numbed limbs, and on March 4, 1921, he was able to accompany his successor, Warren G. Harding, to the Capitol. In 1922, and again in 1923 on Armistice Day, he appeared on his balcony and, in a voice still thickened by paralysis, said a few words to the crowd. He spoke of the shame for America of having remained outside the League of Nations. Finally, on February 3, 1924, he died after prolonged and cruel suffering.

Actions and Reactions

The election of 1920 had a double character. It was in part a vote against Wilson, against the treaty, against the League of Nations. Many Americans felt sorry that they had become involved in European affairs. An adroitly contrived campaign tended to disgust them with their victory, to make them believe they had fought for the bankers, and to supplant their friendship for their former Allies by pity for their former enemies. Wilson's illness and his seclusion had undermined the prestige of the Democratic party. The voters wanted most of all to return to their prewar life, which had been, they believed, a happier one. They had the illusion that a change of leaders and of politics would restore business freedom and the good old times. Since Theodore Roosevelt had died in 1919, the Republican party lacked a hero, but it could have its choice of several distinguished men: Governor Frank Lowden of Illinois, General Leonard Wood, and President Nicholas Murray Butler of Columbia University. After long debate the convention of 1920 nominated Warren G. Harding, a senator from Ohio, who had nothing to recommend him for the office of President except perhaps his very insignificance.

The candidate's fine presence, hatred of Wilson, fear of the Reds, and distrust of men of ideas won the day. The Vice-President was Calvin Coolidge, former Governor of Massachusetts, famous for having suppressed a police strike in Boston and for having declared that the right to endanger the public safety by a strike did not belong to 'anybody, anywhere, anytime.' The right turn made by the Ship of State in 1920 was abrupt and violent.

But the new pilot did not know his trade. Harding was not of presidential caliber. He tried to make up for his incompetence by putting in his cabinet certain able men, such as Charles E. Hughes as Secretary of State and Herbert C. Hoover as Secretary of Commerce. The appointment to the Treasury of Andrew Mellon, one of the richest men in the country, pleased Mellon's millionaire confreres.

Harding, like Grant before him, was innocent of any fraudulent transactions, but he was a weak and pleasure-loving man who had put rogues into office and who therefore bore the responsibility. He realized it, and toward 1923 his handsome face changed visibly. He had to make a trip to Alaska. During the trip he repeatedly asked those around him: 'What can a President do when his friends betray him?' On August 2, while Mrs. Harding was reading to him, he died. 'Embolism,' the doctors said. The public did not believe it. The startling news reached Vice-President Coolidge on the night of August 2, 1923, at his father's farm in Vermont, where he had gone to spend his vacation. His father was a county justice of the peace. By the light of an oil lamp held by Mrs. Coolidge, wearing a hastily donned dressing gown and using the old family Bible, the father administered the oath of office to the son. The nation was delighted by this little scene, in the tradition of the Founding Fathers. It was reassuring to think that the President who had had the worst associates and who had been the least moral in the history of the United States had for a successor a Yankee and a Puritan.

Calvin Coolidge had reddish hair, blue eyes, and the most remarkable nasal accent New England ever produced. It was said that the word *cow*, as pronounced by him, had at least four syllables. But he had a right to linger over his words, for legend has it that he uttered very few of them. His mannerisms became strangely dear to the American people, and Coolidge was a popular President. He had entered the White House as a result of Harding's death; when he ran on his own account in 1924, he received almost all Harding's votes.

Wall Street was bursting with riches. The

PRESIDENT CALVIN COOLIDGE WITH HERBERT HOOVER,
SECRETARY OF COMMERCE AND FUTURE PRESIDENT OF THE
UNITED STATES. *Keystone.*

ALCOHOLIC BEVERAGES BEING
DESTROYED AT THE BROOKLYN
ARMY BASE. During Prohibition,
millions of barrels of alcoholic beverages were smashed in military railroad
yards. An American photographic
news agency published this picture in
August 1926 with the following
caption: '. . . if the ferries navigating
the Upper Bay rock slightly during
the next few days it will be nothing to
wonder about.' *Underwood and Underwood.*

graphs of securities reached vertiginous heights. It
was the Coolidge boom, and he was proud of it.
Not that he speculated himself. Never was there a
more prudent man. But he loved the spectacle of
America 'making money.' 'Work and economize,
economize and work' was the text of one of his
brief speeches, whereby one can see that he was
not afraid of platitudes. On the contrary; he gloried
in being banal. It was this that made him original.
Mrs. Coolidge, a charming and simple woman,
even after a long married life considered her
husband an impenetrable enigma. As for the
country, it was so prosperous that ways of reducing
taxation became the principal concern of the
Treasury. What was the source of all this money?
Pyramided credits. The United States granted
credits to Germany; Germany made use of them to
pay reparations to France and England; France and
England to repay the war debts to America. Thus
the money moved in a circle, and the United States
received back what the United States itself had
poured in at the beginning of the circuit. The
whole country was speculating. Under a silent and
sober President, America was living in a world of
magic.

Many thought Coolidge would be a candidate
again in 1928, and his name was so linked with the
idea of prosperity that he would have had an
excellent chance of election. But when the moment
drew near he issued a statement of ten words: 'I
do not choose to run for President in 1928.' The
convention nominated almost unanimously the
Secretary of Commerce, Herbert Hoover, who had
been as successful in that office as he had been in the
ones he had occupied during the war of 1914.

The period following the election of Hoover has
not yet emerged from the domain of polemics and
entered that of history. The orgy of speculation

[248]

THE WALL STREET CRASH, OCTO-BER 24, 1929. The crowd of small gamblers assembled in front of the New York Stock Exchange in the evening of the famous Black Thursday; in the background, the mounted police are moving in to contain the angry speculators, suddenly robbed of their shares. *U.S.I.S.*

UNEMPLOYMENT IN AMERICA. The Wall Street crash soon brought the Great Depression, and the United States was the first country to suffer. The prosperity of the Coolidge Era, which had spread to many social strata, had not prepared the urban proletariat for such a sudden onset of utter misery. *N. Ringart.*

that had marked the end of Coolidge's Administration necessarily had to bring about an economic crisis of the first magnitude. Contrary to the belief of the optimists, no new era had opened in human affairs; the same causes still produced the same effects, and the excessive rise had paved the way for an excessive drop. The crisis that began in October 1929 was more serious and more prolonged than any that had preceded it. The number of unemployed rose to fifteen million (in 1933), a catastrophic figure. Hoover, like Van Buren before him, had found the nation 'pregnant with crisis' for which he was not responsible; but in the eyes of the voters he was to blame for their misfortunes, and he was not re-elected in 1932. Hoover was not a Wall Street man. During the war of 1914 he had shown his disinterestedness and his philanthropy. But the Depression ruined his political career. Poverty and unemployment inspired the American people with a bitter distrust of those who had controlled the

country for the past ten years. The captains of industry were discredited. As it had in the time of Cleveland, the nation turned to the reformers.

Hoover's successor, Franklin Delano Roosevelt, had been educated as an aristocrat, but was a democrat in spirit. He belonged to the wealthy family of Theodore Roosevelt, which had for a long time been conspicuous in public affairs. He had been educated at Groton and Harvard—the New England sanctuaries. Nothing seemed to predestine him to become the champion of the poor. But he had a taste for politics, an affinity for intellectual adventure, and he had married one of his cousins, Eleanor Roosevelt, who was a friend of the people by temperament and by choice. In his adulthood Franklin Roosevelt was stricken by a dreadful disease, poliomyelitis, which almost completely deprived him of the use of his legs. Suffering drew him closer to those who were suffering; his efforts to rehabilitate his wasted body steeled his will.

[251]

ROOSEVELT ADDRESSING THE
PEOPLE OF GALION, OHIO (1932).
Candidates running for election, and
particularly presidential candidates,
often conduct 'whistlestop campaigns'
on special trains. Here, Roosevelt is
addressing the crowd from the rear
platform. *National Archives. U.S.
Information Agency.*

Although he was able to stand up only by using a metal brace, he had enough courage to campaign for the post of Governor of New York state, and his success as a governor made him a good presidential candidate. He had demonstrated great boldness, personal charm and friendliness, great flair in choosing new men, and a rare political skill. But no one in 1932 would have dreamt of predicting that this affable crippled politician was going to have the longest and most dramatic presidency in the history of the United States, or that he would make his country one of the two greatest powers in the world.

Roosevelt, or F.D.R. as he was called soon by all Americans, inherited a tragic situation. Not only were there nearly fourteen million unemployed demanding help, but six million farmers were crushed under the weight of ten billion dollars in mortgages. Cotton had fallen to five cents; wheat to thirty-seven. Farmers were being evicted by their creditors. Because loans on real estate could not be repaid, thousands of local banks closed. Depositors in the big banks became frightened and withdrew their gold. By the day of Roosevelt's inauguration payment had been suspended in twenty-two states.

There were three possible economic policies: the classical one of *laissez faire*, which would have meant waiting for the play of individual actions to re-establish equilibrium; the socialist and communist solution (an end to the private ownership of the means of production); and finally, a directed or planned economy. It was this last that the new President favored. To raise the price level, he depreciated the dollar by forty per cent. To help the unemployed find work, he had the nation undertake numerous public works that ran all the way from the construction of enormous dams to the adornment of monuments. To raise wages and the workers' purchasing power, he encouraged collective contracts. To protect the public against fraudulent

securities, he instituted a stricter control over banks of issue, prohibiting them from being also banks of deposit, and had them watched over by the Securities and Exchange Commission. To relieve the farmers, he took over, in the name of the government, part of the mortgages and reduced the rate of interest. To check the fall in agricultural prices, he asked the farmers to limit the areas devoted to cotton and wheat growing. To demonstrate that the state could successfully take over and distribute hydroelectric power, he created the T.V.A. (Tennessee Valley Authority), which was at the same time to distribute electricity at low rates, promote rural electrification, produce nitrates, and serve as a standard by which private companies' rates were to be judged.

This policy, which has been given the name of the New Deal, had fanatic partisans and opponents. F.D.R. became the man who was most hated and most loved in the United States; he was loved by the poor, by the oppressed minorities, and hated by the rich, whose fortunes he was slashing and who blamed him for his budgetary deficits (the public debt doubled in six years) and for betraying his class. But the masses supported him, and he was re-elected for his second term in 1936. By then Roosevelt and his team had transformed the political and economic situation of the United States. The state enforced strict rules upon the capitalist economy; the Federal Government became all powerful; Washington had turned into a capital in the European sense of the term.

So far as foreign policy was concerned, President Roosevelt found himself in a difficult position. The campaign against the League of Nations and the question of the war debts had, since 1920, embittered the United States' relations with France and England. Since a moratorium had been granted to Germany

ROOSEVELT SIGNING THE LEND-LEASE ACT IN THE WHITE HOUSE ON MARCH 12, 1941. The law, approved by Congress that year, authorized the Federal Government to make financial aid available to governments whose defense was deemed vital to the defense of the United States. *U.S.I.S.*

by Hoover in 1931, the circulation of money had ceased, the European nations suspending their payments to the United States, which aroused much resentment because the people did not understand that the means of payment no longer existed.

Three neutrality acts were voted between 1935 and 1937. They were designed to strengthen the position of Congress by depriving the President of some of his prerogatives. To prevent the repetition of a tragedy like that of the *Lusitania*, Americans were forbidden to travel on ships belonging to belligerents; transport of arms and munitions on American ships was forbidden; the export of arms and munitions was prohibited. The passage of these laws strengthened Germany in her determination to conquer Europe.

When war broke out in 1939, Congress, at the President's request, lifted the embargo on arms on condition that the countries buying them should pay cash and provide their own means of transportation (cash and carry). American ships were forbidden to sail in the territorial waters of the belligerent countries. It was the time of the 'phony war,' when military operations on the French front were practically at a standstill and when German propaganda was holding out chimerical hopes of an easy peace. The majority of Americans were hostile to Hitler but thought that France and England would be strong enough to stop him. The defeat of France was a terrible moral shock to America. But when Paul Reynaud asked President Roosevelt for help, the latter could promise him nothing, since every decision involving war was the prerogative of Congress and it had always shown itself very jealous of its rights in this matter. In September 1940 the President announced the transfer to Great Britain of fifty over-age American destroyers in exchange for air and naval bases on islands belonging

[255]

FLAG RAISING ON MOUNT SURI-
BACHI, IWO JIMA, FEBRUARY 23,
1945. *U.S. Marine Corps.*

to Great Britain. At the end of the year came the
presidential election. The two candidates, Franklin
D. Roosevelt and Wendell L. Willkie, the Republican, both declared themselves in favor of
aid to Great Britain but not in favor of a declaration
of war: 'All aid, short of war.' President Roosevelt
was re-elected, the first time in the history of the
United States that a President had asked for and
obtained a third term.

The country's endorsement gave the President
full authority to carry out his policy of aid to
England. He was preparing the country, much more
completely than Wilson, in similar circumstances,
had done.

This masked war might have continued for a long
time if Japan, Germany's ally and like her a totali-
tarian state, which had long awaited a chance to
establish her hegemony in the Pacific, had not
attacked without warning the Americans' base at
Pearl Harbor in the Hawaiian Islands (December
1941). The declaration of war against Japan was

quickly followed by declarations against Germany
and Italy. These surprised no one, and the whole
country approved the decisions of the President and
Congress. By the beginning of 1942 it became
evident that American production would ensure
Allied victory. Japan's initial successes in the Pacific
and the loss of the Philippines worried only those
who did not know the United States' overwhelming
industrial superiority.

During the Second World War, America demonstrated its patriotism, discipline, and efficiency. The
conversion from peacetime industry to war industry
was carried out with astonishing speed. Within a
year after Pearl Harbor the factories produced
32,000 tanks, 49,000 planes and 8,200,000 tons of
merchant shipping. This production, which was
greatly exceeded the following year, made it possible
not only to arm the American forces, but also to
help Great Britain, China, and especially Russia,
which was fighting heroically after being attacked
by Germany. The American army and navy carried

military science and power to their highest degree. Agriculture performed miracles, and within fifteen months, seven billion pounds of food were shipped to the Allies. Inside the country, rationing and price controls kept inflation down. The country's unity was remarkable; despite the diversity of races and nationalities, the declaration of war was not followed by opposition or sabotage. The workers produced more than ever; strikes were few and short, war-bond drives were successful. Military expenditures made it necessary to raise the income tax to such levels that earlier differences in ways of life became much less marked and the distribution of wealth became more equitable.

Roosevelt had the wisdom to decide, despite resistance from the western states, that the main effort would be directed first against Germany and Italy. Hence, the conduct of the war may be summarized as follows: (1) retreat in the Pacific; (2) conquest of the approaches to the European fortress;

(3) conquest of Europe; (4) recapture of the Pacific areas. In 1940, long before America entered the war, the President had started political preparations for a possible landing in North Africa. The Normandy coast did not lend itself to frontal attack (Dieppe experience). Algeria and Tunisia offered the best prospects for the first stage of the reconquest of Europe. American advisers who were maintained there for that purpose had secured the promise of some French help. In 1942 General Eisenhower was entrusted with organizing an expedition. It was successful. As Roosevelt had hoped, the French army in North Africa joined the American and British forces. Germany was completely defeated in Tunisia. From Africa, Eisenhower moved on to Sicily, then Italy. The Italian government asked for an armistice in August 1943. General Eisenhower, who was appointed commander in chief of the Allied forces on the western front, used bombing to break Germany's resistance and cut down her

AMERICAN TROOPS LANDING IN
NORMANDY ON JUNE 6, 1944.
National Archives. Navy Department.

THE ATOM BOMB EXPLOSION AT
NAGASAKI. On August 9, 1945,
three days after Hiroshima, a second
atom bomb was dropped, this time
over the Japanese city of Nagasaki
(253,000 inhabitants). The terrifying
weapon prompted the Emperor to
capitulate, thus ending the Second
World War. The after-effects of the
two atomic explosions in Hiroshima
and Nagasaki are still being felt today
through residual radiation, and the
list of casualties is not closed. *U.S. Air
Force.*

production. Meanwhile, he was meticulously preparing the Normandy landing. Two artificial
harbors were built, and a pipe line was laid across
the Channel. On June 6, 1944, the Allied armies,
preceded by airborne divisions, took the Germans
by surprise between Caen and Cherbourg and
after a few weeks of fighting, broke the German
front. A second landing took place between
Marseilles and the Italian border on August 15, 1944.
Despite a few German attempts at counterattacking,
the final outcome was never in doubt. Two incomparably powerful war machines, one in the east
(the Russian army), the other in the west, were
combining to crush Germany, which had already
been broken by the Allied bombings. Hitler committed suicide, and on May 7, 1945, at Rheims
Eisenhower received the unconditional surrender
of all German armed forces. Japan still had to be
defeated. On that front, General MacArthur,
starting in Australia and going from island to island

had, little by little, reconquered lost territory. Then,
under cover of the navy and air force, he had
secured the bases needed to invade Japan. But this
was to be a costly operation, since it required
mounting an attack on armies that were still strong
and eagerly supported by the civilian population.
Hence, the final campaign was expected to be fairly
long. Suddenly the atom bomb was dropped. For
several years Roosevelt had secretly sponsored
huge expenditures for research on the fission of
certain unstable atoms; the objective was to start the
reaction inside a bomb which, when dropped from
an airplane, would produce a dreadful cataclysm.
Roosevelt did not witness the victory he had
prepared. He was already in very poor health
when he was re-elected for a fourth term in 1944,
and he died of a brain hemorrhage on April 12,
1945. He was succeeded by Harry S. Truman. In
July 1945 the first atom bomb, which had been
tested at Los Alamos before officers and scientists,

revealed the terrifying power of the new weapon. On August 6 and August 9, atom bombs were dropped respectively on the cities of Hiroshima and Nagasaki. The enormity of the destruction, casualties, and suffering convinced the Emperor of the futility of continuing the fight. Confronted with such weapons, he could capitulate without losing face. On August 14 President Truman announced the end of the hostilities. The Second World War was over.

Victory Without a Victory

As the end of the war approached, Roosevelt and the American people along with him had entertained great hopes. But this time the difficulties arose abroad. The war had terribly weakened not only the defeated countries, but Great Britain and France as well. Two giant powers remained in presence—the United States and the U.S.S.R. Stalin did not express hostility to the foundation of a United Nations organization, but since each of the 'Big Five' (U.S.A., U.S.S.R., Great Britain, France, and China) had a veto power, the United Nations would be able to act only if the U.S.S.R. trusted the organization sufficiently to cooperate.

Throughout the last phase of the war Roosevelt had tried to promote such trust, even at the cost of dangerous concessions to the Soviet Union. At the Yalta Conference (February 1945) he had permitted the Russians to advance as far as Berlin, and consented to the cession of a large German territory to Poland and to the installation of communist governments in the Balkan countries in the hope of winning Stalin's friendship. Moreover, in exchange for the Soviets' declaration of war on Japan, he had accepted their seizure of Manchuria. On this point he had taken the advice of his military chiefs, who did not believe that the atom bomb would ensure victory in the Far East. Truman inherited that

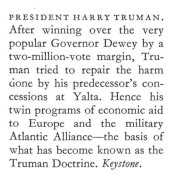

PRESIDENT HARRY TRUMAN. After winning over the very popular Governor Dewey by a two-million-vote margin, Truman tried to repair the harm done by his predecessor's concessions at Yalta. Hence his twin programs of economic aid to Europe and the military Atlantic Alliance—the basis of what has become known as the Truman Doctrine. *Keystone*.

situation and had to confirm all these concessions at Potsdam. The United Nations Charter was adopted in San Francisco in June 1945 by fifty nations. Other international organizations (U.N.E.S.C.O., International Refugee Organization, Bank for International Settlements, etc.) were created or planned. But the spirit of cooperation was absent. At the United Nations Russia immediately used her veto power aggressively. Despite Yalta and Potsdam, Stalin remained distrustful of the capitalist powers, and particularly the United States. This was not real peace; it was given the name of Cold War.

At first, Truman was not thought to possess the qualities of leadership needed especially in these difficult circumstances. He had done good work in the Senate, but in a minor capacity. In the beginning he gathered rather too many of his personal friends from his native Missouri around him. But very soon his responsibilities instead of overcoming

him enhanced the strength of his character. This man who for a long time had lived in obscurity suddenly showed that he had rare courage and strong common sense. In his foreign policy, though, he was hampered by the nation itself, which demanded a swift return to peacetime conditions because it was unaware of the immense dangers of the situation. Prosperity further increased euphoria. Never had the United States been so rich; never had the distribution of the riches been more equitable. Sixty million Americans were employed, against forty-eight million before the war. The production of consumer goods was at least twice as large as before the war. The Eightieth Congress (elected for two years) was hostile to Truman, and he did not seem likely to be elected in 1948.

Governor Dewey, who was nominated by the Republican convention, was a strong candidate; despite opposition from the conservative southern Democrats, Truman was nominated by the

PRESIDENT TRUMAN GREETING
SECRETARY OF STATE GEORGE C.
MARSHALL ON HIS RETURN FROM
PARIS, ON NOVEMBER 22, 1948.
General Marshall gave his name to
the plan for economic assistance to
Europe for which in 1948 Congress
appropriated billions of dollars to help
the nations most seriously hurt by the
war. *U.S.I.S.*

Democratic convention. Even his friends barely helped him because they did not believe he could win. But with amazing zest Truman carried on the fight by himself, touring the country and making speeches in his whistle stop campaign. He received two million more votes than Dewey. This caused very great surprise and considerably enhanced his prestige. He needed it, for the situation abroad was growing increasingly serious. The U.S.S.R. had established communist governments in East Germany, Hungary, Czechoslovakia, Roumania, and Bulgaria. Yugoslavia was communist, but dissident. An 'iron curtain' had cut off Eastern Europe from the West. Stalin's promise of free elections, made in Yalta, had not been kept in a single one of the countries beyond the Curtain. Western Europe was struggling amidst terrible financial difficulties in trying to rebuild after the war. This made her accessible to revolutionary propaganda; moreover, she was almost completely disarmed, hence vulnerable.

In the Far East the situation was even more difficult. A civil war had broken out in 1945 between Chiang Kai-shek and the Chinese communists. During World War Two the Americans had supported Chiang's nationalist government, although its corruption and incompetence were only too well known. At the end of 1945 General Marshall went to China but failed in his attempt to mediate. The Chinese communists armed by the U.S.S.R. then won one victory after another. In 1949 they were the masters of China, and Chiang had to flee to the island of Taiwan with what was left of his army. This meant the annexation of four hundred fifty million Chinese to the communist world, and the ease with which this had been accomplished raised the danger that Stalin might want to take over the whole of Asia. What was Truman to do, and what could he do? At first, he had hoped that the United Nations would draft a disarmament plan and set up an international atomic-energy commission. But Stalin had not accepted any effective control. There were only two ways to stem any further conquests: strengthening the West's military power and improving the economic situation of the

GENERAL MACARTHUR BEING WELCOMED IN CHICAGO. A typical American parade inspired by Roman processions, in which the chariots are replaced by fifty-five powerful open cars. The ticker-tape throwing is peculiar to the United States. *U.S.I.S.*

threatened countries. In the famous Point Four of his inaugural address in 1949 Truman suggested that the United States give technical assistance to economically underdeveloped nations. Then, with his Secretaries of State (first General Marshall, then Dean Acheson), he drafted two programs—one for assistance to Europe, the other for an Atlantic alliance.

The idea he expressed in 1947 with respect to Greece and Turkey has been called the Truman Doctrine. The policy of the United States should be, he stated, to help free peoples to resist attempts to subjugate them made either by armed minorities or by foreign adversaries. The same year General Marshall announced in a speech at Harvard that if the European nations would agree upon a common economic reconstruction program, the United States would assist them. The agreement was concluded at the Paris Conference. The nations beyond the Iron

Curtain had been invited, but refused help from the 'capitalist imperialists.'

The Marshall Plan was approved by Congress in 1948. The program was designed to operate until 1952. During those four years, fourteen billion dollars were distributed by the E.C.A. (Economic Cooperation Administration). The Marshall Plan enabled the countries that had suffered from the war to live through a difficult period. France used the assistance mainly to modernize her industry. But the Plan did not solve the military defense problem.

Therefore, in April 1949, a North Atlantic Treaty was signed by the United States, Canada, Great Britain, France, Italy, Belgium, the Netherlands, Luxembourg, Norway, Denmark, Iceland, and Portugal. It stated that an armed attack against one or several of the contracting countries in Europe or North America would be regarded as an attack

PRESIDENT DWIGHT D. EISEN-
HOWER EXAMINING THE NEW
AMERICAN FLAG. A fiftieth star
was added to the Star Spangled
Banner on July 4, 1959.

against all of them. It was an alliance pact, and it was approved by a large majority of both parties in the U.S. Senate. Now the alliance had to be given means of enforcement. The United States promised military assistance to the member nations. It was decided to create an interallied army to defend Western Europe in case of need. General Eisenhower was appointed its commander in chief, and he established his headquarters (Supreme Headquarters Allied Powers [Europe]—S.H.A.P.E.) at Louveciennes, near Paris. His objective was to build an army of at least fifty divisions to make aggression difficult if not impossible. The task was a gigantic one. Countries that had almost exhausted their resources had to be asked for substantial contributions; officers of diverse languages and traditions had to be induced to work together. Eisenhower's personality helped in this respect. Not all the objectives that had been set were reached, far from it; but by the end of 1952 great progress had been made.

Meanwhile, in Asia things were going from bad to worse. In 1949 the American forces had evacuated South Korea, leaving in power a local government headed by Syngman Rhee; the withdrawal resulted in an invasion of the area in 1950 by North Korean communists prompted by the Chinese, who joined them a little later. This aggression, coming after so many others, aroused anger in the West. Taking advantage of the Russians' absence from the United Nations Security Council (which they were boycotting because nationalist China had retained her membership), Truman obtained a condemnation of North Korea's action and asked the other members for their support. Actually, European and South American help was mainly symbolic, and the brunt of the Korean war fell on the United States. But the principle of collective resistance was vindicated, and General MacArthur took command in Korea in the name of the United Nations. In a remarkable campaign he succeeded in expelling the aggressors from South Korea and pursued them into North Korea, although several member nations would have preferred him to have stopped at the border. In November 1950 MacArthur predicted that the war would be over and the soldiers back home by Christmas. But a large Chinese-communist force intervened; the United Nations forces were pushed back, then they recaptured the territory they had lost. Finally both armies established themselves along fortified lines in what became a war of attrition.

[*The text that follows is by Malcolm Cowley.*]

For a long time President Truman and General MacArthur had bitterly disagreed over Far Eastern policy. MacArthur, with the support of a powerful political faction, demanded priority for the war in Asia. He asserted that he could bring the war to a rapid close by bombing airfields in Chinese territory and by reinforcing his army with Chinese Nationalist troops from Taiwan. General Omar Bradley, then chairman of the Joint Chiefs of Staff, and President Truman both feared that this might lead to another world war. The President called MacArthur back and replaced him with General Matthew Ridgway. It was thought for a time that the recall of MacArthur might stir the country, and indeed he was given an enthusiastic welcome. When he entered the Republican primaries, however, the enthusiasm was not translated into votes.

In the presidential election of 1952, the Democratic Administration was faced with a new adversary, General Eisenhower, who had accepted nomination by the Republican convention. His rival there was Senator Taft, who was preferred by the party stalwarts; but the Republicans had been out of power for twenty years, and most of the delegates felt that Eisenhower's immense prestige could bring them back by rallying large numbers of independent voters. Truman had announced that he would not run for re-election. The Democratic convention nominated Adlai Stevenson, a cultivated man with a brilliant mind who promised to continue Roosevelt's and Truman's liberal policies. Eisenhower was elected by a majority of more than six million votes, which was largely owed to his personality and fame, but was doubtless increased by his promise, made during the last weeks of the campaign, to go to Korea and do what he could to stop the war.

Still another factor in the campaign was the suspicion that the Democrats, during their many years in office, had been 'soft on communism.' There had been a number of court trials involving accusations of espionage and treason. Senator Joseph McCarthy of Wisconsin had charged that the State

Department was infiltrated with 'card-carrying Communists.' When the Republicans assumed control of the Senate after their victory in 1952, McCarthy became chairman of a Permanent Investigations Subcommittee and pursued his crusade against subversives by increasingly flamboyant methods. Many officials of the foreign service were discharged or forced to resign for what would later seem to be frivolous reasons. McCarthy then shifted his attack to the Department of the Army, which he accused of concealing evidence of espionage. The Army brought countercharges, and these were investigated by the Senate, which exonerated McCarthy and his aides. President Eisenhower had taken no stand in the controversy, but he was an Army man, and he must have been relieved when the

ASTRONAUT EDWARD WHITE'S
TWENTY-MINUTE WALK IN SPACE
DURING THE GEMINI IV FLIGHT.
The close race for the conquest of
space is intensifying, since today a
nation's technological achievements
and scientific progress are the key to
its prestige in the eyes of other
nations. A large portion of the United
States budget goes into the space
program. *U.S.I.S. U.P.I. Telephoto.*

[269]

DEMONSTRATION FOR SCHOOL INTEGRATION IN SAINT LOUIS. Negro children and their parents carrying posters. The federal law no longer permits racial discrimination, in particular in the schools. But state governors, overtly or covertly, have on occasion opposed enforcement of the law, and this has caused clashes between the local police and federal authorities. *U.S.I.S.*

Senate, acting on a motion of censure, voted to 'condemn' McCarthy for contempt of a Senate elections subcommittee, for abuse of certain Senators, and for insults to the Senate itself. After that vote, in December 1954, McCarthy's influence rapidly declined.

Meanwhile Eisenhower had kept his promise in regard to the Korean War. Negotiations with North Korea, which had dragged along since 1951, were prosecuted with more vigor, and an armistice was signed six months after he became President. It was a peace without victory, but South Korea was safe from being invaded. Relations with Russia had become still more confused, but somewhat less tense, after the death of Stalin in March 1953. New leaders, headed by Malenkov, announced a more flexible policy toward the West. Malenkov, however, was

soon eliminated in favor of a Bulganin-Khrushchev team; then Khrushchev alone took over. The new head of the country was an intelligent man of peasant stock, with a sense of humor. He was less bloodthirsty than Stalin, but no less ambitious, and he proved to be a wily imperialist. Under his leadership Soviet diplomacy attempted an immense turning movement through the Middle East, Egypt, and even Central Africa, aimed at isolating the West. The steady growth of Soviet military power increased the danger of this policy for the United States and Western Europe. Russia had exploded an atom bomb in 1949 and a hydrogen bomb in August 1953. She was working at top speed to develop an arsenal of long-range rockets with nuclear warheads.

In 1955 the President suffered a heart attack that led to grave concern for his life. But he recovered, resumed his duties, and was unanimously renominated at the Republican convention of 1956. Once again the Democratic candidate was Adlai Stevenson. He waged a vigorous campaign that was hopeless from the beginning as a result of Eisenhower's immense popularity. In the election Eisenhower carried all but seven states and won a popular majority of nine and a half million votes. Richard Nixon, his Vice-President in both terms, had come to be regarded as the heir presumptive.

Foreign policy remained in the hands of John Foster Dulles, the Secretary of State, who was faced with international crises before and after the 1956 election. The newly elected president of Egypt, Colonel Nasser, had adopted a neutralist position, abhorrent to Dulles. On July 19 Congress voted not to extend him funds with which to build the Aswan High Dam. Seven days later Nasser seized the Suez Canal and announced that he would not permit the passage of cargoes bound to or from Israel. The British and the French were deeply perturbed by the threat to their own supplies of oil from Arabia and Persia. On October 29 the Israelis invaded the Suez Peninsula and rapidly defeated Nasser's army. Two days later Britain and France, after an ultimatum, moved to occupy the Suez Canal. The Russians threatened to send 'volunteers' to help the Egyptians. But simultaneously the Russians were having trouble in Europe, where a revolt of Hungarian patriots was crushed on November 4 by Soviet tanks.

In the United Nations, the United States voted with the majority to condemn Soviet intervention in Hungary, but voted with the Soviet bloc—this for the first time—to demand the withdrawal of British, French, and Israeli troops from Egyptian soil. It was a somewhat paradoxical position, intended to restore peace in the world, but leading to resentment in Western Europe and strengthening the Soviet position in the Middle East. The President tried to repair the damage by proclaiming the Eisenhower Doctrine, which promised economic and military assistance to Arab nations threatened with communist subversion. The only military result of the Doctrine was the landing of Marines on the beaches of Lebanon (July 1958), a farcical interlude in which the Marines were greeted, not by machine-gun fire, but by small merchants peddling Coca-Cola. As for

Egypt and Syria—joined for a time as the United Arab Republic—they showed a preference for Soviet arms and advice.

The entire field of military weapons was undergoing immense changes, with long-range missiles taking the place of bombing planes. In October 1957 the Russians launched Sputnik I, an artificial satellite, thereby displaying an unexpected advantage in the new science of rocketry. They had already announced that they possessed an intercontinental ballistic missile (ICBM) capable of striking selected targets in North America. The first American reaction to Sputnik was one of dismay, combined with irritation against the three armed services and against an educational system that was not producing a sufficient number of highly trained scientists. Researches and experiments now went forward rapidly. An American ICBM was tested in November, and an artificial satellite, Explorer I, was fired at the end of January 1958. Something close to a balance of terror was being maintained on both sides. During the last two years of Eisenhower's Administration, there was a partial thaw in the Cold War. Khrushchev paid a visit to the United States in 1959, and arrangements were made for a summit conference to be held in Paris on May 16, 1960. But meanwhile the United States had been sending high-flying planes over Russia to report on the progress of Russian military technology. One of the planes was shot down on May 1. Khrushchev angrily demanded an apology for the flights, and the summit conference collapsed.

At home the chief issue was racial integration of the public schools, as ordered by the Supreme Court in a famous decision of the year 1954. The decision had been obeyed in many of the border states, but everywhere in the Deep South it was meeting with angry resistance. Eisenhower, always a moderate, tried to avoid federal intervention. Nevertheless he sent troops to Little Rock, Arkansas, to end the disorders that followed the admission of nine black students to a local high school. The country was generally prosperous during his two Administrations, although the gross national product (GNP) was increasing at a slower rate in the United States than in Russia, Japan, and many West European countries. In 1954 and 1958 it declined, in token of mild recessions, and there was another mild recession

Skaggs
DRUG
CENTER
SKAGGS
FREMONT
CASINO
The
MINT
GIFTS JEWELRY
SOUVENIRS
FREMO

◀ NEON SIGNS ON BROADWAY. *John Craven photo.*

A POOR NEIGHBORHOOD IN NEW YORK. Fire escapes, generally made out of metal, are one of the most familiar sights in New York as soon as one has left the fashionable sections. *John Craven photo.*

in 1960 and 1961, when unemployment temporarily rose to eight per cent of the labor force. The country was losing part of its immense store of monetary gold, as a result of deficits in the balance of payments with Europe. All this would combine with international rivalries to create problems for a new administration.

At the Democratic convention of 1960, John F. Kennedy of Massachusetts was nominated on the first ballot. He surprised everyone by choosing his principal rival, Lyndon B. Johnson of Texas, as his running mate. The Republican candidate, also nominated on the first ballot, was Richard Nixon. The most dramatic feature of the campaign was a series of televised debates between Nixon and Kennedy, image facing image; the Kennedy image was judged to be more persuasive. Still, the election was the closest in history, with Kennedy ahead by a popular majority of only 118,000 votes—a 'tremendous landslide,' he called it derisively (and ungrammatically), 'that swept the Vice President and I into office by one-tenth of one per cent.' At forty-three he was the youngest man ever to be elected President, and the first Roman Catholic.

He did not preside over a Catholic Administration; in fact the Church exercised rather less influence on

THE NEGRO MARCH ON WASHINGTON.
AUGUST 28, 1963. This peaceful demonstration in which many whites (writers,
scientists, painters, actors, and actresses)
took part was also the first 'news picture'
relayed by Telstar. *U.S.I.S.*

his policies than on those of some earlier Presidents. His three years in office did a great deal toward banishing the religious issue from American politics, but they reintroduced a conflict of generations. Youthful in fact and spirit, Kennedy offered a contrast with Eisenhower, who sometimes reminded people of wise old General Kutuzov in *War and Peace;* he had the same habit of delegating responsibilities to his staff and of letting events take their course. Kennedy was an activist, as were the young men he brought to Washington. These were serving on what he called the New Frontier, and they remembered the slogan on which he had based his campaign for office: 'Let's get the country moving again.'

Many of the young men were on leave of absence from the faculties of famous universities, with Harvard providing more than its share. The Pentagon, citadel of the armed forces, was invaded by 'whiz kids' from the Harvard Business School. Though Kennedy resembled Roosevelt I in his activism, he was more like Roosevelt II in the use he tried to make of the intellectual community. Indeed, the use was wider in his case, since most of the New Dealers had been lawyers or economists, whereas the New Frontiersmen also included sociologists, physical scientists, political scientists, and historians. They did not include poets, painters, or novelists, but these received a form of recognition. Many of them were sent abroad on cultural missions and others were invited to formal dinners at the White House—good dinners, too, cooked by a French chef. Washington became a livelier place than it had been since the First New Deal.

In the economic field, Kennedy's central purpose was to restore full employment while keeping wages and prices at a reasonable level. He tried to stimulate production by fiscal measures, that is, by increased government spending and by levying smaller taxes on capital invested in new factories. When these measures, though partly successful, still fell short of achieving his purpose, he recommended a general reduction in taxes, which Congress approved soon after his death. Congress had already given him authority to reduce import duties by as much as 50 per cent, thereby expanding international trade. To prevent an inflationary rise in wages and prices, he announced 'guidelines' for both. These did not have the force of the law, but it was sometimes costly for labor unions or businessmen to disregard them—as the United States Steel Corporation discovered in 1962, when it announced a rise in prices that Kennedy regarded as unreasonable. Governmental pressure was brought to bear and steel prices went back to their former level. But Kennedy had projects for the country that went far beyond these efforts to maintain stable prices and encourage economic growth. Among the measures he strongly recommended were federal aid to education, medical care for the aged under social security, and expanded civil rights for Negroes. All the measures were delayed in Congress by a coalition of Northern Republicans and Southern Democrats, but they were ready for passage and they were all enacted shortly after he died.

The Cold War reached a climax during the Kennedy years. Beginning with his first months in office, the new President faced a succession of crises during which he acted, in effect, as his own Secretary of State. The first crisis was over Cuba, whose new ruler, Fidel Castro, had seized American property, denounced American imperialism, and taken steps toward joining the Soviet bloc. Meanwhile the Central Intelligence Agency (CIA) had trained and equipped a band of Cuban exiles who swore to liberate their country if landed on its shore. Eisenhower had approved the project. Kennedy was dubious, but after listening to arguments from the CIA and the Joint Chiefs of Staff, he decided to go ahead. Wisely he ruled against the use of American troops. The landing, made at the Bay of Pigs in April 1961, was a disastrous failure. Kennedy accepted the blame for it; 'This is where the buck stops,' he said. He had learned a lesson of caution from the disaster and another lesson too: that the Chiefs of Staff and the CIA were not infallible.

The second crisis followed an unsatisfactory meeting with Khrushchev in Vienna (June 1961) and was caused by Khrushchev's efforts to frighten the United States into withdrawing its forces from West Berlin. He threatened to isolate the city and there was talk of nuclear war. With Kennedy displaying firmness, but taking no rash steps, the crisis slowly melted away, leaving as its only memorial the Berlin Wall. But a third crisis followed, after a relatively peaceful year. The CIA had been reporting that the Russians were active in Cuba. On October 16, 1962, it submitted aerial photographs to the President that showed men at work on launching pads for nuclear missiles and even showed one of the missiles. This had a range of one thousand miles and hence could hit any target south of a line drawn from Memphis to Norfolk. Later it was discovered that there were forty-four of these missiles in Cuba, with still longer-range missiles scheduled to arrive.

There was a weeklong conference in the White House. The threat to the country was immediate, and many of the President's advisers held that the only possible answer was an air raid big enough to destroy every launching pad in Cuba and every plane capable of carrying nuclear weapons. Kennedy adopted a less drastic course of action that would give the Russians a chance to withdraw without blood being shed. On October 22 he announced to the country that he was ordering a naval quarantine of Cuba in order to halt the passage of vessels bearing offensive weapons. On October 25 half of the ninety Russian vessels then on their way to Cuba turned about and steamed for home. On October 28 Khrushchev drew back from the threat of nuclear catastrophe; he told Kennedy that his men would stop work on the missile sites and that men and missiles would be returned to the Soviet Union.

What followed those two anxious weeks was a loosening of tension that led to negotiations and later to a treaty which banned the atmospheric testing of nuclear devices. The treaty was ratified by the Senate in September 1963. Meanwhile Kennedy had been winning other diplomatic victories in Africa and Latin America. He had done less well in Southeast Asia and the Middle East, but still it had been a long time since the United States had had so many friends abroad as during the last two months of his presidency. When he was shot and killed by an assassin during a visit to Dallas, Texas (November 22, 1963), people all over the world mourned his death as that of a man who had revived their hope for peace.

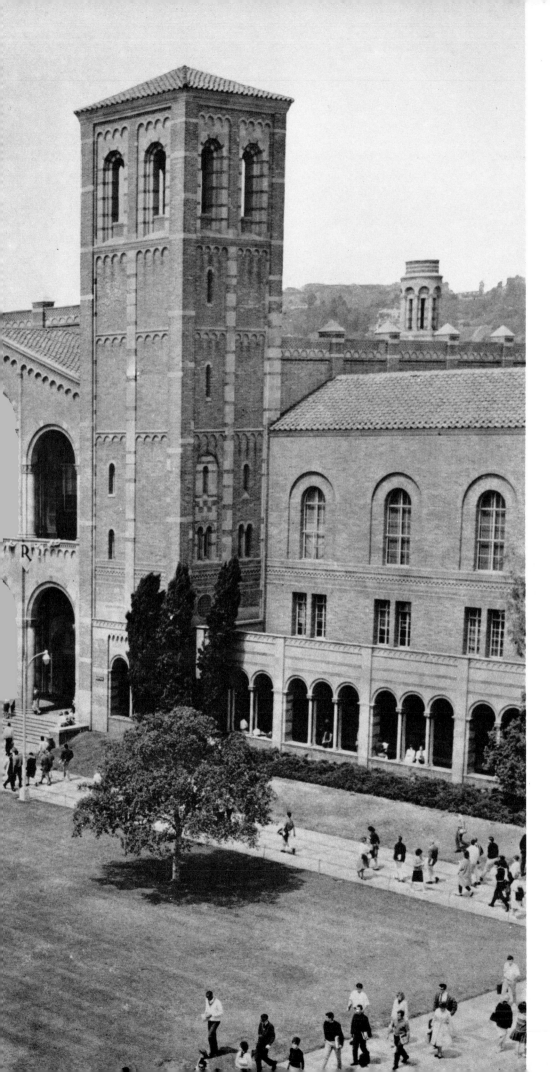

A UNIVERSITY CAMPUS. The campus is the central square and yard in American colleges and universities. Its Latin name reflects the determination, or even the need, of the American intellectual to maintain his contact with the cultural past of the Old World; another example of this is the archaic pseudo-Romance style of the façade. *John Craven photo.*

ERNEST HEMINGWAY. Great ▶
traveler, man of action, a picturesque
figure, Hemingway—unlike Faulkner,
for example—won universal fame and
even popularity among a wide variety
of people of different ages and cultural
backgrounds. *Agence France-Presse
photo.*

MARK TWAIN. S.L.Clemens, a
humorist, was also famous for his
fighting spirit and independence. All
his life he was the butt of the resentment of the self-righteous Average
American. Twain was one of the
first writers who started withdrawing
American literature from English
influence. *Underwood and Underwood.*

The New America

The United States has undergone vast changes since 1940, but most of them have depended on one essential change: the accelerated growth of the country in population and wealth. 'America, I love you! And there's a hundred million others like me!' crowds used to sing during the Liberty Bond campaigns of World War I. A hundred million seemed an incredible figure in 1917, but it was close to being accurate. There would be 106 million Americans in 1920, 123 million in 1930, and 132 million in 1940, when the decennial increase had fallen to its lowest figure of hardly more than seven per cent; that was the result of immigration quotas and a reduced birth rate during the depression years. But then the rate of growth began to rise again: in 1950 there were 151 million Americans, and in 1960 there were 179 million, an increase in ten years of nineteen per cent, owed chiefly to a rise in the birth rate after the war. In 1967 the Census Bureau announced that the population had passed 200 million, having doubled in forty years.

Growth was by no means uniform over the country. There was an immense movement of population from east to west. There was a smaller but substantial movement from the Old South to the North, though Florida, the southernmost state, was an exception because of its mild climate; the population there had increased by 161 per cent from 1940 to 1960. California had an increase for twenty years of 127 per cent, and by 1967 it had become the most populous state. Two new states, Alaska and Hawaii, the forty-ninth and fiftieth, had been admitted during the Eisenhower years; their populations were small but growing. On the other hand, four of the central states and one Appalachian state, West Virginia, had fewer inhabitants in 1960 than they had in 1940.

Another vast movement of population was from countryside to city, and from smaller cities to what were called the Standard Metropolitan Areas. By 1960 there were 225 such areas and twenty-four of them each had more than a million people. The farm population was rapidly decreasing, and this was

especially true of the Southern black peasantry, which was streaming into Northern cities. Seventy per cent of all Americans lived in cities or suburbs. A city-world, or megalopolis, was taking shape on the Atlantic coast; it stretched in an almost unbroken arc from Portland, Maine, to Norfolk, Virginia. Another megalopolis spread eastward from Chicago along the southern shore of the Great Lakes, and still another occupied almost all the habitable land in southern California.

The increase in population led to an even greater increase in consumption. The United States had become incomparably the best market for everything consumers needed, or could be made to think they needed. Here was a nation of fairly uniform tastes, which could be changed in a uniform fashion by advertising based on motivational research. Here people were gathered by millions in convenient centers of distribution, and the centers were bound together by a superb network of railways, highways, airways, waterways, pipe lines, and power lines, with the result that everything could be produced in quantity, attractively packaged, cheaply distributed, and efficiently merchandised as if in a nationwide supermarket.

By 1965 the gross national product had increased to $685 billion—it would be nearly $900 billion three years later—and there were buyers for everything produced. Prices had risen, taxes had risen—especially local taxes—but wages and income from investment or speculation had risen even faster. The most perplexing problem of many people was how to spend their money. Each year at Christmas time, the spending season, magazines were full of advertisements for articles of no possible utility and little charm except their preposterous cost. 'A good wife knows how to be an expensive mistress' was the message of an advertisement for Russian sable coats. 'Are you so busy being devoted to your husband you never make reckless demands? That's a mistake. Try acting spoiled now and then. Simply *have* to have some wildly beautiful extravagance.' The wives of wage earners were cajoled to make less expensive but, for them, equally reckless purchases: color TV, for example, usually bought on the installment plan. As a result of installment buying and the wide use of

KENNEDY'S ASSASSINATION. It was during a visit to Dallas, Texas, that President Kennedy was slain. Although he was rushed to a hospital, he died within a short time. Here, a few moments after the shooting, Mrs. Kennedy leans over her husband's body, *U.S.I.S.*

a new device, credit cards, consumer credit had reached a disturbingly high figure. Still, with rising wages and the high rate of employment, it seemed likely that most of the payments would be met. There were 75.5 million wage and salary earners by 1967. Even the unemployed (2.9 million) and the unemployable had purchasing power as a result of social-security measures and welfare allowances. The employed had vastly more of it, and by 1968 the median family income had risen to $8,000 a year.

Wealth breeds wealth. The gulf between American riches and the poverty of undeveloped countries was becoming deeper year by year. In the United States rich corporations were taking over poorer ones—often on generous terms, since the losses of the latter could be applied as credits against the corporation tax. Three of the giants—General Motors, Standard Oil of New Jersey, and Ford— had an aggregate gross income that was larger in 1965 than that of all the farms in the country. The hundred largest manufacturing firms had one-third of all the sales in their respective fields. Under the antitrust laws, the government forbade mergers that would create monopolies or near-monopolies, but another sort of merger was still permissible. To quote from a 1968 issue of *The New Republic*:

> The new expansion device is conglomerate mergers (i.e., mergers in unrelated fields). . . . The thing is spreading. Last month [October] the previous high record of 3,000 such mergers in a year had already been passed. United Fruit (bananas) is joining Textron (zippers, helicopters); Dow Chemical joins Hartford Fire Insurance; Loew's Theatres marries Lorillard Tobaccos.

Not all these mergers would be profitable in the end or would lead to an increased volume of business for the merged companies. Some expressed a rage for mere bigness or were merely an excuse for maneuvers on the stock exchange. But in general they were based on sound principles, namely, that the merged companies would have more working capital; that they could pay for more efficient management; could rationalize, computerize, and spend more for R & D, research and development, which had come to be the accepted pathway to new products, new methods, and new customers. The new giants of business moved quickly into foreign territory, where they set up new factories and were regarded as a threat by the smaller native firms. The United States had come to be the greatest exporter not only of manufactured products—a field in which West Germany and Japan were vigorous competitors—but even more of capital, managerial techniques, and fashions of life.

The new Americans lived by preference in single-family houses; it was their principal concession to the individualism of the pioneers. In the 1960s nearly a million one-family houses were built each year, most of them in housing developments outside the central cities. The household usually consisted of a nuclear family: husband, wife, and children under the age of eighteen. It was seldom that one found three generations under the same roof. Older couples lived alone, each in a house that had sheltered five or six persons, or else they retired in their sixties to communities planned for 'senior citizens.' The houses where younger couples lived were full of labor-saving devices—clothes washers and dryers, electric toasters and grills, electric dishwashers, vacuum cleaners (besides the omnipresent TV)—but the wife had no one to help her except the baby sitter who appeared, or failed to appear, on the evening when she and her husband planned to go bowling together.

Wives complained, often with good reason, of being overworked. Many of them added to their burdens by finding outside employment as soon as all the children were of school age. In small towns most of the schoolteachers were married women. Husbands usually worked at a distance from their homes. Since public transportation was inconvenient or totally lacking (except for schoolchildren), most of them drove to work, and they spent more time on the road than earlier Americans who had walked to work. Hardly anyone walked in the late 1960s, when there were nearly a hundred million motor vehicles, five-sixths of them passenger cars. In spite of morning and evening traffic jams, the new Americans—at least the men—had vastly more leisure than their fathers. The working day had shortened to eight hours or less (not counting overtime) and the five-day week was almost universal. How Americans were using their leisure was a subject for argument, but certainly not so much of it was devoted to public activities (watching parades, going to big picnics, sitting in movie palaces, rooting for the home team) and more to drinking beer in the living room while watching some of the same events on television.

In general the new Americans were not a strongly religious people. The Protestant ethic that ruled the country during the nineteenth century had softened into a vague idealism or liberalism. Dancing, drinking, and playing cards—even playing house—were no longer regarded as sins except by southern Baptists and by Mormons in the mountain states. The Protestant Churches had invested too much of their moral authority in the Prohibition Amendment (1919), and they had lost it when the amendment was repealed in 1933. Church membership had increased after World War II and continued to be high; in the late sixties there were about seventy million American Protestants. But church attendance was low, and idealistic young ministers often preached the social gospel to empty pews.

About 5.6 million people were members of Jewish congregations, whose rabbis often worried about problems of unbelief and assimilation. Catholics, 47.5 million in 1968, had great success in holding the loyalty of their communicants; also the birth rate among them was higher than among Protestants or Jews and assured the Church of a steady growth. There was a rapid change in the public status of Catholicism after the middle of the century. Since its most pious adherents had usually been poor people descended from Irish, German, or Polish immigrants—with the Italians less pious but generally faithful—and since there had been certain clubs and public offices for which Catholics were not considered, they had come to regard themselves as a somewhat persecuted minority. That self-image had been weakening for some time, and it disappeared almost from the beginning of the Kennedy Administration. During the 1960s *Who's Who* and *The Social Register* were full of Catholics. Priests served beside ministers and rabbis on welfare committees. The only public issue on which the Church stood in opposition to other religious communities was that of birth control, and here the Church itself was divided. Some of the great Catholic universities—even including their theological faculties—were strongholds of liberal thought.

The new Americans of whatever faith, or none, were paying much more in local taxes for the education of their children. As a result of the baby boom in the 1950s, thousands of schools had to be built in the new suburbs and around the new industrial centers, where most of them had the functional look of new factories. In each of eleven consecutive years more than four million children entered the first grade. They would, on the average, spend many more years in school than earlier Americans. Most of them would finish high school, while the number of college graduates in the adult population had almost doubled in fifteen years. The total school population at all levels had risen by 1966 to 55.1 million.

When the Russians launched Sputnik I in 1957, they gave a shock to American education that would be felt for many years. American youth, so it seemed, had been poorly trained in science and mathematics: Why else should the Russians be first to achieve this scientific miracle? Thereafter high-school students were asked to work harder in specific fields instead of taking vague courses supposed to encourage good citizenship or 'life adjustment.' All the famous colleges, now besieged with applicants for their freshman classes, imposed higher standards that the high schools tried to meet. Thus, as a result of Sputnik and College Board examinations, boys and girls in the 1960s were studying a little more than their predecessors of the early 1950s. Meanwhile the college population was growing rapidly; in 1966 it was 6.4 million, after an increase of fourteen per cent in a single year. The rate of growth was even higher in graduate schools, which year by year kept offering scores of new programs. College campuses were full of raw excavations which—one was told above the din of riveting hammers—would be the site of an expanded library or a new science building.

The sale of serious books had increased, partly because they were assigned in college courses, partly because they were read by widening circles of college graduates, but also because college libraries were receiving subsidies from the Federal Government. Novels—including the serious ones if they were widely discussed, but more often the sexiest and most sensational—might reach millions of readers in paperback editions sold everywhere on the news-stands. To some extent paperback books had taken the place of the general or 'family' magazines, most of which had been discontinued. Another group, the cheaply written pulp-paper magazines of earlier times, had disappeared, as had the weekly 'comic books' that followed them; both had lost their readers or nonreaders to the superior mindlessness of TV. A few magazines, for the most part profusely illustrated and containing no fiction, had prospered immensely. Those with the largest circulations in 1967 were *Reader's Digest* (17.3 million), *TV Guide* (12.7 million), *McCall's*, largest of the old-line women's magazines (8.5 million), and *Look* (7.8 million), an illustrated fortnightly that had drawn ahead of its weekly rival *Life* (7.4 million). For those seeking information not to be found in local news-papers, there were the news weeklies, of which the oldest and most widely read was *Time* (3.7 million). For serious or sophisticated readers, a smaller but growing audience, there were *The New Yorker*, *Esquire*, *Saturday Review*, *Harper's*, *The Atlantic*, and the liberal *New Republic*, all exerting a considerable influence on styles of thinking and living.

Newspapers had increased in circulation but decreased in number. Competition in the field had practically disappeared, most cities being left with one morning and one afternoon paper. Chicago had two of each and New York had three in all (not counting the energetic suburban dailies on Long Island). Most newspapers were politically conservative, but in a rather colorless fashion, since they tried to speak for a whole community. A few, including the liberal *New York Times* and the conservative *Wall Street Journal*, had acquired a national influence greater than that of any magazine.

In the literary world the era of naturalistic novelists and playwrights (Dreiser, Lewis, O'Neill) was followed by that of the Lost Generation, whose leading members (Hemingway, Faulkner, Fitzgerald) were not lost at all, but merely venturesome in life and art. Dos Passos, Steinbeck, and Richard Wright were spokesmen for the 1930s. After World

War II one looked for their successors, but these were slow to appear. It seemed for a time that the literary discoveries were being made not by novelists or playwrights—not even by poets, though some were gifted—but rather by critics attached to the great universities. Fiction and poetry reflected the cautious and critical temper of the times; but the temper changed after 1960, when experiments of every sort came back into fashion. The new poetry was loose and swinging; the new fiction was likely to be expressionistic. The names one heard mentioned with respect were Bellow, Cheever, Mailer, and among the poets Roethke and Lowell.

The new writers could, practically speaking, say anything they pleased. In earlier times there had been certain subjects, including sexual intercourse, that could not be directly treated in fiction. There had been certain words that could not be spoken in mixed company or written in books intended for general circulation. Any book that violated the rules was unmailable under the postal laws and, if printed abroad, was confiscated by the Customs Bureau when tourists tried to smuggle it into the country. A series of court decisions, beginning with one by Judge Frederick Bryan in the famous case (1959) against *Lady Chatterley's Lover*, struck down the prohibitions one after another. By the late 1960s almost any situation could be presented in writing of almost any level (except children's books). Any word could be used, and the once forbidden words were used so often in some books that they gave an effect of stupefying monotony. Readers were learning that fornication and fellatio are as dull as any other subjects if treated in a dull fashion.

The repeal of provisions against pornography was one feature of a 'culture explosion'—as it was called to make it seem as momentous as those other 'explosions' in population, production, and armaments—that began with the Kennedy Administration. For the first time government was actively sponsoring the arts, and its example was followed by some of the great private foundations, notably Ford and Rockefeller. The performing arts received most of the money. Lincoln Center in New York City, which provided a whole collection of auditoriums for opera, ballet, symphonies, and plays, was a vast monument to private benefaction. Another huge center for the performing arts was started in

Washington with some help from the government, and lesser centers were being planned throughout the country. There were more than two thousand symphony orchestras in the United States, though few of their programs featured American music. Every ambitious city tried to have its own museum of modern art. In New York there were four of these, each trying to assemble exhibitions that would draw bigger crowds than those assembled by its rivals. New York had produced its own school of painters with international reputations, sometimes gained for work that was more audacious than lasting; still, it brought high prices in a market where works of art were bought as speculative investments. The commercial theater was living through a lean period, with only half as many showcases on Broadway as during the 1920s, but new informal theaters were being started in Greenwich Village and were giving lively performances. Everywhere the impression was one of bustle, novelty, excitement, impermanence, and mingled with all this a hope that some genius would come forward to give shape and meaning to the age.

The picture has a darker side. All this frenzied growth in population and wealth, in consumption goods and cultural activity, had involved a vast expenditure of the resources provided by nature. Fuels and ores were being used up, but that was only part of the wastage; now it extended to the three basic resources: land, water, air. Its results were being felt in the lives of ordinary Americans.

More and more of the land, millions of acres each year, was being ruined for tillage. Some of it was being washed or blown away; some was pushed aside by gigantic earth movers to uncover the coal beneath it. Freeways ran on high embankments over what had once been fertile fields. But the great devourers of land were the Standard Metropolitan Areas. Besides rising toward the sky in the fashion of earlier American cities, which depended on vertical transportation, they spread horizontally into the countryside behind squadrons of bulldozers that uprooted the orchards, leveled the hills, and left behind them a desert of asphalt streets lined with upturned strawberry boxes. There were famous agricultural regions of the past—the Hartford Basin, the Santa Clara Valley—that now grew almost nothing but children.

Pure water, like fertile soil, was becoming a scarcer commodity. In much of the West it had always been scarce, but now it had to be piped from greater distances. Wells had to be sunk deeper year after year, and many of them were beginning to pump brine. In the East there was still plenty of water, but much of it—including three of the Great Lakes—was polluted with sewage and industrial wastes. In every big city the air itself was poisoned by the fumes from hundreds of factories and hundreds of thousands of automobiles.

The cities were being ravaged like the countryside. By day their streets were jammed with traffic moving slower, in many cases, than horse-drawn carriages at the turn of the century. Men and women waited in line for places at quick-lunch counters. At night the business district was almost deserted and people feared to walk there alone. As urban life became noisier, smellier, and more dangerous—except for the rich in their apartments high above the streets—more and more families of average means took refuge in the suburbs. Sometimes their former dwellings were razed and the sites used for parking lots. Much oftener the dwellings were occupied by the poor, usually black or Puerto Rican, who had more children to educate and many of whom were on relief. That placed an always heavier burden on city governments, which had to spend more on education and welfare while deriving much of their income from a shrinking middle class.

More ominous than the decay of central cities was the increasingly open conflict between blacks and whites. The conflict had always existed in the background of American life, but it had been easy to disregard—at least in the North—for the simple reason that the blacks were too weak politically to do more than complain in low voices. A campaign for Negro rights started in 1954, when the Supreme Court ruled that racially segregated public schools were forbidden by the Constitution. In the first phase of the campaign, the slogan was Integration, a word that was used in its broadest sense. White and black liberals both dreamed that when Negroes had achieved an equal place in society, they would be integrated into the general population and the color problem would disappear. There was little violence in those early years, except of white mobs preventing black children from entering newly integrated schools. A second phase, marked by more breaches of the peace but not by wide disorder, started in 1960. This time the slogan was Civil Rights, and Negroes were trying to win the rights by holding massive but peaceful demonstrations. In August 1963 a rally in Washington was attended by more than two hundred thousand demonstrators, black and white. The rally was superbly organized by Negroes and was addressed in moving words by Dr. Martin Luther King, who a year later was awarded the Nobel Peace Prize.

Black Americans had by then gained several important victories, though still without achieving equality in their daily lives. In 1965 the campaign entered a new phase, with the slogan this time of Black Power. It was taken to mean that Negroes should cease to depend on the help of white liberals and instead should move toward 'getting it together' —that is, toward uniting as 'soul brothers' and taking control of the areas they inhabited. A few zealots preached that a black government should rule over a separate black nation. As a slogan Black Power was not intended as a call to violence, but still, beginning in 1965, riots broke out in the Negro sections of one city after another. They reached a climax in April 1968, during the week after Dr. King was killed by a white sniper. The National Guard was called out in several states and Washington itself was patrolled by federal troops.

Meanwhile a foreign war continued in Vietnam, where more than half a million Americans were serving on active duty. Since the war was costing billions of dollars each year, the government had less money for fighting poverty or solving the problems of decaying cities. There was wide opposition to the Selective Service Act, under which most of the soldiers in Vietnam had been drafted. The act was unfair in many of its provisions, and these were interpreted in different fashions by four thousand local draft boards. College students were granted deferment, with the result that poor boys were more likely to be drafted than those of the middle classes.

PHOTOGRAPH OF THE EXPENDED SATURN IV-B STAGE OVER THE ATLANTIC OCEAN OFF THE COAST OF ▶
CAPE KENNEDY, FLORIDA. Taken from the Apollo 7 spacecraft during its eleven-day flight in October 1968. *NASA*.

Negroes complained that they were providing more than their fair proportion of combat soldiers. Many younger men of both races complained that they were being forced to fight in a war not of their making, whereas everyone over twenty-six was exempt from the draft. Thus, a war in Asia had intensified most of the conflicts in American society, including a revived conflict between the young and the middle-aged.

That battle of the generations might have been prophesied far in advance by anyone who reflected on the probable effects of a rising birth rate after World War II. The postwar babies were now coming of age, more than three million of them each year—soon more than four million—and they were likely to assert their new standards, whatever these might prove to be, by simple force of numbers. It was the nature of the standards that surprised and shocked an older generation. Young people by tens of thousands were rejecting what their elders regarded as the American way of life. Born in comfortable homes, reared permissively, showered with electrical toys, expensively educated, and granted more privileges than any earlier generation, they nevertheless revolted against what they called 'the whole bankrupt system'—in some cases by 'copping out,' living in squalor, and wearing outlandish clothes; in others by marching, submitting demands, and shouting for a revolution. Some of their behavior was childish and some was suicidal; it was a time of hippies, yippies, and Black Panthers; of drug taking, communal sex, undernourishment, and student riots. It was also a time when many older Americans had a feeling of unease, wondering as they did whether the conflicts in society could be resolved before a whole culture shattered apart. Others—and they included this writer—felt that the rebellion of these youngsters, foolish as it was in some of its manifestations, was still a token of vitality and outraged idealism. It might be followed by a serious effort to abolish the conflict of races, rebuild the cities, stop the wastage of natural resources, and create a peaceful America in which every man had leisure, dignity, and his own voice.

The Presidents of the United States

PRESIDENTS	TERM OF OFFICE		POLITICAL AFFILIATION
1 George WASHINGTON	1789–1793	1793–1797	Fed.
2 John ADAMS	1797–1801		Fed.
3 Thomas JEFFERSON	1801–1805	1805–1809	Dem. Rep.
4 James MADISON	1809–1813	1813–1817	Dem. Rep.
5 James MONROE	1817–1821	1821–1825	Dem. Rep.
6 John Quincy ADAMS	1825–1829		Dem. Rep.
7 Andrew JACKSON	1829–1833	1833–1837	Dem.
8 Martin VAN BUREN	1837–1841		Dem.
9 William Henry HARRISON	1841 (*deceased*)		Whig
10 John TYLER	1841–1845		Whig
11 James Knox POLK	1845–1849		Dem.
12 Zachary TAYLOR	1849–1850 (*deceased*)		Whig
13 Millard FILLMORE	1850–1853		Whig
14 Franklin PIERCE	1853–1857		Dem.
15 James BUCHANAN	1857–1861		Dem.
16 Abraham LINCOLN	1861–1865	1865 (*assassinated*)	Rep.
17 Andrew JOHNSON	1865–1869		Dem.
18 Ulysses Simpson GRANT	1869–1873	1873–1877	Rep.
19 Rutherford Birchard HAYES	1877–1881		Rep.
20 James Abram GARFIELD	1881 (*assassinated*)		Rep
21 Chester Alan ARTHUR	1881–1885		Rep.
22 Stephen Grover CLEVELAND	1885–1889		Dem.
23 Benjamin HARRISON	1889–1893		Rep.
24 Stephen Grover CLEVELAND	1893–1897		Dem.
25 William MCKINLEY	1897–1901	1901 (*assassinated*)	Rep.
26 Theodore ROOSEVELT	1901–1905	1905–1909	Rep.
27 William Howard TAFT	1909–1913		Rep.
28 Thomas Woodrow WILSON	1913–1917	1917–1921	Dem.
29 Warren Gamaliel HARDING	1921–1923 (*deceased*)		Rep.
30 Calvin COOLIDGE	1923–1925	1925–1929	Rep.
31 Herbert Clark HOOVER	1929–1933		Rep.
32 Franklin Delano ROOSEVELT	1933–1937	1937–1941	
	1941–1945	1945 (*deceased*)	Dem.
33 Harry Shippe TRUMAN	1945–1949	1949–1953	Dem.
34 Dwight David EISENHOWER	1953–1957	1957–1961	Rep.
35 John Fitzgerald KENNEDY	1961–1963 (*assassinated*)		Dem.
36 Lyndon Baines JOHNSON	1963–1965	1965–1969	Dem.
37 Richard Milhous NIXON	1969–		Rep.

The Formation of the Fifty States

STATE	CAPITAL	ENTRY INTO THE UNION
Alabama	Montgomery	1819 14 December
Alaska	Juneau	1959 3 January
Arizona	Phoenix	1912 14 February
Arkansas	Little Rock	1836 15 June
California	Sacramento	1850 9 September
Colorado	Denver	1876 1 August
Connecticut	Hartford	1788 9 January
Delaware	Dover	1787 7 December
Florida	Tallahassee	1845 3 March
Georgia	Atlanta	1788 2 January
Hawaii	Honolulu	1959 21 August
Idaho	Boise	1890 3 July
Illinois	Springfield	1818 3 December
Indiana	Indianapolis	1816 11 December
Iowa	Des Moines	1846 28 December
Kansas	Topeka	1861 29 January
Kentucky	Frankfort	1792 1 June
Louisiana	Baton Rouge	1812 30 April
Maine	Augusta	1820 15 March
Maryland	Annapolis	1788 28 April
Massachusetts	Boston	1788 6 February
Michigan	Lansing	1837 26 January
Minnesota	Saint Paul	1858 11 May
Mississippi	Jackson	1817 10 December
Missouri	Jefferson City	1821 10 August
Montana	Helena	1889 8 November
Nebraska	Lincoln	1867 1 March
Nevada	Carson City	1864 31 October
New Hampshire	Concord	1788 21 June
New Jersey	Trenton	1787 18 December
New Mexico	Santa Fe	1912 6 January
New York	Albany	1788 26 July
North Carolina	Raleigh	1789 21 November
North Dakota	Bismarck	1889 2 November
Ohio	Columbus	1803 1 March
Oklahoma	Oklahoma City	1907 16 November
Oregon	Salem	1859 14 February
Pennsylvania	Harrisburg	1787 12 December
Rhode Island	Providence	1790 29 May

STATE	CAPITAL	ENTRY INTO THE UNION
South Carolina	Columbia	1788 23 May
South Dakota	Pierre	1889 2 November
Tennessee	Nashville	1796 1 June
Texas	Austin	1845 29 December
Utah	Salt Lake City	1896 4 January
Vermont	Montpelier	1791 4 March
Virginia	Richmond	1788 25 June
Washington	Olympia	1889 11 November
West Virginia	Charleston	1863 20 June
Wisconsin	Madison	1848 29 May
Wyoming	Cheyenne	1890 10 July

Index

(Numbers in bold type refer to subjects illustrated)

[293]